Joined-up Life

For Alison (and Jack),
who showed me how
to start joining up my life

Andrew J. B. Cameron

Joined-up Life

A Christian account of how ethics works

ivp

INTER-VARSITY PRESS
Norton Street, Nottingham NG7 3HR, England
Email: ivp@ivpbooks.com
Website: www.ivpbooks.com

First published 2011
Reprinted 2011

British Library Cataloguing in Publication Data
A catalogue record for this book is available from the British Library.

ISBN: 978-1-84474-515-9

Set in Monotype Garamond 11/13pt
Typeset in Great Britain by Servis Filmsetting Ltd, Stockport, Cheshire
Printed and bound in Great Britain by Ashford Colour Press Ltd, Gosport, Hampshire

Inter-Varsity Press publishes Christian books that are true to the Bible and that communicate the gospel, develop discipleship and strengthen the church for its mission in the world.

Inter-Varsity Press is closely linked with the Universities and Colleges Christian Fellowship, a student movement connecting Christian Unions in universities and colleges throughout Great Britain, and a member movement of the International Fellowship of Evangelical Students. Website: www.uccf.org.uk.

CONTENTS

PART 3 JESUS VERSUS ETHICS

PART 4 FIVE THINGS THAT MATTER

PART 5 LIVING OUR LIVES

PART 6 LIFE-PACKAGES

PART 7 SIX HOTSPOTS

LIST OF FIGURES

PREFACE

Where I live, everyone has something to say about sport. When it comes to Grand Slam tennis, Test Cricket, Formula One, the Australian Football League or the World Cup, anyone can offer an opinion. Everybody has something to say. No one gets to pull rank, because everyone is already an expert.

The topic of this book is a bit like that. Everyone knows something about living. We all have to work out what to do next based on what we want, who we're with, and some tussles about right and wrong (about 'ethics'). We're all in the business of living, so maybe everyone is an expert on the topic of this book.

Why then would I presume to write about a *joined-up life* and about *how ethics works*? I could try to point to my credentials. I'll tell more of my story soon; but in brief, I'm an ordained Anglican minister from the 'Reformed' and 'evangelical' wing of that denomination. I work in a theological college in Sydney, Australia, and over the past ten years have tried to help budding pastors and people in churches to live well as Christians. They call this kind of thing 'ethics' (which, as I'll go on to explain, is not really my favourite word for it).

But so what? If I were you, those 'credentials' would not particularly impress me. Plenty of ministers are just plain hard work. It might turn out that my own expertise is no greater than your own. You face situations where I'd be clueless, cowardly or wrong. Just by being human we're all in the same boat. We impress ourselves when we do something properly. Yet our lives are often conflicted, fragmented and inconsistent. We find bad ways to be good and poor ways to do well. Mostly we just muddle along. 'Being in the same boat' doesn't qualify me to write about how ethics works, and I certainly can't claim to have cornered everything about good, bad and living well.

So I'll state my goal up front. This book is about finding our best humanity in Jesus Christ. It's about how to understand ethics as springing from Jesus. It seeks to show how *identifying with Jesus Christ brings order and clarity to human life.* In a world where everyone is an expert on right and wrong, this book tries to show how Jesus *unifies* the best of what you hear. *He joins up messy lives.*

You may have had 'Jesus Christ' attached to experiences and claims you want to forget. Something about Jesus (or his overeager people) has threatened your sense of who you are. But your worries would have surprised him. He thought he could set people free (Luke 4:18). He thought he could give people 'rest' (Matt. 11:28–30). He may still turn out to solve some of your life's concerns.

My interest in ethics began with some confusion. I enjoyed Christianity's message of *grace* – the open-handed kindness by which God accepts and loves people, including me, despite all my flaws and failures. But if grace was so important, why did Christians often seem anxious, guilty, work-obsessed or stern? I also loved Christianity's 'big picture': that since prehistory, God has worked to introduce Jesus Christ, the human worth watching. But why did Christians often seem unclear about life's details? I was young, and my perceptions might have been wrong. I can't quite tell in hindsight. I was probably only seeing myself in those around me. I was certainly too harsh on people who were themselves still learners. I later found people discussing these confusions under the heading of *ethics.* I also discovered that this heading is misleading, because Jesus (and his followers) thought that a lot of what we call 'ethics' would *not* set us free, nor give us any rest.

This book is the result of my journey through those puzzles. You won't find a history of ethics here (although you'll find some historical moments). You won't find answers to every ethical question (although there may be some). You won't find many moments of arbitration about moral dilemmas (because I don't think ethics primarily works that way). You won't find a rigorous treatment of social ethics here – that is, of those issues where we worry about what laws and policies a government should enact and uphold.[1] I think

---

1. You could however visit the site of a group I'm involved in: <http://www.sie. org.au>.

of this book as a reappraisal of our cluttered, tumultuous lives, and I'll try to get you to see your life through a different lens:

- Part 1 considers some common ways of thinking about ethics (e.g. rules, rights, values and results).
- Part 2 considers some arenas we're unaware of, but which have a huge impact on how we live.
- Part 3 shows how Jesus Christ becomes a better main category than ethics for determining who we are and what we do.
- Part 4 builds a 'unified field', shaped in response to Jesus Christ, by which we can orient ourselves to whatever is around us.
- Part 5 examines some means by which we approach the daily details of life within this overall orientation.
- Part 6 looks at some aspects of our life-package, or 'vocation', to see how they're located within the 'unified field'.
- Part 7 visits some areas of discussion that cause great disagreement between Christians and others, and tries to show why.

I hope to offer you some new thoughts and practices. There are other excellent introductions to Christian ethics, some of which I mention at the end of this preface. But I've borrowed the format of this book from another author, who in frustration makes a comment that fits my own experience: 'I've lost count of the number of times I've tried to introduce this subject.'[2] His method for handling his complex field was so clever that I copied it.

You don't have to read this book 'linearly' from left to right. Each part contains several self-contained chapters that address some specific aspect of Christian thinking about ethics and life. Each chapter will be peppered with references to other key chapters, such as the chapter on identity 'in Christ' (ch. 14), or to key concepts referenced to a specific page (e.g. *gestalt*, p. 72; or *discernment*, p. 312). *You should feel free to dip into any chapter you like.* (This method means I continually return to words and phrases from previous chapters. I apologize to linear readers who find that repetitive.) Some readers find it helpful to keep a finger in the contents while they read, to stay oriented within the bigger picture.

I considered starting every chapter with some statement like this: 'It's ridiculous to imagine that this subject can be addressed adequately in the space of this chapter . . .' But the refrain became so monotonous that I'll say

---

2. David Crystal, *How Language Works* (London: Penguin, 2006), p. xi.

it just once here. Every chapter of this book *is* ridiculous. I remind myself of a man driving a bus through a car park, sideswiping everything just to get to the other side. There are library shelves devoted to matters I barely touch upon. I'm sorry for the inevitable deficiencies. But because I believe people need these topics drawn into one overview, I've aimed for short or middle-sized discussions of each area. I've tried to make each chapter digestible in a sitting or two, in the hope that they synthesize a bigger picture of life.

The book is not for professional thinkers about ethics, but I've tried to distil some of their best thoughts. I've not mentioned every relevant book or article though. Some footnotes will offer a little more detail to readers who like that. I'll also list further readings at the ends of some chapters. These readings are eclectic, and some may be hard to find. Where an important work on ethics is absent, that's not necessarily a condemnation of it. (I may not have read it.) The readings that do appear are my best guess as to what might offer some further help, and many point to other relevant readings. Of course, I don't agree with everything they say. Asterisks show the level of the reading:

* a short or light summary
** of a style or at a depth similar to this book
*** requires serious concentration

I pepper the text with references to the Bible, whose context I may not pause to discuss. You might occasionally stop and look up some of these in a modern translation of the Bible, to get a sense of what its authors said. Along the way, I'll completely ignore several arguments among biblical scholars. Some of these interest me, but most don't, and you haven't picked up this book for them. As much as I can get away with, I'll tell you what I think and move on.

I have, due to a theological conviction and a social reality, assumed that the biblical literature offers a coherent 'story' of ethics. The theological conviction is that God somehow masterminded the activities of the separate biblical authors, which would lead us to expect some coherence, even if it's complex. (I consider this complex coherence when I speak of the Bible's 'story arc', ch. 19.) The social reality is that in the experience of Christian people the Bible comes at them as a whole. Its parts accumulate over time to create a moral vision.

I flit between several Bible translations. As I wrote, I checked them against original language texts. Sometimes I chose the one that seems closest; but the major translations are all quite good, so I usually just picked whatever sounded nicest in English. In this process, I so regularly chose the excellent Holman

Christian Standard Bible (HCSB) that it became my 'default'. You're reading the HCSB when the translation isn't noted. (I've retained its odd capitalizations.)

There are so many people to thank that my intellectual debts are everywhere. I remind myself of another author, who said, 'it may be more true to say I am the editor of this book than to say I am its author'.[3] The wisdom and teaching of my doctoral supervisor, Professor Michael Banner (while he held the position of F. D. Maurice Professor of Moral and Social Theology at King's College, London), has helped me greatly. He has an extraordinary capacity to see beyond all the superficial chatter around him, and to bring past theological treasures to bear upon the present. In Australia, among many good and faithful teachers, I must name my first mentor in Christian ethics, Rev. Michael Hill. He so clearly understands that our relationships are not the white noise against which we conduct our lives, but the reasons for our lives.[4] I remain deeply appreciative of Archbishop Peter Jensen's expansive, Christ-centred theological tutelage, and of his persistence in encouraging me to develop my knowledge of ethics. (I wouldn't have had the imagination to do so otherwise.) The writings of Professor Oliver O'Donovan (of the University of Edinburgh Divinity School) have also had a formative influence on me. I've borrowed liberally from all of them and from several others. I think of this book as my way to bring some of their thoughts to a wider audience. I don't want to embarrass them by aligning them too closely with it, though; its mistakes, oversimplifications and omissions are entirely mine.

I've been very dependent on research support provided by Des Smith, Lisa Watts and Andrew Ford. Several kind readers have worked through various drafts of this book: Tim Adeney, Matt Andrews, Josh Apieczonek, Kim Baker, Sarah Balogh, Brian Brock, Chew Chern, Rick Creighton, Andrew Errington, Andrew Ford, Olivia Kwok and Lisa Watts. The text would have been incomprehensible without their invaluable and generous feedback. IVP's Philip Duce has given warm and patient encouragement.

My wife, Mary-Anne, has been long-suffering and patient as always, and her intelligent and loving eye has enabled me to see this project, and myself, in a way I could never have seen alone. She's helped me to join up my wobbly life. My children, Amy and Thomas, have given far more warm interest and encouragement than I could rightfully expect of any two teenagers. (Several

---

3. Dale S. Kuehne, *Sex and the iWorld* (Grand Rapids: Baker, 2009), p. 17.

4. For an appreciation of Michael's work, see Andrew J. B. Cameron and Brian S. Rosner (eds.), *Still Deadly: Ancient Cures for the 7 Sins* (Sydney South, NSW: Aquila, 2007).

pages of the book resulted from all the eggs Thomas cooked to keep me going.) Delightful people surround me.

I stress again that I say too little about every area. But the intention of this book is to offer a cumulative overview of ethics, as understood by a Christian. I'll be glad if the book affects and enriches your 'moral imagination' (chs. 2, 10), but I'll be gladder if Jesus' new way to be human becomes your own.

Andrew J. B. Cameron
Moore College, September 2010

Further reading

These books offer useful and very different Christian overviews of ethics:

** Banner, Michael C., *Christian Ethics: A Brief History* (Chichester: Wiley-Blackwell, 2009).

** Fedler, Kyle D., *Exploring Christian Ethics* (Louisville, Ky.: Westminster John Knox, 2006).

** Hill, Michael, *The How and Why of Love: An Introduction to Evangelical Ethics* (Kingsford, NSW: Matthias Media, 2002). Online: <http://www.matthiasmedia.com>, <http://www.thegoodbook.co.uk>.

** Hollinger, Dennis P., *Choosing the Good: Christian Ethics in a Complex World* (Grand Rapids: Baker Academic, 2002).

*** O'Donovan, Oliver M. T., *Resurrection and Moral Order: An Outline for Evangelical Ethics*, 2nd ed. (Leicester: Apollos, 1994).

** Volf, Miroslav, *Against the Tide: Love in a Time of Petty Dreams and Persisting Enmities* (Grand Rapids: Eerdmans, 2010).

PART 1 AWARENESS

When and where does 'ethics' hit you in the face? This section looks at our initial awareness of ethics – the ways in which matters of right and wrong first present themselves to us in late-modern Western culture.

I'll look at the word *ethics* itself, and then go on to consider where it often hits us. Ethics often arrives in the form of a *decision* we must make, sometimes urgently. We often think about *rules, rights, values* and *results*. They form our immediate awareness of right and wrong.

Ethics can make people quite tense. Decisions are often hard; and rules, rights, values and results can leave us jaded and cynical:

- We've suffered under rules that stifle innovation, create meaningless paperwork and cover someone's behind.
- We've battled for ages to uphold someone's rights, or to resist someone's claim to a right.
- The group we belong to holds some values that mean nothing to us, but we have to act as if they really matter.
- We work with someone who's obsessed by results. They never notice the damage they do while achieving them.

As it happens, I don't think that rules, rights, values and results make complete sense of right and wrong. I lead with them mainly because most people think of them first. From where I sit, the surprises start to unfold in Part 2 and you should feel free to begin there.

We may have negative associations with ethics that go back further. We may remember young experiences of being a 'bad boy' or a 'bad girl', and the stupid hoops we had to jump through to become 'good'. For some of us, 'goodness' was never reachable, always receding like a mirage.

If you don't experience the negative associations I've described, you may have received the best applications of rules, rights, values and results. Each of these can have a place in ethical thinking – as long as it 'knows' its place (cf. ch. 27), and isn't pressed into service to solve every problem.

1. WHAT IS 'ETHICS'?

In Part 1 we're considering our initial awareness of ethics — how matters of right and wrong first present themselves to us. This chapter begins to unpack the strange and broad word 'ethics'.

A kind of talk about life surrounds us every day:

- 'Eric, you mustn't *ever* run onto the road! A car could kill you!'
- 'Matilda, share the toys with your brother.'
- *The values of this school are responsibility, respect, care, honesty, a fair chance for all, excellence, democracy, inclusion, understanding and tolerance.*
- 'Good morning, and thanks for having me to your school. We're talking today about drugs. They feel great, and you'll feel a lot of pressure to join in. But illegal drugs will leave you jailed, or sick, or desperate, or dead.'
- *New students must understand rules relating to intellectual property. Students must sign a declaration promising to submit their own work, and must acknowledge their sources.*
- 'For vegans, it's wrong to kill and use animals for food and for other purposes. Consuming dead bodies repulses some. Others think that no human has the right to destroy an animal's life.'
- 'This community keeps sex for marriage. Married men and women

devote their sexual energy to their wife or husband. Networks of close relationships among singles are freed from the jealousies and distortions of sexualized relationships.'

- 'The right to bear arms is fundamental to a free society.'
- *The section manager, Zeke, turned up with that deadline-look in his eye. He handed me a folder. 'Ben, the bosses want to sign this afternoon. But if the client's going to bite, those figures on page 9 have to be lower. Over to you.' I froze over inside; I only had a vague idea of the figures, but guessed what was going down. I replied with the only answer I had at that moment. 'No, Zeke. I can't: I'm an honest person.'*
- 'Corrupt police are using Tasers with excessive force against racial minorities. This injustice is endemic, and must stop.'
- 'We cannot continue to consume fossil fuels and heat the planet. We're exploiting natural resources, destroying ecologies, assaulting developing-world communities and stealing from our children.'
- 'I've worked hard for this. I've spent my entire working life doing things for others, and I've earned a break. No one is going to tell me what to do with our money. If I want to sell it all and travel around the world, I don't care what my kids think.'
- 'Mum, I *can't* put you into a nursing home. After everything you've done for me? I really can't. You're *not* a "burden". Please, let's care for you here a little bit longer.'
- *The deceased has consented to donate all his bodily tissues, with the exception of his brain tissue, for scientific and medical purposes.*

These 'quotations' are all semi-fictional, but you'll recognize something in most of them. They'll remind you of uncertainties in your own life, and of discussions important to others. These are those situations and conversations where *something matters* to someone and the stakes are high. If he or she acts (or doesn't act), something is protected and something precious may be lost. Several features of the list above are worth noticing:

1. They range in *focus*. Some concern what individuals do. Others are about how to handle one-to-one relationships. Yet others are about how we should act as a group. The non-human world also features highly.
2. Most seem to be about how what we do now affects people (or the planet) *in the future*.
3. Different forms of *language* are at work: commands and rules; best guesses about future results; settled habits of action and feeling (e.g.

'care', 'honesty'); and weighty abstract terms (e.g. 'right', 'injustice', 'freedom', 'exploitation').

4. Many *areas* of life are included.

It seems quite mad to try thinking about all this at once. The ways we think and act as individuals, in relationships and as groups, such widely ranging language, informed guesswork about the future, and all in so many different areas of life – how could anyone sum up all that? Yet whether or not we realize it, we each attempt to do so all the time. This activity goes by the name of *ethics*.

Although 'ethics' is a plural noun, it's used as a singular since it encompasses all this activity. The Oxford English Dictionary tells me that ethics is 'the science of morals'. So I dig around under 'moral', 'morals' and 'morality' and find, among other things, that the 'moral' is 'ethical', and 'morality' is about 'ethical wisdom'.[1] Hmmm.

Looking further under 'ethics', I find that it's 'the department of study concerned with the principles of human duty'. Looking further under 'moral', 'morality' and 'morals', I find that these concern 'character or disposition, considered as good or bad, virtuous or vicious' and 'the distinction between right and wrong, or good and evil, in relation to the actions, volitions or character of responsible beings'. (At least 'morality' isn't just about sex!)

Some make a distinction between ethics and morality. They think *morality* refers to *specific norms* held by particular people and their communities – their list, if you like, of what matters most. They think that *ethics* refers to the general study of right and wrong, beyond specific norms. This distinction may be helpful in some contexts, but most now ignore it. For better or worse, most people use these words synonymously. So I reckon it's simpler to say that ethics and morality *describe and analyse our thoughts and feelings about right and wrong acts and conditions*. (This arena used to be called 'practical reason' – our thoughts about our practices. This label unfortunately also sidelined the *feelingful* aspect of these thoughts.)

But although I've risked a simple definition of our subject, I don't think ethics or morality is simple. I think this area is complex (ch. 10). By 'complex' I don't mean 'impenetrable', or 'only for experts and clever people'. Normal, everyday people do complex things all the time. Even breathing, scientists tell me, is complex. So is walking, talking and having relationships. Rather,

---

1. *Oxford English Dictionary Second Edition on CD-ROM* (v. 4.0) (Oxford: Oxford University Press, 2009).

I mean that it cannot and should not be oversimplified. Unfortunately, people attempt to oversimplify ethics all the time. For example:

1. 'I did my duty. I did what anyone should do in that situation.' *Deontology* makes ethics into the search for the general set of requirements that apply to all people.[2]
2. 'I do what the law requires. You can't expect more than that.' *Legalistic* deontology reduces ethics to obedience to some pre-existing list of rules.
3. 'Just follow God's commands; he's all you need.' *Divine command* deontology presents ethics solely as obedience to rules declared by God.
4. 'I was following orders. That's what I do.' *Authoritarianism*, yet another form of deontology, sums up ethics as obedience to some human authority.
5. 'I'm in tune with nature. I protect what's natural, and do what nature intended.' *Natural law* pictures ethics as our response to whatever we think the planet and our place in it was meant to be.
6. 'Respect each other's rights, and everything else will follow.' *Human rights* thinking reduces ethics to the identification and defence of elementary entitlements called 'rights'.
7. 'This organization values innovation, loyalty and excellence.' *Values* thinking simplifies ethics into a list of settled habits and patterns of action and feeling that we call our 'values'.
8. 'I didn't hurt you, because I don't do that. I'm a kind and gentle person.' *Virtue ethics* frames ethics primarily as a description of our regular personal habits.
9. 'I take my lead from the people around me. My community shows me what's right.' *Communitarian* thinking defines ethics as the norms, practices and agreements arising from stories told by those alongside whom we live, work or worship.
10. 'I live by my own code. No one tells me what to do.' *Voluntarism* limits ethics to the activity of our will to choose what matters.
11. 'I did nothing wrong; I meant well. I can't help how it turned out.' *Intentionalism* (a form of *idealism*) reduces ethics to the motivations and plans we bring to our actions, as if performance and results don't matter.

---

2. My insertion of some technical terms in italics risks oversimplification. Please think of each bullet point as a stick-figure sketch of each technical term. I also recognize that the terms in this list overlap. It mixes apples and oranges in philosophical talk about ethics.

12. 'It doesn't matter how we get there, as long as we get the right result.'
    Consequentialism reduces ethics to the way 'ends' justify 'means'.
13. 'Whatever floats your boat, honey; just do whatever makes you happy.'
    Eudemonism, a kind of consequentialism, simplifies ethics to the quest
    for personal happiness.
14. 'We have to find a policy that satisfies as many preferences, for as
    many people with preferences, as we can.' *Utilitarianism*, a kind of
    consequentialism for groups, simply describes ethics as the best
    way to please as many as possible.

Each simplification is *reductive* or *reductionist* (which is a kind of swear word among scholars). Reductionists believe that some necessary truth can suffice to explain everything.

Yet at various times in life, some point on the list above offers the best explanation or suggestion about what to do. If there's a 'kernel of truth' to everything listed (and I think there is), it isn't surprising that people try to make each into the key that unlocks every door.

But the danger of ethical reductionism is in what it misses:

- If I follow only duty or rules, I may fail to see someone's rights.
- If I do only what my community does, I may fail to see when the group is destroying the natural habitat that sustains it, or is forgetting helpful rules, or is victimizing and bullying a few people within it.
- If I define myself by my values or virtues, I may fail to examine the actual actions that make up my days and my life.
- If I focus on achieving happiness or good results, I may ignore and destroy the relationships of trust and loyalty essential to a well-lived life.

So by saying ethics is complex, I mean that we do better when we keep an eye on everything in the list (and perhaps on other things as well).

People often find ethics boring, depressing and terrifying. They're bored when people start throwing around words like 'complexity' and 'reductionist', rather than just being practical. It's depressing when it seems to be more about what we do wrong than what we do right. (When was the last time you felt good about yourself in a conversation over climate change, money or child rearing?) It becomes terrifying when we suddenly find ourselves in rapidly unfolding real-time situations where *we don't know what to do*.

I've felt all of these, and don't always love thinking about ethics. I don't think of myself as an expert, because I often feel as mixed up, discouraged and confused about ethics as the next person. I'm not sure I even believe in 'ethicists', if we imagine them to be a class of people with a monopoly on wisdom. At best, this book is part of a conversation between limited humans who are trying to discern what's best. Ethics is an arena where we really do need each other.

However, I'm also optimistic that, given time and a bit of reflection, our ethical deliberations can make more sense. Maybe I'm cheating slightly to have this optimism, because I think that Christianity offers a sort of 'unified field theory' for ethics (Parts 3–6). But even if Christianity isn't (yet?) a part of your journey, please don't be discouraged, fearful or contemptuous. We may still be able to travel together, conversing and learning along the way.

2. DECIDING

In Part 1 we're considering our initial awareness of ethics – how matters of right and wrong first present themselves to us. We may think ethics is simply about deciding what to do. But this chapter raises three problems for that view, and invites us to expand our 'moral imagination'.

When I chat to people about ethics, they usually focus upon some *decision* they need to make. In these moments of decision, our awareness of ethics is often at its most acute:

- 'Should we smack our toddler?'
- 'Should we send our child to a government or to a non-government school?'
- 'Should I stay with that difficult husband or wife?'
- 'Should I buy a Pontiac Firebird?'
- 'Should a surrogate mother bear our child?'
- 'Should we turn off father's life-support machine?'
- 'Should we tax carbon emissions?'
- 'Should the Internet be censored?'
- 'Should we turn away asylum seekers if they're "illegal immigrants"?'

I feel tense just looking at these questions. Each represents a high-stakes moment in the life of a person or his or her community. We often have to make these decisions within a limited period. A different future hangs on the outcome.

Deciding 'what I/we should do' seems most obviously to be the core-business of ethics. Surely 'ethicists' (if we believe in such beings) should be experts at perusing some situation and then offering excellent advice about what to do. If ethics cannot finally decide, then surely it hasn't earned its keep. But is ethics *really* all about making difficult decisions?

I suggest you'll do yourself a disservice if you think that ethics only, or even mainly, concerns decision-making. Now this will seem a strange claim for anyone raised in the modern West, where ethics mainly concerns *acts* – specifically, those acts we're obliged to do or not to do. In the list of questions above, the clue to this mindset is in the repetition of the word 'should', one of English's most serious obligation-words.

I can think of three ways in which this approach to ethics malfunctions. The first problem is *decisionism* (a word also found in other contexts and with other meanings), where we simply make any decision for the sake of it. We give up trying to think through a difficult decision, and in frustration exclaim, 'It doesn't matter what I decide – I just have to decide *something*!' That exasperation is understandable and 'just deciding' may be quite valid if there are two or several good courses of action (as is often the case). It may also be valid if we're keen to avoid the passivity of non-decision, which can in turn become the way we make decisions. But if deciding hardens into a habit where the priority is *only* on deciding and acting, we become 'decisionist'. Decisionism short-circuits the task of reflecting upon and carefully deliberating over what's actually *right*.

The second problem, *analysis paralysis*, seems to me far more common. Most people I know are not 'decisionist': they don't pride themselves on their power to decide and act without thought. To the contrary: they agonize over thoughts in dozens of different directions. Their agony consists, it seems, in uncertainty. They imagine themselves taking various courses of action, and then think of several reasons why each may be wrong. (This comment, sadly, doesn't apply so much to political discussions, where we could wish each side were more ready to imagine itself wrong.)

What's gone wrong here? I don't mean to be unkind to anyone wracked by such agonies. But their mistake has been to pack *all* of their serious think-ing about ethics into these moments of decision. They're not only thinking through the decision itself – they're straining to do a lot of catch-up thinking about *how ethics works*.

In reality, our decisions are the proverbial tip of a much larger iceberg. Most of what we bring to a decision occurs subconsciously. Whether we realize it or not, each of us has a *moral imagination* (or a *moral vision*). Currents around us constantly shape it. We then bring this imagination to every decision. It furnishes us with the options and tools available to us when working through a decision.

When no decision is at stake, most people are not very interested in the shape of their 'iceberg', and even less in reshaping it. That is, people don't take the time to consider what gave them their moral imagination, and whether to expand, change or challenge that moral imagination. When they need to make a decision, they're constrained by its limits, even though they work desperately to expand it while the clock is ticking on the decision itself.

The concept of a moral imagination enables us to see the third problem. In the first, I make decisions too quickly. In the second, I make decisions too slowly. Both share the third problem, where I think my decisions are the *only* arena for doing my moral thinking. This problem is a *failure* of moral imagination.

What could it mean to have 'a failure of moral imagination'? Our moral imagination contains the options and tools that may help to solve a problem. But if I never read or discuss such options and tools when no decision is at stake, I cheat myself out of liberating new possibilities. I may never have heard that others have helpfully considered some dilemmas. I may never discover that in some decisions there's such a thing as two right answers. I may fail to imagine a better way to frame the entire decision. I may never be in a position to question, challenge or abandon the entire project that generates the decision. It may never occur to me to try changing the conditions that shape my life, or that of the group around me. 'A failure of moral imagination' describes a way of wandering through life without stretching or challenging the way I wander through life.

An old adage describes military combat as 'weeks of boredom punctuated by moments of terror'. An overemphasis upon decisions turns ethics into something similar. There will always be acts to get right and decisions to make. But we do well to imagine ethics as a terrain far more rich and wide-ranging than mere decision-making.

The pages that follow are an attempt to help us discover that terrain, and so to stretch our moral imagination. I'll continue to refer to our moral imagination or vision, and to how we may expand it. The term isn't meant to imply that we should dream up unheard-of, *imaginary* moral solutions. It refers to the moral inheritance we bring to each scenario (or 'moral field', ch. 10): the options and ways of thinking that are at our disposal. I'll contend that Christianity expands our moral imagination by giving us *deeper* insight into problems, and *more* solutions to work with, than the moral inheritance given to us by whatever other background we've come from.

3. RULES AND CODES

In Part 1 we're considering our initial awareness of ethics — how matters of right and wrong first present themselves to us. We've seen that the need for decision often drives ethical thinking. The next chapters consider the kinds of bases upon which people make their decisions. The first of these are the rules and codes that surround us.

Our earliest awareness of 'ethics' often begins with rules, usually issued by a mother, father or some other carer:

- 'Eric, you mustn't *ever* run onto the road! A car could kill you!'
- 'Matilda, share the toys with your brother.'

What makes these rules work? In Eric's case (above), the rule quickly transmits wisdom. Parental safety rules save children's lives. These rules act like a 'wisdom pill', compacting years of experience into a small packet. The child receives a way to function that saves him much trial and error (including errors leading to death). Eric has been 'vaccinated' with a rule-shaped shot of ethics.

However, Eric's mother also included a quick glimpse of the reasoning behind the rule. ('A car could kill you!') At that moment she not only brought to bear the force of her authority, but also initiated Eric into rational discussion about it. The rule is good due to its good reason.

Matilda (above) also receives a wisdom packet, but its reasoning is different.

If she's reached the 'why' stage ('but *why* do I have to share, Daddy?'), then Daddy has a tough job. For Eric, self-preservation on the road obviously seems like a good reason. For Matilda, the 'good' of curtailing her desires (ch. 7) for the sake of her brother is much more contestable. What could her father say in response?

1. He could draw upon his authority: 'Because I said so, Matilda.' She'll comply if she fears his punishment – *or*, if their previous relationship has grown such great trust in him that she feels sure the instruction is for her best, even if she cannot quite see how.
2. He could include her in a communal family norm. 'Matilda, sharing is what we do around here.' This response widens the rule, making it applicable to all. Matilda may simply calculate that at least she'll benefit when her brother and father also follow it; or she may so want to identify with and belong to the group that its norms shape her own identity.
3. He could risk a full philosophical claim about what's inherent in her as a human. 'Matilda, honey, although it doesn't always feel like it, people aren't built to think only of themselves. Everyone is precious, and we're made for each other, to help each other. When you live like that, you'll become happier because the people around you are happy.' If she can follow this argument, Matilda might suspect that he's spinning a powerful yarn (a 'metanarrative') to control her; or that he's named something she recognizes to be deeply true within her own experience of being human.

Matilda and Eric's cases raise several questions:

• Why does it seem better to attach a reason to a rule, and what makes some reasons better than others?
• Why are self-preserving reasons instantly clearer to us than other-person centred, society-building reasons?
• Are any of the father's reasons obviously superior?
• If he opted for point 3 above, how could he *know* all that? Indeed, why not rather say to Matilda, 'Take those toys from your brother, honey. Only the strong get ahead in this world' (ch. 11)?

You may now pause to consider: what rules confront you? If I asked you to list all the rules that come at you every week, you could immediately list dozens or hundreds. At the 'small' end of the spectrum are the rules we observe in our domestic lives with others, such as we saw for Eric and Matilda. The 'heaviest' are the laws that surround us. In the middle are all sorts of packages of rules: policies, regulations, protocols, professional codes, directives, standing orders, council ordinances, house rules, pool rules, dress codes and 'enforced etiquette' (such as on a Sydney bus, where I can sit in a red seat until a person with a disability or an elderly person needs it).

(We could even expand the net to those 'unwritten rules' we only gradually become aware of. My wife and I visit a food co-op that sells 'organic' products grown locally. Although thin people who buy tiny amounts of food populate it, we fatties buy lots of food for our family. We gradually became aware, without anyone saying so, that the thin people consider this practice quite wrong. But such 'unwritten rules' are hard to get a grip on, so I'll save this kind of experience for when we think about social influence, ch. 8.)

Many people believe that the Bible is loaded with rules (ch. 23). However, if we could put the biblical authors into a time machine and show them around our world, they'd probably pity us. 'How can you possibly function under *so many rules?*' they might ask. They'd be incredulous and appalled. Incredulous, because there are literally millions more rules in our lives than what they proposed for the good life. Appalled, because they had a clear sense of how limited in usefulness rules really are.

Of the published rules that surround us, a recent phenomenon is the rise of the professional 'code'. These lists of rules guide our activities in our work role. In my own case, I'm required to live by a code called *Faithfulness in Service*, which has been in national use by the Anglican Church in Australia since 2004 (with additions made by my local patch of Anglicans in 2007).[1] It first appeared to stop sexual abuse by church workers, but has grown to become a guide to church workers in many areas. Here are a few clauses from this code:

- 'You are not knowingly to make statements that are false, misleading or deceptive.' (6.9)
- 'You are to avoid situations of conflict between your personal financial interest and your pastoral ministry responsibilities.' (8.8)

1. Anglican Church of Australia, Diocese of Sydney, *Faithfulness in Service: A National Code for Personal Behaviour and the Practice of Pastoral Ministry by Clergy and Church Workers* (Sydney, 2007). Online: <http://www.sds.asn.au/assets/Documents/ handbooks/FaithfulnessInService2007.pdf> (accessed 12 Sept. 2010).

- 'When engaged in pastoral ministry you are not to administer corporal punishment to children . . .' (5.11)
- 'You are not to disclose confidential information received in pastoral ministry . . .' (4.8)

This code is now quite long, with some twenty pages covering pastoral relationships, relationships with children, personal behaviour, sexual conduct and financial integrity. It's useful and was necessary. We could muse about what went wrong to make such detailed codes necessary for those once regarded as community leaders in ethical integrity, but that story is too complex for me to tackle here. (I comment on church sexual abuse in ch. 34.) Rather, and moving now beyond the specific example of this particular code, what do we learn about 'morality' by the existence of such codes in our professional worlds?

- First, codes highlight how our work exists *for* others, not for fulfilment, reputation or consumption (ch. 41).
- Secondly, codes attempt to illuminate where we're most prone to self-deception by highlighting those desires, drives and impulses that tempt us to exploit and harm others (chs. 7–9).
- Thirdly, when codes address a variety of circumstances they highlight the complexity of morality (ch. 10), and seek to address and anticipate that complexity in advance.

In short, these codes are moral documents that help us see our profession's proper place in society, and the personal forces we carry at our worst. The code's multiple rules try to help us through potentially complex and chaotic moral situations.

But even if they're necessary, they're insufficient. A code alone isn't rich enough to tell us what our profession is *for*; indeed the code writers may not have taken the time to consider the matter deeply (or even shallowly). The rules in a code may highlight the desires and drives that tempt us, but cannot burrow deep into our psyche to change them. Ironically, the code may even inflame them. And however many situations a code tries to address, some novel combination of factors will always confront us. We then either act in the 'spirit' of the code, or dodge through those gaps we call 'loopholes'.

Rules seem unpleasant, and we often indulge our impulse to get around them. We can imagine that robots may follow rules simply and easily, but humans generally don't. As with Matilda and the toys, we've strong and fixed ideas about what's best for us, *and these have deep emotional roots*. But rules slice sharply across these desires (ch. 7).

In his tract *What Is Enlightenment?* the eighteenth-century German philosopher Immanuel Kant issued a clarion call against 'heteronomy' (which
he describes as any ethical claim 'imposed' upon us by another) in favour of
'autonomy' (where we use our own reason to determine right from wrong).[2]
Modern Matildas and Erics find it a whole lot harder to obey a rule if they
cannot see its reasoning for themselves. (Of course, this attitude has been
helpful in running democracies because we can now have public discussions
about the reasons for laws, as was actually Kant's intention.)

What would a Christian account of the Bible's rules have to say about heteronomy? In the Bible, rules are not stand-alone entities. They're embedded in
a total picture of reality (ch. 23). We do well to know this reality, and how the
rule emerges from it. As in Matilda's father's third option, the biblical authors
continually unpack this account of reality and how we humans inhabit it.

2. Immanuel Kant, 'What Is Enlightenment?', tr. Lewis White Beck, in *On History*, ed.
Lewis White Beck (Indianapolis: Bobbs-Merrill, 1963), p. 3. Online: <http://www.
fordham.edu/halsall/mod/kant-whatis.html> (accessed 15 July 2010).

4. RIGHTS

In Part 1 we're considering our initial awareness of ethics — how matters of right and wrong first present themselves to us. This chapter considers one basis upon which people make decisions and form rules: those lists of good things we defend for each other and ourselves, now known as our 'rights'.

People need to make decisions (ch. 2), and rules can be useful guidelines (ch. 3). But deeper reasoning has to come from somewhere, and people draw on various discourses to give that reasoning. One of those is the language of rights, as in these examples:

- 'You have no right to take my things.'
- 'Everyone has the right to life.'
- 'No! Every woman has the right to choose.'
- 'Everyone has a right to employment. Employers have no right to discriminate on the basis of gender, race, sexual orientation or disability.'
- 'No! Employers have the right to hire whoever they choose to pay, and to fire whoever they choose not to pay.'

Rights have become a powerful and popular language for moral discussion. (For simplicity in this chapter, from now on when I say 'rights' I'll generally mean 'universal human rights'. But technically, there are rights that hold only for some in some situations, and are not universal; and some argue for the rights of non-humans.) Philosophers and theorists argue about what a right is, and how to define it. I'll try to do so in a roundabout way.

What makes you 'you'? That's quite an abstract question, yet we do have some clear hunches. I'd cease to be me if someone sliced me in half. The problem isn't just that I'd be dead, but that I'd have lost something essential to making me 'me'. Similarly, some believe I'd no longer be 'me' if my brain was damaged and I lost some skill I'd honed over a lifetime, or if I lost all my memories.

Now I'm glossing over a lot of complex discussion here, because 'me-ness', 'you-ness' and identity in general are notoriously difficult to pin down.[1] But I simply want us to notice the way we think of ourselves as composed of various things that help make us who we are. We think we've a proper claim to keeping them.

A right is a *moral* part of that profile. To have a right to liberty is a way of saying that liberty is *also* necessary to make me 'me', so I've a proper claim to liberty. Rights are a shorthand way of quickly pointing to what we may reasonably and properly claim if we're to be properly human. I could equally say I've a right to my memories, to some skill I've honed, or to the left half of my body. I could also do so on your behalf, observing that you have a right to these things. Therefore, when we make a list of rights, we make a list of good acts or states to which someone is entitled. Beneath every rights-claim is a view of what's essential to our humanity and of what we want to defend and keep. As legal expert Leif Wenar puts it, 'rights are entitlements (not) to perform certain actions or be in certain states, or entitlements that others (not) perform certain actions or be in certain states'.[2]

We all have views of what's essential to our humanity. Some Fijian gold miners, too tired to enjoy sex at night, thought they had a right to a 'sex break' during the day. Some University of Massachusetts students thought they had a right to a unisex toilet. An old Japanese man sued against a skyscraper based on his right to sunshine. A man who underwent a sex change argued for the right of men who undergo sex changes to compete in women's athletic

---

1. Indeed, this book will question some of our conceptions of identity. Perhaps my memories, skills, body and whatever else I care to list do not suffice to define my identity, if it is only known truly by God and found in Jesus Christ (ch. 14).

2. Leif Wenar, 'Rights', *Stanford Encyclopedia of Philosophy*. Online: <http://plato. stanford.edu/entries/rights> (accessed 18 Apr. 2010).

competitions.[3] Slightly embarrassingly, the 1948 United Nations Declaration of Human Rights (UNDHR) defends the right to 'periodic holidays with pay' (Art. 24). People of the world: note that you have an Australian Prime Minister to thank for this insertion.

We can lampoon the concept of rights by using examples like these, but the critique is mistaken. In these cases, the mistake is what each claimant thinks is essential to his or her humanity, not necessarily in the term 'right'. (I'm not even sure the Japanese man was being at all silly.) People often draw the boundary too widely around what they think of as essential to their humanity, but it doesn't follow that *nothing* is essential to each person's humanity. More serious rights-language consists in an agreement among different people about what's essential to humanity. After the Nazi atrocities, UNDHR signatories agreed that life, liberty, security and equal protection before the law were essential and should be defended and upheld. They also spelt out some opposites. We each have the right *not* to be enslaved, tortured, cruelly or degradingly punished, or arbitrarily arrested or detained. For philosopher Nicholas Wolterstorff, the language of rights is 'for bringing the patient- or recipient dimension to speech. Rights-talk is the language one needs to speak up for the wronged of the world.'[4] In other words, Wolterstorff views the terminology of rights as essential if we're to discuss justice, because it often describes what the recipient of justice lacks. (As important as the 'patient' is, I don't believe that such a primacy of rights can sufficiently arbitrate justice for a harmonious *community*. See further the readings below.)

You'll notice that over the last few paragraphs my exposé of rights has inexorably drifted into the direction of law and justice. We can and do use rights-language in everyday moral discussion. I could say to my wife, 'You have no right to talk to me like that!' My friend could say to me, 'Tell me what they said about me: I've a right to know!' Such rhetorical outbursts pack a punch in everyday life, but we don't often sit down to analyse them. They may or may not work; the discussion moves on. But rights-language gains traction and becomes more significant in the realm of law and justice, and it isn't easy to talk about rights in abstraction from this legal realm.

---

3. These examples are from Warren Lee Holleman, *The Human Rights Movement* (New York: Praeger, 1987), p. 5.

4. Nicholas Wolterstorff, 'How Social Justice Got to Me and Why It Never Left', *Journal of the American Academy of Religion* 76.3 (2008), p. 671. See also Nicholas Wolterstorff, *Justice: Rights and Wrongs* (Princeton: Princeton University Press, 2008), p. 7.

Unfortunately, it's quite hard to sum up all the issues here. I'll simply make a few general observations.

Several other legal instruments have followed the UNDHR, which seek to outline rights in more detail. This body of thinking has eventually made its way into the legal structures of some UN members' states. In general, they list goods to defend, and stipulate how to test other laws against that list.[5] For a range of technical reasons, the human-rights laws of these member states have varying degrees of effectiveness.

Proponents of such charters hope they'll defend the weak and marginalized, and give lawmakers a moral compass. Opponents object that each 'fuzzy' right doesn't sit well with the precision of the rest of the law. They also object to the way only one set of goods becomes frozen into legislation. There are many other arguments for and against. I'm an opponent, but I'm not very useful to other opponents, because I find it quite hard to attack the proponents' hope for a just society and for better law.

I'm also an opponent for a smaller, local reason. A human-rights charter in a neighbouring state excludes 'abortion or child destruction' from the right to life (see n. 5, below). This exception suggests that in my part of the world the game is rigged. The charter purports to interrogate all existing law, except those laws that the ruling elite decide are too precious to risk scrutiny. We're asked to believe in 'universal human rights'; yet no 'right' can be permitted to upset our fetish for excluding the unborn from our moral community (cf. ch. 22). This episode leaves me somewhat sceptical about rights-law.

Many Christians vehemently oppose this kind of law. They worry that it may be used against freedoms of religious belief and practice, even though it's supposed to uphold these. They also have some philosophical concerns.

---

5. For example, the Australian state of Victoria's *Charter of Human Rights and Responsibilities Act* (2006) sets out to defend these rights: to recognition and equality before the law; to life (although amazingly, not including 'abortion or child destruction', §48); to protection from torture and cruel, inhuman or degrading treatment; to freedom from forced work; to freedom of movement; to privacy and reputation; to freedom of thought, conscience, religion and belief; to freedom of expression; to peaceful assembly and freedom of association; to protection of families and children; to take part in public life; cultural rights; to property ownership; to liberty and security of person; to humane treatment when deprived of liberty; for children in the criminal process; to fair hearings and in criminal proceedings; not to be tried or punished more than once; and against retrospective criminal laws.

A conception of a created moral order (ch. 22) no longer controls rights-language, so it can press for special interests without reference to wider concepts of justice. These claims become hard to arbitrate in comparison to other claims. For these reasons, many Christians cannot endorse human rights.

But other Christians enthusiastically promote human-rights law, because Christian theology defends human life and various familial and communal interactions. These defences are expressed in the Bible, match the God-given natural moral order (ch. 22) and have been repackaged as human rights – a spectacularly successful popular reassertion, they think, of some key elements of the moral order. For these reasons, many Christians cannot oppose human rights.

My own view is that rights-language has descended partly from Christianity's account of a created moral order (chs. 22, 27), naming some of what each precious person needs to function. But attempts by individuals to define their own identity without reference to others have also driven rights-language. Therefore, I try to avoid the language of rights, but recognize that increasingly I'll have to do business with those who use it. I might agree with some uses of it, and disagree with others, but I won't know until they use it. My agreement or disagreement will depend on whether these uses make sense, within the 'unified field' (Parts 3–6, especially ch. 26) by which I orient myself to life and society.

Further reading

*** O'Donovan, Oliver M. T., 'The Language of Rights and Conceptual History', *Journal of Religious Ethics* 37. 2 (2009), pp. 193–207.
*** Wannenwetsch, Bernd, 'But to Do Right . . . Why the Language of "Rights" Does Not Do Justice to Justice', *Studies in Christian Ethics* 23.2 (2010), pp. 138–146.

5. VALUES

In Part 1 we're considering our initial awareness of ethics – how matters of right and wrong first present themselves to us. In this chapter we consider the way the term 'values' is used both to describe 'ethics' in general, and to name settled patterns and habits of action and feeling that form part of our identity.

Matters of right and wrong are often now referred to under the heading of 'values'. It's become a summary word for morality and ethics. (If I send a child to one school instead of another for her to 'learn some values', then I'm saying I want her to receive some ethical instruction.) But confusingly, morality can also refract into lists of discrete 'values'. For example:

- *The values of this school are responsibility, respect, care, honesty, a fair chance for all, excellence, democracy, inclusion, understanding and tolerance.*

These 'values' have been borrowed from the Australian State school system. They're an amalgam and paraphrase of values-lists put out by the Commonwealth, New South Wales and Victorian educational authorities. They gained some prominence during a public and political discussion in Australia about values in schools. Some perceived that independent religious schools were the place where a child might learn some values. Government school systems countered this view with lists like the one above. It strongly emphasizes the quality of relationships in a community: all the values listed make sense only when other people are around. The list assumes that every person in the school is equally precious. However, we could imagine a completely different list, where other people are peripheral and their importance not as obvious:

- *Kandii's values are assertiveness, self-fulfilment, achieving her potential, self-esteem, independence, autonomy, personal productivity and self-acceptance.*

Which of these lists – the schools' or Kandii's – is 'best'? The concept of 'values' alone cannot tell us, for technically each list describes only what someone, well, values.

We all have an inner list of what matters to us. As Jesus once put it, 'where your treasure is, there your heart will be also' (Luke 12:34; cf. p. 195). The term 'values' appeared much more recently, to articulate these internal treasures that differ for all of us.

Therefore, simply to speak of values doesn't enable us to decide between the schools' list and Kandii's. On the face of it, whether or not any of those values are better or worse is impossible to tell. Each list only tells us what Kandii and the educational authorities treasure. A person (let's call her Carmen) could equally say:

- *My values are meals with friends, tennis, the natural environment, free-range chickens, skydiving, Mozart, cuddles and Smirnoff.*

Of course, you may not agree that a person could 'equally' list these as 'values' alongside 'honesty', 'autonomy' or 'tolerance'. You may argue that although the items on Carmen's list are 'valuable' to her, we mean something bigger than individual preferences when we refer to 'values'. Carmen has listed only her preferences. If you think Carmen's preference-list differs from Kandii's and the schools' value-list, then why does it? Where does the difference lie? I suggest the lists differ in two respects. The first is *personal* and the second *cosmic*.

The personal reason for why they differ is that Kandii has listed *settled patterns of action and feeling* describing how she generally thinks, feels and acts. Carmen has told us what she likes, but nothing tells us how often she enjoys each thing, if at all. In contrast, Kandii claims her values are what you would see driving her if you watched her for a few days. We often describe the overall summation of these settled patterns of action and feeling as her *character*. Similarly, the schools' organizers want to see settled patterns of action and feeling among school children, which would give a school a particular character (or *culture*, as we're more likely to say of a collective).

You may also have a cosmic reason for thinking that the schools' and Kandii's lists differ from Carmen's. 'Respect', 'honesty', 'independence' and 'autonomy' in Kandii's and the schools' lists all seem much weightier than Carmen's love of tennis and chickens, for they rely on reasons beyond personal preference to explain what makes them good. For example:

- 'We respect each other, because everyone is equal and their diversity is precious' *or* 'because everyone is made and loved by God'.
- 'We're honest because we need relationships; but relationships cannot survive if we deceive each other.'
- 'Independence and autonomy enable people to function as well as possible without interference or exploitation by others.'

Each of these reasons relies on something bigger than the value-holder. Something about *reality itself* makes sense of each value. We may disagree about which reasons, and whose account of reality, are correct. But at least we would agree that to understand morality you would also have to understand something of the reality we inhabit together.

We would therefore be *moral realists* or *morally objective*, because we believe that morality describes something beyond us all that claims us all, in which we all participate together (ch. 22). Of course, some people think that values are *only* a list of preferences like Carmen's, that nothing cosmic is involved and that we can find no meaningful agreement about reality itself and how it shapes morality. This view is *moral relativism* or *moral subjectivism*.

These settled patterns are a different approach to ethics than 'rules' or 'rights':

- They tell us more about *who a person is* than what they do.
- They're 'fuzzy' or 'vague'.[1] They describe a person's 'vibe'. They're about a person's style, but they don't predict specific actions.

---

1. I do not use the terms 'fuzzy' and 'vague' as a put-down. A word is fuzzy or vague when we're unsure of its 'edges', even though it points to something real. We cannot be sure where 'hot' begins, yet it's still helpful. Even Mount Everest is 'vague': no one quite knows exactly where it starts (or, in a blizzard, where it stops!). So it is with a virtue term such as 'kindness' – it may be hard to describe where it starts and stops (cf. p. 195), but we know it when we see it.

So because of Kandii's assertiveness, independence and self-acceptance, she'll reliably deal with shopkeepers, bus drivers and bureaucrats differently than she would if she'd valued submissiveness, patience and politeness. Her values describe something of her character, and give a general 'ballpark' of her likely and unlikely actions.

If we went back as little as two centuries, people did not talk of values. Yet they were *very* interested in settled patterns of action and feeling. They would describe a person's character as courageous, temperate, prudent or just. Or people could be described at more length, as when Jane Austen characterizes the humble but attractive Mrs Smith: 'here was that elasticity of mind, that disposition to be comforted, that power of turning readily from evil to good, and of finding employment which carried her out of herself'.[2]

What we call 'values', they called *virtues*. Virtues were not matters of personal preference; they were patterns of action and feeling that *should* arise in response to our world. But at the end of the nineteenth century the German philosopher Friedrich Nietzsche (ch. 11) asserted that a virtue 'has to be *our* invention, *our* most personal defence and necessity'.[3] Here we begin to see a shift from an idea of virtues as applicable to all, to the modern idea that we each have self-chosen values.

Christianity has its virtues (ch. 30). These, say the biblical authors, are good and right for us all, and bring personal meaning and joy. In fact, 'joy' is one of the settled patterns of action and feeling that Christians begin to discover (Gal. 5:22). The 'treasures' of our 'heart' (p. 195) that we now value (ch. 7) can move, shift, change and grow into something the Bible calls 'love' – for God, each other and the world around us.

When that happens, we see some merit in the values of the Australian school system. We also begin to suspect that Kandii has missed the significance of the planet and of the people who surround her, even though she may be right to rejoice in how good it is to be a free agent.

I've suggested, then, that what we know of as values have their ancestral root in what were once known as virtues. I'll go on to suggest that virtues, in turn, are ultimately indebted to the character of God (ch. 21).

---

2. Jane Austen, *Persuasion* (London: David Campbell, 1992), p. 153.

3. Friedrich Nietzsche, *The Anti-Christ*, tr. Reginald J. Hollingdale (London: Penguin, 1990), p. 133 (§11); emphasis original.

Further reading

** Himmelfarb, Gertrude, *The De-Moralization of Society: From Victorian Virtues to Modern Values* (New York: Knopf, 1995).

6. RESULTS

In Part 1 we're considering our initial awareness of ethics — how matters of right and wrong first present themselves to us. We've seen that the need for decision often drives ethical thinking, and have considered the kinds of bases upon which people make their decisions. This chapter addresses an approach called 'consequentialism', where good results determine right and wrong. We also consider how this approach differs from simply being future-oriented in our practices.

Plenty of people I know would have no patience for this book. 'Stop junking everything up,' they object. 'Let's keep it simple. It's all about results.' For them, ends really do justify means. The way to test the rightness of some policy or action is simply to look at its outcome:

- 'I had to leave that woman. I've never been happier.'
- 'The US had to detonate the A-bombs over Japan, or millions more would have died in the war.'
- 'If the Guatemalan military had not made its opponents disappear, the Communists would be in power by now.'
- 'We'll live together for as long as it works. A piece of paper isn't going to make any difference.'
- 'Waterboarding is necessary for intelligence gathering and national security.'

- 'I take my brother's attention-deficit medication so I can study longer and perform better in exams. I'd only stop if it was shown to result in brain damage.'
- 'We should destroy human embryos, if embryo research cures disease.'

Each of these is an example of *consequentialism*, where some action is justified by its future result. The desired future state varies: happiness, less war-dead, the absence of Communism, a relationship that 'works', national security, academic performance, health. In each case, other considerations (such as justice, faithfulness, rules or rights) are irrelevant. In consequentialism, 'the proof is in the pudding'. If my action somehow leaves the world a 'better' place, then I've acted well.

Consequentialism is a scriptwriter's dream. In the police drama *The Shield*, lead detective Vic Mackey (played by Michael Chiklis) kills his colleague, who threatens to expose Vic's corruption. But Vic believes he acts for a greater good – to minimize community suffering through his own particular style of policing. In the film *The Watchmen*, the death of fifteen million people is justified by the world peace that follows.

At this point I'll declare my hand, and quite rudely. (I'll then backtrack and qualify my rudeness a little.) Consequentialism is a shallow and lazy approach to life. It's very important for a consequentialist not to think about anything other than the goal he seeks. He's like a driver who defines his home as the only good worth considering, and must get there at all costs. It doesn't matter what he destroys along the way. He doesn't think these are moral considerations, because he's decided in advance to ignore them. Once he's home, he must have driven well, because he's home. This driver has not even evaluated his future happiness very well, because he's failed to imagine how unpleasant home becomes once police, lawyers and angry relatives are banging on the door. Like an addict, he must then engage in a new round of consequentialism to get out of the mess.

At its worst, consequentialism has nothing to do with ethics. It simply describes someone getting what they want by doing whatever they have to. When I'm driven by some craving (ch. 7), I dignify my actions by claiming that the end justifies the means. The Nazi Adolf Eichmann drew up timetables for the trains that freighted Jews to the death camps. He simply wanted to belong (ch. 8) by doing his job well. Instances of consequentialism are not all as bad as Eichmann's, but we can easily resemble him. We convince ourselves that some imagined future state justifies 'whatever it takes' to get there.

Consequentialism has a rather odd attitude to these future states. Happiness, security, health, relationships, knowledge, prosperity and every other desirable future state are good. The consequentialist is very motivated by this good – but she doesn't pause to analyse what *makes* it good, and whether her actions to get it will damage some key ingredient of its good. Nor does she pause to consider whether other 'goods' will be ruined by her actions.

So I lie to get ahead but find that once 'ahead', I'm lonely, because good relationships need trust, and trust needs honesty. Or we carelessly kill civilians to win a war, so that those who are left hate the 'freedom' and 'justice' we say we offer. Or I refuse to 'complicate' my relationship to a partner with any promises, but then find we cannot prosper, because we needed assurances of fidelity all along. These absurd failures of moral imagination (p. 25) are every bit as bad as we saw in the driver above. At its worst, consequentialism masquerades as thoughtfulness, but is a thinly veiled concoction of craving for future fantasies alongside the failure to imagine well.

The fourth-century theologian Augustine replied to a buffoon called Consentius, who had a grand plan to return ex-Christians to Christianity through an elaborate deception. These former Christians had been lied to by a charismatic leader, so Consentius thought it might be clever to bring them back to Christianity though trickery. Augustine's response turned into an attack on consequentialism in general. We can all imagine situations where it seems right to commit a small evil to stop someone else doing a bigger one. We then become willing to commit a few large evils to stop many smaller ones. Before long, argued Augustine, all boundaries are torn up and evil reigns. To be 'wise' in this sort of way – 'what's it but to lose one's wits', asks Augustine, 'or rather, to be downright mad?'[1]

Augustine could be picturing a prison hellhole, or a deranged and toxic corporate culture (such as the last days of Enron), or total war. Consequentialism looks easy and simple, but fails to notice that its own real consequences are more likely to be the dissolution of the structures, habits and practices that makes life in society worth living.

I said above that scriptwriters love this stuff. In the second season of the television series *24*, Jack Bauer (Kiefer Sutherland) threatens a terrorist's family with death, forcing the terrorist to give up the whereabouts of a nuclear bomb. But by the seventh season, Jack's consequentialist excesses have become a habit. At 3.25 p.m. he advocates threatening to kill the wife and child

1. Augustine, 'Against Lying', in *Nicene and Post-Nicene Fathers of the Christian Church*, vol. 3, *Moral Treatises*, tr. C. L. Cornish, ed. Philip Schaff (Grand Rapids: Eerdmans, 1988), §20. Online: <http://www.ccel.org/ccel/schaff/npnf103.v.vi.html> (accessed 15 July 2010).

of a corrupt Secret Service agent to make him talk. Two FBI agents baulk at his plan, but Jack mocks them: 'When are you people going to stop thinking everyone else is following your rules? . . . You've got one of two choices. You can either phone the President and explain to her that your conscience won't allow you to do what's necessary . . . or you can simply *do what's necessary*. Pick one!'

The problem is that by Season 7 of *24*, Bauer's world has disintegrated around him, despite his good intentions. FBI Agent Larry Moss, like Augustine, tries to point out this pattern. 'Look at yourself. You've lost everyone and everything you ever had by doing what *you* think is necessary. . . . Jack, the rules are what make us better.' 'Not today,' Jack replies. Ironically, Jack's 'not today' has become his motto every day on *24*. In this way, the show cleverly explores the long-term consequences of consequentialism.

The time has come to qualify my rude rejection of consequentialism. First, the problem with consequentialism isn't its interest in the future. Everyone who wants to live well has to consider the future. Even Immanuel Kant, the German philosopher and arch-opponent of consequentialism, who valued duty above all else, had to consider the future. (He tried to find what his duties were by asking 'what would happen if everyone did what I'm about to do?' This diagnostic question is future-oriented.) Those who defend rights calculate the future effects of policies and actions upon our rights. Those who think ethics is primarily about people becoming 'virtuous' think futurewards about what kind of person they're becoming. Christians are future-oriented when they act as 'retrievalists', seeking to retrieve and maximize as much good as possible on all fronts, even in horrendous situations.[2]

Consequentialism's flaw isn't that it's future-oriented. It's flawed because it excludes too many relevant considerations. It doesn't train us to evaluate the merits of rules, or to discern whatever our 'conscience' is trying to protect, or to consider what kind of person our action might make us. It doesn't contemplate what makes various rights worth defending. It can be careless with the existing structures of our social and natural environments, and is poor at considering longer-term effects upon those environments.

Secondly, a subspecies of consequentialism deserves marginally more respect, because it isn't so reckless. *Utilitarianism* began life as an objection to the elitism and injustice of eighteenth-century England. Social reformer Jeremy Bentham cut through incoherent laws with a clarion call of appealing

---

2. The concept of retrieval comes from Michael Hill, *The How and Why of Love* (Kingsford, NSW: Matthias Media, 2002), pp. 132–134.

simplicity: that the greatest happiness of the greatest number is the foundation of morals and legislation. Bentham used this principle to identify good social policies and just laws. Utilitarianism has been refined since Bentham. For example, the Australian ethicist Peter Singer seeks to maximize preference satisfaction among as many sentient beings (not just humans) as possible.

I'll not outline or comment on utilitarianism here, although I think it suffers from many of consequentialism's deficiencies. I simply want to concede that this version of consequentialism sets out to find the best for a society, and that utilitarians are not necessarily selfish and thoughtless.

Further reading

* Cameron, Andrew J. B., 'Utilitarianism: Whatever it Takes', in *A Spectator's Guide to World Views*, ed. Simon Smart (Sydney South, NSW: Bluebottle, 2007), pp. 85–101.

*** Smart, J. J. C., and Bernard Williams, *Utilitarianism: For and Against* (Cambridge: Cambridge University Press, 1973).

PART 2 UNAWARENESS

The previous section has visited some arenas of ethical discussion. Our awareness of ethics and morality most likely comes from these arenas.

But there are undercurrents in our lives. We're barely aware of how they pull and push us, and they carry us far from where we began. We don't often notice or talk about these areas of *unawareness*, yet they deeply affect what we think, what we do and who we are.

Australians love the ocean surf beaches that pepper our coastline. We learn as youngsters about the undertows and rips that form after the waves break and as seawater drains back to the deep. These broad, strong currents are hard to spot from the beach, and almost impossible to notice when we're in one. We can splash about for many minutes, all the while thinking that we're in control of our situation. But in a way that has escaped our perception, our 'frame of reference' has slowly shifted – until suddenly we realize we're out of our depth, or on the rocks.

This section looks at *our desires and emotions*, the undertows that surge within us. It also looks at *systems of social inclusion*, the undertows that surround us. We examine a biblical term, *flesh*, that describes a way of living oblivious to these undertows. I then suggest that partly because of these undertows, ethical thinking is more *complex* than we realize. I end with a small tangent, asking whether psychopaths have it right. Perhaps we should simply *give up imagining ourselves as anything other* than the sum total of our desires and of our standing with a group.

Ethical discussions rarely acknowledge these matters. But we cannot live well if we don't deal with them. They affect every decision we make. Rule-making, rights-defending, future-thinking or values-orienting alone cannot protect us, and can become the ethical equivalent of thinking we're in control as we splash about making decisions – all the while being swept silently toward the rocks or the deep.

7. DESIRE

In Part 2 we're considering some generally unacknowledged 'undertows' in human experience. We're often unaware of them, but they have a dramatic effect on how we think ethics works and upon our practices. This chapter is about our emotions, our desires, or what one theologian called our 'loves'. This good aspect of us tragically becomes our downfall.

Most people think ethics has something to do with being good. But if we're honest, it doesn't attract us. Anything concerned with 'being good' can leave us a bit nauseous. People will sometimes pay lip service to sets of 'values' they *should* value, but really don't, because these things quite bore them. (Think about how you feel when your boss tells you that your workplace values 'integrity', 'excellence' or 'service'.) Similarly, rules often annoy us; the rights of others often mean less to us than our own rights; and thinking about results easily degenerates into getting the result *we* want. That we often have little interest in the so-called 'values' we're supposed to espouse shows that our real loves lie elsewhere. Why are we like this? Something about our emotions drives these reactions. The life of our emotions is the great untold story in ethics. I'll approach it with the help of two philosophers and a theologian.

The eighteenth-century German philosopher Immanuel Kant spoke of 'souls so sympathetically attuned that, without any other motive or self-interest they find an inner satisfaction in spreading joy around them and can take delight in the satisfaction of others'. That sounds like a brilliant way to be.

But Kant goes on to assert that 'in such a case an action of this kind, however it may conform with duty and however amiable it may be, has nevertheless *no true moral worth* but is on the same footing with other inclinations'.[1] In other words, if we *feel* like doing something, we cannot really count our action as 'ethical'. For Kant, ethics is a matter of 'reason' alone, and our emotional inclinations can throw no light upon our understanding of right and wrong. For decades after Kant many believed *real* ethics was about obedience to duty. If we felt like doing something, or if we enjoyed the result, then it couldn't really count as a good act. (Sadly, many Christians still think this way.)

In contrast, the ethical emotivist C. L. Stevenson argued in the 1940s that our ethical judgments are *only* emotional dispositions, and are largely unrelated to our thoughts. As such, we cannot really give 'reasons' for our ethical judgments. They're simply manifestations of mysterious emotional 'attitudes'. (He did not analyse where these 'attitudes' came from.)[2]

Kant and Stevenson totally disagree about how to determine right and wrong. For Kant, we can only think our way to ethical truth, rather than feeling what's good. For Stevenson, good and bad are *only* a feeling, rather than something we think about. But they both agree on one key point: *that our thoughts and feelings are separate*. The seventeenth-century philosopher Descartes led the way in compartmentalizing thinking and feeling, a habit that has dominated the West until recently.

But what if our thoughts and feelings are *always woven tightly together*? This better account of the relationship between 'thoughts' and 'feelings' is re-emerging in many disciplines. (I say 're-emerging' because we can find ancient versions of it.) Different parts of the brain probably govern our cognitions and emotions; but these parts are highly interconnected. As a result, many of our thoughts lead immediately to emotions, and many emotions have their own powerful logic.

The fourth-century theologian Augustine understood this interweaving of thought and emotion. He thought there were three basic attributes of humanity: we *exist*, we *know* and we *love*.[3] These capacities are inherent in us. While

---

1. Immanuel Kant, *Groundwork of the Metaphysics of Morals*, tr. Mary J. Gregor, in *Practical Philosophy*, ed. Mary J. Gregor and Allen W. Wood (Cambridge: University Press, 1996), p. 53; emphasis added.

2. Charles L. Stevenson, *Ethics and Language* (New Haven: Yale University Press, 1944).

3. Augustine, *The City of God against the Pagans*, tr. R. W. Dyson (Cambridge: University Press, 1998), p. 488 (§11.28).

alive, we cannot stop existing, knowing and loving. Augustine thought that the philosophers and thinkers of his day were obsessed about existence and knowledge, but never stopped to consider the many ways in which we *love*.

He didn't mean we necessarily love other people. Rather, each of us simply has a capacity for love and delight, which we direct everywhere. Augustine is referring to the whole range of our interests: our desires, cares, concerns, attractions, lusts, and so on. Our knowledge-relationship to the world is irreducibly touched and tinged by these 'loves'. We cannot help it. This is how we respond to something good: we love it, want it, desire it, yearn for it and hunger after it. We inhabit an ordered ecology of goods, and *respond* with the various desires, interests, cares, concerns and attractions Augustine is content to call 'love'.

We could try to list everything 'good' and would fail:

- Skiing at dawn
- A woman singing
- The care of friends
- Dancing
- The beautiful complexity of biology, mathematics or physics
- Lego with children
- Banquets
- Washing a dog
- Weddings
- Lovemaking
- Problem-solving
- Fine acting
- Magnificent craftsmanship
- The alien beauty of distant planets
- The familiar beauty of mountains at sunset

After a hundred pages, we would still have failed, so loaded is our habitat with everything good. Our loves grip and carry us into all this goodness around us, in a basic and inalienable response central to being human. We can be no other way. According to Augustine, human existence is unintelligible without love.

But something goes wrong.[4] One of Western culture's most famous

---

4. For a more general investigation of the way our desires turn into obsessions and of how theology can help us, see Andrew J. B. Cameron, 'Augustine on Obsession', in *The Consolations of Theology*, ed. Brian S. Rosner (Grand Rapids: Eerdmans, 2008).

depictions of what goes wrong appears early in the Bible, in that famous scene where a woman stares at a tree and its fruit. Reading this text, we *watch and feel with her* as desire swells and swells. She's surrounded by trees 'pleasing in appearance and good for food' (Gen. 2:9), but she can see only one: a single, off-limits tree. Desire so fills her that she can think of nothing else. She 'saw that the tree was good for food and delightful to look at, and that it was desirable for obtaining wisdom' (Gen. 3:6). In this masterful presentation, as readers we long for the tree with her. She's us; we're her; and in the grip of desire, she's turned endless abundance into a problem of scarcity, as we so often do. So the God who gives seems evil, because *we cannot have what she wants*.[5]

Augustine strongly identified with this woman, in an experience also involving a fruit tree. Spying a farmer's pear tree with a group of friends, they decide to jump his fence and steal the pears. The desires welling up to motivate this act later perplex him, for 'of what I stole I already had plenty, and much better at that, and I had no wish to enjoy [them.] . . . We took away an enormous quantity of pears, not to eat them ourselves, but simply to throw them to the pigs.'[6]

It's as if God has made his world too good. We attach to parts of it with an intense and voracious selectivity that blocks out everything else. Augustine's incident with the pears is a good example. The longing to belong (ch. 8) drove him, he later concludes. In this way, one desire (belonging) eclipsed all other goods from his mind (such as the preciousness of the farmer and his living).

Augustine was very moved by the apostle John's diagnosis of our mangled love (1 John 2:15–17). John may be reflecting on that old story of failure with the off-limits tree when he instructs his readers not to 'love the world' (v. 15). At first, he seems to disagree with God's own assessment of the world as good. But he doesn't locate humanity's problem within God's good world. It's

---

5. According to a standard objection, this scenario is sexist, because it seems to make a woman responsible for the failure of humanity. But the man also fails spectacularly, although differently. God charges Adam to avoid the tree, but Adam simply complies with the social influence upon him (ch. 8). Paul later names Adam as the prime mover in humanity's failure (1 Cor. 15:22; Rom. 5:12–19). The Gen. 3 scenario may also seem to suggest that desire enslaves women and not men. But no biblical author makes this conclusion. In the Bible, men and women fall headlong into their own desires. Paul later uses the deception of Eve to warn men and women alike (2 Cor. 11:3).

6. Augustine, *Confessions*, tr. R. S. Pine-Coffin (Harmondsworth: Penguin, 1961), p. 47 (§2.4).

located behind our eyeballs, not in front of them, when John mentions 'the lust of the flesh, the lust of the eyes, and the pride in one's lifestyle' (v. 16). Desires for good things derange humanity, and the 'world' John depicts is *the way humans thanklessly and voraciously misappropriate God's good world*. We attach to aspects of it too hard: voraciously, intensely, obsessively and destructively:

- The young man loves sex and freedom so much that he won't give himself to a woman to welcome her babies, and a sex industry and the strange logic of cohabiting relationships emerge, to give him what he wants.
- The young woman loves her independence so intensely, or an older woman her existing children so fiercely, that both live in terror of being pregnant, and an abortion industry emerges to give them what they want.
- The scientist craves so much for new cures and for the recognition that would come to him that he must never allow himself to see the human embryo as personal, and a bioethics industry emerges to argue for what he wants.
- We love productivity and independent mastery so passionately that we cannot bear to admit that too much fossil fuel may be going up in smoke, or that the planetary atmosphere is compromised, and a rhetoric of 'economic growth' enables us to defend what we want.

In each case, someone defends something good. But it fills the horizon, and the desire for it displaces other desires worth having. Instead of abundance, all we see is scarcity; and in the hungry state that follows, we believe God doesn't bless us and is against us. Yet we also believe other people's loves are mere hobby horses, fads and political posturing. Any love for others or for environmental goods worth defending are swept away. We become people who cease to care, except for those few values (ch. 5) and desires *we* decide matter to *us*.

But ironically, our desires also enslave us. Augustine could be speaking of Hitler's obsession with race, or Stalin's or Mugabe's paranoid addiction to power, when he observes that 'the bad man is a slave even if he reigns'. These people are slaves 'not to one man, but, what's worse, to as many masters as he has vices'.[7] The apostle Peter writes similarly of those religious manipulators who use sensual passions to seduce people. (I think of Jim Jones in Guyana during the 1970s or of David Koresh in Waco, Texas, in the 1990s.) 'They

---

7. Augustine, *City of God*, p. 147 (§4.3).

promise them freedom, but they themselves are slaves of corruption, since people are enslaved to whatever defeats them' (2 Pet. 2:19).

The problem isn't confined to manipulative leaders. We're often unaware of our longings, but they create an undertow that affects what we think and do.

- Some good thing fails to move us. We run from the plight of the developing-world poor. We know that the company we work for destroys communities or wrecks the environment, but we don't care. We make a promise, and then hate the thought of keeping it. In each case, some other love moves to centre stage and mesmerizes us.
- An obsession so dominates us that 'ethics' becomes irrelevant. A married man or woman craves intimacy or security, and leaves spouse and children. The son of a sick old woman rationalizes her killing as 'euthanasia', but his interest in her money drove him. A judge lies and lies all the way to prison, because he cannot bear the impact upon his pride of a seventy-seven dollar speeding fine (true story).

We regularly live 'in the passions of our flesh, following the desires of flesh and senses' (Eph. 2:3, NRSV; see ch. 9 on 'flesh'). Again, the objection isn't that people are attracted to good things such as food, sex, pleasure or belonging. It's rather that *we bank everything* on these goods, and then fall prey to such beliefs about scarcity that we become 'captives of various passions and pleasures, living in malice and envy, hateful, detesting one another' (Titus 3:3).

Christianity challenges and confronts these addictions. It interrogates how we express our loves. People therefore accuse Christianity of opposing desire itself; but that charge won't stick to Christianity's founder, Jesus Christ. He's frequently moved to action by powerful compassion; he looks at people, then responds to them in love (Mark 19:25); he 'fervently desires' to eat a last Passover with his friends (Luke 22:15). Jesus had a fully functioning emotional world. Augustine observed that 'good and evil men alike feel desire, fear and joy' but that 'the good feel these emotions in a good way, and the bad feel them in a bad way, just as the will of men may be righteous or perverse'.[8] Jesus is this kind of good man. His emotions power an overall human 'package' that's good. He really does love what's good. We glimpse such moments in each other:

---

8. Ibid., p. 596 (§14.9).

- We're desperate for our missing child or boyfriend to reappear. We want a relationship to find its way from tortured pain into peace and affection. We want to save the last few of some species of frog or tiger. We strive passionately to see a disease banished, an excluded person cared for or for a nation's corrupt bureaucracy to change.

The task of genuine ethical enquiry, then, will include the identification of goods we've missed and are failing to love, and the articulation of the loves we pursue and defend. We cannot begin to answer ethical questions until we have some conception of how our longings interact with our ethical judgments.

We may even begin to find our loves are not set in stone. We move in a culture that imagines our loves to define who we are. On this view to change what we love is impossible or unthinkable.[9] But perhaps our loves *can* change, over time. Perhaps we can begin to love what we didn't care about, and hate or grieve over whatever threatens it. We might begin to see why someone's view of what's right is worth our love (e.g. biodiversity, justice, loyalty, constructive efficiency, sexual purity). We may even find that we begin to love people whom we thought were unlovable. We may find ourselves defending and fighting for people and principles others have abandoned.

Christianity challenges our loves in these kinds of ways. Oddly, those of us who've lived through this challenge wouldn't have it any other way. We've caught the aroma of love that comes 'from a pure heart, a good conscience, and a sincere faith' (1 Tim. 1:5). In other words, we catch a whiff of what it was like for Jesus to think, feel and act.

And we like it.

Further reading

* Elliott, Matthew, *Feel: The Power of Listening to Your Heart* (Carol Stream, Ill.: Tyndale House, 2008).
** Elliott, Matthew, *Faithful Feelings: Emotion in the New Testament* (Leicester: IVP, 2005).
** Roberts, Robert Campbell, *Spiritual Emotions: A Psychology of Christian Virtues* (Grand Rapids: Eerdmans, 2007).

---

9. See the brief comment on *emotional essentialism* below, p. 198.

8. SYSTEMS OF INCLUSION

In Part 2 we're considering some generally unacknowledged 'undertows' in human experi-
ence. We're often unaware of them, but they have a dramatic effect on how we think ethics
works and upon our practices. This chapter is about our need for social connection –
another good desire that can ruin us.

At what point did you become a 'social' being? Of course, none of us can
remember such a time. We're each born into networks of human relationships, and our lives mainly consist of a constant interplay between others and
ourselves. People sometimes live 'solo' for a time, but most people interact
with others most of the time. We call this fundamental aspect of humanity
our *sociality*.

If someone points at and laughs at us in a group, a deep reflex surges a red
blush to our skin. Whistling is contagious: within seconds we echo someone's
whistle without thinking. Our clothing often has more to do with the habits
of a wider group than with climate. In each case, social interaction is the major
trigger for what we do. These and many other effects happen because we're
'hard-wired' to interact with others. Every waking moment several parts of
our brain monitor our interactions with the groups around us, and adjust our
actions accordingly.

Oddly though, this constant element of our lives usually drifts into unawareness. We imagine ourselves to be ruggedly individual, choosing and

planning our destinies as if we're not materially and mentally dependent upon those who surround us. Even more amazingly, the study of ethics generally fails to reckon with the complexities inherent in our sociality. Many approaches to ethics (such as the forms of ethical 'reductionism' we saw in ch. 1) assume we're each a free and rational agent. They picture us each making independent, logical choices. The main argument then becomes which approach generates the most logical choice. Similarly, *social ethics* (where we consider how groups should live well together) imagines free, logical and independent people gathering and contracting some ethical agreements that will enable the well-being of all. In this way, it's claimed, a society is forged, as if individuals *chose* sociality.

But these are the silliest of conceits. The influence of others upon us is always quite evident. We're not really very free. Our desires, including our desire to belong, are so powerful that we're often not very rational or logical (unless we admit that emotions have their own logic, ch. 7). And the notion that we somehow *create* society through systems of agreement is plainly absurd. (As Bertrand de Jouvenel once remarked, theories of 'social contract' must be the views of men without familial connections, 'who must have forgotten their own childhood'.[1]) The groups around us assist and confound our ethical judgments. Groups don't just act like individuals. They are not individuals writ large and they're not simply the sum of individuals. If I put myself into a group, I'll *change*.

Groups can exhibit collective virtues (ch. 30) such as generosity and mutual care, friendliness or concern for other communities. Groups can foster creative synergy, problem-solving and originality. In a minority stand, a smaller group resists the majority and gradually carries everyone with them (as when Wilberforce and his circle took down slavery; or as when a small group of Australian politicians opposed their party and sacrificed their careers to end draconian government policies against refugees). People find new courage in groups to enable them to do hard things they wouldn't do alone (such as preaching about Christ, or caring for the marginalized). Groups can become hives of cooperative, gift-based service that organize events, protect and improve environments or feed entire populations. So when I go on to list several ways in which groups can make us bad, my intention isn't to attack our sociality as such. That would be as pointless as attacking any other aspect of our created being. We can gratefully accept our sociality as good.

But *every group we ever join becomes a school of moral formation*. Every kind of

---

1. Bertrand de Jouvenel, *The Pure Theory of Politics* (Cambridge: Cambridge University Press, 1963), p. 45.

social inclusion we give ourselves to or find ourselves in – friendships, work-places, universities, corporations, political parties, professional organizations, Internet forums and states – will expect us to love as it loves (ch. 7). They'll package these loves as rules to keep, rights to uphold, values to promote and results to work for, all reified in the language of the group. If we're not alert to this process, we simply undergo this moral formation. Modern Westerners like to pretend that families, childhood schools and religious organizations are the only groups that attempt to form us morally. I deny that conceit. *All* groups morally form us if we let them. I expose myself to change whether I join a university, a professional society or a church.

Sadly, we clearly see the moral effects of groups upon individuals when groups make people bad. Army units, lynch mobs and political parties can enable uses of violence that most individuals wouldn't consider alone. (The soldiers involved in the My Lai massacre of civilians during the Vietnam War cannot account for their complicity that day.) Groups can exhibit conform-ism, illicit compliance to authority and mass stupidity in a phenomenon often referred to as *groupthink*. (Groupthink nurtured Nick Leeson's destruction of Barings Bank, the ludicrous accounting procedures that inflated then collapsed Enron, and the degrading practices seen at Abu Ghraib prison in Iraq.) Groups can exhibit 'collective sins' such as pride, greed, carelessness and neglect. (Church groups often use self-aggrandizing rhetoric, or pursue grandiose building projects, that they wouldn't condone for an individual member.) As a small tangent, I'll now share five different excursions into the negative effects of groups. I'm saddened yet fascinated by each one.

1. In the 1950s, social psychologist Solomon Asch placed lone volunteers in one of several groups, each of which included seven others, to perform a simple perception test. The volunteer thought the other seven were also volunteers, and was naive to the fact that Asch had rigged a unanimous majority. When asked which of a set of three lines was longest, the seven would brashly give an obviously wrong answer. (In Asch's control groups, everyone answered quietly on paper.) Asch was surprised at how easily the naive individual would simply agree with the majority. There were almost no wrong answers from the control groups, but one third of naive subjects gave wrong answers in the rigged groups. When pressured to change, only one in four subjects held out against the majority.[2] In even a tiny task with

---

2. Solomon E. Asch, 'Effects of Group Pressure Upon the Modification and Distortion of Judgments', in *Groups, Leadership and Men: Research in Human Relations*, ed. Harold Guetzkow (New York: Russell & Russell, 1963), pp. 181–182, 185–186.

unknown people, we've a strong desire to conform to the opinions of a group.

2. Authority magnifies the effect. In Stanley Milgram's frightening 1963 experiment, volunteers asked an unseen 'learner' questions. The volunteer gave the learner an increasing electric shock for each wrong answer. A white-coated 'researcher' sat behind the volunteer. Volunteers thought it was all an experiment in education, but the setup was rigged. The learner was an actor, the shock was a fake, and the researcher was actually studying the volunteer. Learners often answered wrongly, and the researcher told volunteers to deliver ever-harsher electric shocks. Learners would complain, yell and moan; volunteers would query the researcher whether to continue; but the white-coated researcher simply intoned, 'The experiment must continue.' So continue it did. Volunteers escalated the (fake) shocks to near lethal levels. Milgram instructed learners to cry out, to claim heart trouble, to plead for freedom; yet the volunteers still obeyed the researcher. The preference to comply with malevolent authority deeply disturbed Milgram. 'A substantial proportion of people do what they're told to do, irrespective of the content of the act and without limitations of conscience, so long as they perceive that the command comes from a legitimate authority.'[3]

3. Philip Zimbardo's 1971 Stanford Prison Experiment used a mock prison to create a realistic incarceration scenario. Young volunteers became 'prisoners' or 'guards'. Within hours, guards began bullying, intimidating and humiliating prisoners using behaviours that rapidly escalated in intensity over the next few days. Prisoners quickly lost the will to resist. But the situation did not drift out of control solely due to the behaviour of the young men. Every *older* person associated with the scenario – Zimbardo himself, the parents of the young men involved and even a priest – became so swept up in it that they did not think to question, challenge or stop the behaviour of the guards. Zimbardo's fiancée came to the situation later and saw it for what it was, and only her intervention enabled Zimbardo to snap out of 'groupthink' and end the experiment. The experience so disturbed him that he took nearly three decades to write about it.[4] Zimbardo draws parallels between what he saw at Stanford and the events of Abu Ghraib.

4. German academic Elisabeth Noelle-Neumann has studied the *bandwagon*

---

3. Stanley Milgram, *Obedience to Authority* (London: Pinter & Martin, 1997), pp. 205, 206.

4. Philip Zimbardo, *The Lucifer Effect* (London: Rider, 2007). Online: <http://www.lucifereffect.com> (accessed 28 Jan. 2010).

effect, where many suddenly and unpredictably switch to one side or the other just before an election. She observed how highly attuned we are to diffuse attitudes that accumulate to form 'public opinion', and concludes that 'individuals experience fear of isolation continuously'.[5] Because of this fear of isolation, we constantly try to assess the climate of opinion and censor our public behaviour – particularly our expressions or concealments of opinion. Noelle-Neumann calls this process 'the spiral of silence'.

5. When Jewish philosopher Hannah Arendt attended the trial of Nazi war criminal Adolf Eichmann, she sought to discover the nub, the essence, the core of evil. What would make a man so efficiently able to draw up timetables for trains bearing hundreds of thousands of Jews to their deaths? To her horror, Eichmann's reasons were as bland as those that drive us. He wanted to belong, and to advance in his career by impressing friends and superiors. She journeys into the heart of darkness, merely to discover the corrupted preoccupation of social impulse that drives us all. Her awful conclusion gradually dawns on her, of 'the fearsome, word-and-thought-defying *banality of evil*'.[6]

All of these examples highlight the way groups become schools of moral formation. They're the tip of the iceberg. A vast amount of research in several disciplines now studies how others affect and shape us (e.g. sociology, social psychology, social anthropology, social neuroscience, cultural studies and marketing). The ancient world also frankly observed this theme.

The biblical authors note several classic moments of group behaviour. A civil war in early Israel pivots on a point of group pride. It turns out that members of the warring tribes pronounced differently the insignificant Hebrew word *šibbolet* (meaning 'grain' or 'stream'). It was the only way to tell friend from foe, yet sufficed to enable one group to kill the other (Judg. 12:1–6). This episode has become an archetype of how easily people will use an insignificant group-marker to drive bullying, persecution and division.

For me, the most salient Old Testament reflections on group behaviour and influence appear in its wisdom literature. The call to avoid false inclusion introduces the entire psalter:

---

5. Elisabeth Noelle-Neumann, *The Spiral of Silence*, 2nd ed. (Chicago: University of Chicago Press, 1993), p. 202.

6. Hannah Arendt, *Eichmann in Jerusalem: A Report on the Banality of Evil*, rev. and enl. (Harmondsworth: Penguin, 1977; originally publ. New York: Viking, 1964), p. 252; emphasis original.

How happy is the man
who does not follow the advice of the wicked,
or take the path of sinners,
or join a group of mockers!
(Ps. 1:1)

Psalmists wrestle with the tempting yet terrifying groupthink of wickedness
(e.g. Pss 2:1–3; 3:1–2; 26:4–5; 64:1–6; 94:3–7; 141:4), and Proverbs teaches
how to discern the best and worst sociality:

The one who walks with the wise will become wise,
but a companion of fools will suffer harm.
(Prov. 13:20) (Compare also Prov. 17:17 and Eccl. 4:8–12 to Prov. 22:25–26 and 28:7.)

We see remarkable moments of 'groupthink' among Jesus' twelve disciples, as when they bicker about greatness, and then wish destruction upon
a village (Luke 9:46, 52–56). Episodes of crowd caprice are also recorded,
where a group's interest in Jesus morphs into menacing hostility (Luke
19:36–40; 23:18–21; John 6:24, 41–42, 52, 60, 66). As the early church emerges,
it's affected from within and without by a variety of group dynamics: ethnic
friction (Acts 6:1), politico-religious envy (Acts 13:44–45) and even a wryly
observed instance of riot behaviour (Acts 19:28–29, 32). In an emerging discussion about the nature of freedom, the apostle Peter buckles under peer
pressure (Gal. 2:11–13), just as his fear of others and his need for inclusion
around a fire had previously caused him to deny Christ (Luke 22:54–62).

Paul notices the way groups give each other permission and courage to
practise and promote greed, envy, murder, deceit, slander, arrogance and
other patterns we call 'vices' (ch. 30). Groups endorse and reify what God
condemns (Rom. 1:29–32). Then, as now, people were unaware of the effects
of groups upon them, so Paul warns 'don't let anyone lead you astray', adding
an ancient proverb for good measure: 'Bad company corrupts good ways'
(1 Cor. 15:33, NJB).[7]

---

7. The New Jerusalem Bible numbers the verse as v. 34. When these translators
   render the Greek word *ethos* as 'ways', they recall the ancient origins of our word
   'ethics'. An *ethos* was a set of habits or patterns of life, whether good or bad. Other
   modern translations render the verse as bad company corrupting good 'morals' or
   'character'. These are higher-order concepts, representing the sum of a person's
   'ways'. Our 'ways' coagulate into settled patterns and habits of action and feeling

These moments highlight the Bible's consistent recognition that we're deeply social beings. God's creation of an 'image' of himself consists in the creation of a (male and female) 'them' (Gen. 1:27); and in the complementary creation account, the only blot on an excellent creation is a lone human who needs another (Gen. 2:18). These verses are important for the Bible's story arc (ch. 19) on marriage (ch. 37). They also highlight human sociality and have implications for singleness (ch. 36). When we discover that the Godhead consists of three Persons who dwell in unity, some wonder if that community is the key respect in which humanity is in God's image. (Here I touch on a controversy among theologians, for neither should we imagine the Godhead as some easy equivalent of good human society.) Sociality is one of human-ity's best and most exciting features. But according to the Bible's story arc, it becomes corrupted, warped and ruined. The fourth-century theologian Augustine observes how 'the desire to be feared or loved by other men, simply for the pleasure that it gives'[8] then shape-shifts into temptations that con-stantly confront him. Like us all, he experienced the problem from childhood. He reflects on the incident (mentioned above) where he and some friends stole pears that he neither liked nor wanted. He recalls their

> friendship of a most unfriendly sort, bewitching my mind in an inexplicable way. For the sake of a laugh, a little sport, I was glad to do harm and anxious to damage another; and that without thought of profit for myself or retaliation for injuries received! And all because we are ashamed to hold back when others say 'Come on! Let's do it!'[9]

But this kind of false inclusion ultimately shapes his adult life, in a career dominated by social expectations. 'I was preparing a speech in praise of the Emperor,' he confesses, 'including that it should include a great many lies which would certainly be applauded by an audience who knew well enough how far from the truth they were. My ambitions', he continues, 'had placed a load of misery on my shoulders and the further I carried it the heavier it became' – until, walking along the road one day, he passes a drunken beggar. With a shock Augustine realizes that the beggar isn't stuck in a cloying, grasp-

---

     – the 'virtues' and 'vices' that could also be called our 'morals'. 'Character' is the overall 'summary' of us that emerges from our virtues and vices (ch. 30).

8. Augustine, *Confessions*, tr. R. S. Pine-Coffin (Harmondsworth: Penguin, 1961), p. 244 (§10.36).

9. Ibid., p. 52 (§2.9).

ing network of distorted inclusion. He's happier and freer than Augustine is.[10]

I find the most masterful treatment of these distortions in the work of the English literary academic and Christian apologist C. S. Lewis. He describes our 'quest for the Inner Ring'[11] – the longing to socialize with circles of people who currently exclude us. In one story, young Mark Studdock has begun work at 'Bracton College', and longs for acceptance into its various inner circles. Eventually he becomes involved in a plot by the National Institute for Controlled Experiments (NICE) to deliver Britain over to eugenics, involuntary sterilization, ethnic cleansing and fascism. But Studdock's *inner compulsion to be on the inside* is what erodes him, not the programmes themselves.

'Of all the passions,' says Lewis, this 'passion for the Inner Ring is most skilful in making a man who is not yet a very bad man do very bad things.'[12] These rings are very informal: only a particular slang and a certain style of conversation mark those who are 'in' and those who are not. But they control people through the lure of inclusion and the threat of exclusion. Before long a cycle has captured us: envy at others' belonging, an aching yearning to belong, exultation when we're accepted, then boredom, and envy of the *next* ring. The cycle can destroy us, because the promise of inclusion usually includes a subtle challenge to our morality, all 'disguised as a triviality and sandwiched between two jokes'. Later the demand will be 'something a little further from the rules . . . but all in the jolliest, friendliest spirit. It may end in a crash, a scandal, and penal servitude: it may end in millions, a peerage and giving the prizes at your old school. But you'll be a scoundrel.'[13]

'My main purpose', Lewis concludes, 'is simply to convince you that this desire is one of the great permanent mainsprings of human action.'[14] This

---

10. Ibid., p. 118 (§6.6).

11. For a more detailed account of Lewis's thought about 'The Inner Ring', see Andrew J. B. Cameron, 'C. S. Lewis – Inner Circles and True Inclusion', in *The Trials of Theology*, ed. Andrew J. B. Cameron and Brian S. Rosner (Fearn, Ross-shire: Christian Focus, 2010).

12. C. S. Lewis, 'The Inner Ring', in *Essay Collection*, ed. Lesley Walmsley (London: HarperCollins, 2000), p. 319. Online: <http://faculty.millikin.edu/~moconner/in150/lewis2.html> (accessed 15 July 2010). For the rise and fall of Studdock, see C. S. Lewis, 'That Hideous Strength', in *The Cosmic Trilogy* (London: Pan, 1990).

13. Ibid., pp. 318–319.

14. Ibid., p. 318.

need to belong will drive everything we do, if we let it, and every ring we need to belong to *will* become *our school of moral formation.*

These systems of false inclusion surround us. We think they set us free, but they bind and diminish us. One of my hobbies is to read about the last days of Enron, the gigantic Houston energy company that collapsed in 2001. I picture myself among the throngs of people both inside and outside the company, its brash confidence and faux strength fooling everyone. I wonder what it would take to see through the groupthink that suppurated through every floor, branch and unit. I shudder, because I cannot imagine myself seeing differently from everyone else. How can we become free of this undertow – this subtle capacity of a group to form us morally? We cannot ever evade our intrinsic sociality.

But when Asch added a *second* naive subject in his rigged groups, the number of wrong answers they gave dropped to only 5–10%. There's a hint in this: we can only overcome false and distorted inclusions with the power of a better one.

So as this book unfolds, I'll describe where our yearning for inclusion can find a better home (chs. 12–14), and where we can begin to participate in a different school of moral formation (chs. 18, 25, 34). For, according to Christian thought about ethics, the *only* hope of seeing differently is to side with someone who always saw differently, and who wasn't swept up in the groupthink of those around him. Yet he remained so socially connected and involved that he modelled a new way to a sound sociality. He offers a new, true inclusion (ch. 14).

I don't mean that by siding with him we become immune from false inclusions. I'll persistently repeat that Christians remain flawed and limited, and prone to many failures. But even so, this book is about beginning to find a better way to be included.

Further reading

** Arendt, Hannah, *Eichmann in Jerusalem: A Report on the Banality of Evil*, rev. and enl. (Harmondsworth: Penguin, 1977; originally publ. New York: Viking, 1964).
** McLean, Bethany, and Peter Elkind, *Smartest Guys in the Room: The Amazing Rise and Scandalous Fall of Enron* (New York: Penguin, 2003).
** O'Donovan, Oliver M. T., *Common Objects of Love: Moral Reflection and the Shaping of Community* (Grand Rapids: Eerdmans, 2002).

9. 'FLESH'

In Part 2 we're considering some generally unacknowledged 'undertows' in human experience. We're often unaware of them, but they have a dramatic effect on how we think ethics works and upon our practices. This chapter introduces a biblical term, 'flesh'. Without denigrating our embodied material existence, this term describes how we commonly live as if desire and inclusion are all that matter.

Most respectable modern thought about humanity uses a standard approach. The human sciences – psychology, economics, cultural anthropology, politics and myriad other investigations into personal and social functioning – examine us in terms, say, of the choices we make in order to be happy, or in terms of what enabled our ancestors to survive in our ancient origins, or of what makes our groups function best. There are plenty of disagreements, but when we set foot on a university campus today, we find that humanity apparently consists only in the bodies and brains of individuals, their collectives, and the processes and practices arising from these. These views of humanity focus on our straightforward instincts, thoughts, desires and social inclusions (chs. 7–8).

At its best, this way of watching humanity is entirely defensible. Science watches the relationships between things, describes what makes one thing lead to another, and attempts to make helpful generalizations about these observations. Human sciences need be no different. We do have bodies, brains and collectives; we do have an intricate relationship with the non-human material order; and these result in various desires, behaviours and modes of organization. It's helpful to describe and generalize the interactions arising from this complexity.

Imperceptibly, however, we cross from this method of observation into the belief that *we need nothing else* to understand how to be human. The scientist who observes what we *do* then generates and imposes upon us some final theory of what humans *are*. Important aspects of ourselves become 'totalized' to become the *only* aspects of ourselves that matter. The biblical authors have a name for this conclusion. They often speak of 'flesh'.[1]

The basic architecture of 'flesh' is good. In the Old Testament, 'flesh' encompasses the needs of our bodies and brains, including our deeply felt emotions and our longings to belong. The term affirms our fragile but wonderful mode of being. Likewise, the New Testament authors gladly receive our embodied life on the planet and our creaturely cohabitation with the material order all as the good and precious gift of God. Unlike later Greek thinkers, they have no objection to our material life, even despite the regular sufferings that led other Greeks to condemn 'flesh' as a problem. Christ's physical resurrection emphasizes the goodness of embodied life.

But the New Testament authors hold that it's incomplete to think of 'flesh' as all there is to humanity; and it becomes evil to live as if 'flesh' is all there is to humanity. They speak of regarding humanity 'according to the flesh', which seems to involve looking no further than what's 'primal', 'natural' or 'to be expected' from our physical being. I think that they would say that our totalized modern accounts view humanity 'according to the flesh'. They preferred to view humanity a second way: 'according to the Spirit' (ch. 17).

In two major extended discussions, the apostle Paul contrasts these two ways of viewing humanity, and the lives that spring from each (Rom. 8:1–38; Gal. 5:15 – 6:10). The first discussion asserts that 'the mind-set of the flesh is death, but the mind-set of the Spirit is life and peace. For the mind-set of the flesh is hostile to God because it does not submit itself to God's law, for it is unable to do so' (Rom. 8:5–6). This negative assessment sounds harsh, but

---

1. This English word simplifies a cluster of ancient biblical words. Note also that the NIV translation usually uses the phrase 'sinful nature' instead of 'flesh'. This phrase protects us from the conclusion that the biblical authors hated the body or the creation. But it also creates the unhelpful impression that 'sin' comes from some abstract principle other than simply from our short-sighted loves, including our need to belong (see main text following).

Paul is really only observing two different kinds of awareness. In the mindset of 'flesh', our bodily and social desires become our way of engaging with what surrounds us. Naturally, we resist any interrogation of these desires.

His second discussion colourfully portrays the patterns of action and feeling (ch. 30) that arise when life is lived as mere 'flesh':

> Now the works of the flesh are obvious: sexual immorality, moral impurity, promiscuity, idolatry, sorcery, hatreds, strife, jealousy, outbursts of anger, selfish ambitions, dissensions, factions, envy, drunkenness, carousing, and anything similar. (Gal. 5:19–21)

The depiction is a generalization. Those who view humanity as 'flesh' sometimes act well. But Paul is making a deeper main point: that when we make the instincts of the body, brain and social inclusion the sum total of being human, we're taken into a range of self-interested behaviours that seem deeply and convincingly good to us.

Our sexual thoughts and feelings are obvious candidates for totalizing. It's easy to live stretches of our life as if sex is what we're here for, so that its pursuit justifies and explains much of what we do. Many believe that 'flesh' is a prudish code word for sex. However, in the list above 'flesh' mainly gives rise to *social* malfunctions such as hatred, jealousy and envy, selfish ambition and factionalism, outbursts of anger and drunkenness (ch. 28). In these failures, our basic need for social connectedness (ch. 8) has spiralled out of control in a variety of ways.

Yet all the behaviours listed above *can* be justified by reference to human loves and collectives – by reference, that is, to 'flesh'. Envy helpfully creates competitive markets. Ambition enables us to find our potential. Multiple sexual partners are a lifestyle choice for those who want to show their love. Factions are merely like-minded communities banded together to protect against others. Black magic is simply a nice expression of human diversity. Drunkenness (ch. 28) is our reward for a hard week's work, and our outbursts of anger (ch. 28) protect our interests and identity. Such justifications flow easily.

What I've been calling our 'unawareness' in Part 2, our tangled desires (ch. 7) and systems of inclusion (ch. 8), is summarized in this language of 'flesh'. Three concerns follow.

First, it may seem that despite our claim to celebrate material and embodied life, Christians really only attack human desires and social inclusions. But they're not the true target. It isn't bad that people have desires and need to belong. Indeed, immediately after the vices listed above there appears a list of virtues, each laced with desire and belonging ('love, joy, peace, patience, kindness, goodness, faithfulness, gentleness and self-control', Gal. 5:22–23, NIV). Rather, the target is *our lack of moral imagination* (chs. 2, 10), where we construe goodness solely based on our desires and social inclusions. According to Christianity, our only way to address this unawareness becomes the discovery of *an entirely new identity* 'in Christ' (ch. 14).

For (secondly), if we condemn 'flesh' it isn't obvious what people might do or be instead. What else could humanity possibly be, other than our instincts for survival, our choices to be happy, and the collectives we share? But if Jesus reveals *truest* humanity, then perhaps we discover how to be human *mainly* by observing him. Observations of other bodies, brains and collectives may not be a reliable guide. For Jesus inhabited his flesh beautifully, and enables the second way to view humanity ('according to the Spirit', ch. 17). He gives back to humanity the best of human desires and social inclusions.

But (third) religious Christians can sound superior, as though 'flesh' only condemns *other people's* desires and social inclusions. But paradoxically, Paul's discussions claim that even *religiously motivated rule keeping* is another self-interested activity of 'flesh'. He attacks legal pieties, which enable no exit from the mindset of 'flesh'. They don't enable love, joy, peace, patience, kindness, goodness, faithfulness, gentleness and self-control. 'Against such things there is no law,' he sarcastically asserts against those who try to curb 'flesh' by use of rules (Gal. 5:23).

Christians cannot piously evade or transcend the thoughts and practices of 'flesh'. We'll discover that churches are not places where good people gather (ch. 34). Those who identify with Christ take time to catch up with their new identity (p. 98), and constantly experience a 'flip-flop' between the 'flesh' and 'Spirit' ways of inhabiting their humanity. 'The flesh desires what is against the Spirit, and the Spirit desires what is against the flesh; these are opposed to each other, so that you don't do what you want' (Gal. 5:17). In this passage and in others like it, the New Testament authors may be in dialogue with the ancient Greek notion of *akrasia*, the perplexing human experience of double-mindedness. Those who identify themselves as 'in Christ' (ch. 14) often know that horrible experience where we say, 'I don't know what came over me; I became someone else; I couldn't believe what I was doing.' (See my account of my rage, ch. 28.) Such utterances don't always seek to evade responsibility. They point to my amazement at how convincing it seemed when my rage, lust, jealousy or exultation propelled and justified some action, even while I was morally culpable for it.

The majesty of the Christian gospel is that even at our worst, and when we need him most, we may safely identify ourselves as being 'in Christ'.

But obsessions and false belonging regularly come over Christians, and to pretend otherwise is an arrogant fantasy that insults our neighbour and belittles Christ's death (ch. 15). We're constantly called away from the conceit that we've grown out of our 'flesh'.

All humanity, whether Christian or not, is deeply predisposed to function according this deep mode of unawareness, the 'flesh'. According to the New Testament authors, the only solution is to *participate in a rescue* from this 'body of death' (Rom. 7:24).[2] This book begins to describe how we may go about this participation.

Further reading

** Deenick, Karl, 'Who Is the "I" in Romans 7:14–25?', *Reformed Theological Review* 69.2 (2010), pp. 119–130.

** Ten Elshof, Gregg, *I Told Me So: Self-Deception and the Christian Life* (Grand Rapids: Eerdmans, 2009).

*** Jewett, Robert, *Paul's Anthropological Terms: A Study of their Use in Conflict Settings* (Leiden: Brill, 1971), ch. 3.

*** Wolff, Hans Walter, *Anthropology of the Old Testament*, tr. Margaret Kohl (London: SCM, 1974).

---

2. Some will be aware that Rom. 7:7–25 powerfully addresses the experience of *akrasia*. But I have not majored on this passage due to a long-running disagreement over whose experience Paul describes: his own as a representative Christian; his own as representative of someone prior to their identification with Christ; or, more poetically, Israelite society. He may even be describing a human experience that crosses all those categories. Those not involved in this debate can find it irritating, but there are valid reasons for it. I simply thought it wisest not to pivot anything on this passage, even though it is significant. For a most helpful overview and conclusion (that the 'I' is the Christian Paul), see the article by Deenick in 'Further reading'.

10. COMPLEXITY

In Part 2 we're considering some generally unacknowledged 'undertows' in human experience. We're often unaware of them, but they have a dramatic effect on how we think ethics works and upon our practices. This chapter outlines a different kind of unawareness, where we fail to reckon with the complexity of ethics. When we accept that complexity, we can begin to grow our moral imagination.

We've seen (chs. 3–6) that ethics has something to do with rules and codes, rights, values and results. (There are other ways to approach ethics, but these are the most popular.) I've suggested that each has its place, but that none can suffice to explain everything about right and wrong. We've also seen the undertow of our desires, and of the effects that groups have on us (chs. 7–8).

If I'm right to suggest that each of these should find a place in any account of ethics, then ethics is complex. But people are often unaware of ethical complexity, and our approach to ethics often relies upon some reductionist scheme (ch. 1).

The complexity of ethics adds to our cognitive and emotional load. Sometimes I cannot bear to hear any more about biodiversity loss, or the plight of the global poor. Fights about who should divorce, marry, remarry or adopt children leave me feeling sad and drained. Social policies (e.g. for tolerance in a multiculturally diverse society, or for managing agricultural landscapes altered by changing climate patterns) are so hard to fathom, and finding justice is so hard. It's no wonder we tend only to focus on our immediate surroundings. We feel we can handle that.

But pretending away complexity does no one any favours. Reductionist approaches smooth out complexity, but can leave us blind to what else matters. People with straightforward and clear-cut views of right and wrong have populated some of the worst regimes in history.

This book works on the assumption that we can handle a lot of moral complexity. We already do quite well in other complex areas: swimming, reading, singing, cooking, having friendships (ch. 39), doing science, starting businesses, running governments, and so on. Ethical thinking is complex, because it is *an art of pattern recognition and response*. Since every pattern is a little different, the called-for response will be a little different. We can never quite know what it needs until we get there. An analogy might help to picture what I mean by 'an art of pattern recognition and response'.

I've spent the last few years living with a vegetable gardener. Mary-Anne has not always been a gardener – she's discovered it only in the last few years. She's read and practised a lot of gardening during that time. She knows vastly more than I do, although like anyone with growing expertise, she's quite humble about what she knows and quickly points to what she doesn't know.

Permaculture principles, where complexity is an asset for a garden, have also informed her. I won't attempt to explain these principles, because I know next to nothing about the subject. But I'll point to two aspects of permaculture.

It opposes 'monoculture', where only one crop is grown in an area. Permaculturists know that monoculture temporarily increases yield. But it strips the soil of nutrients, and is a free kick to bugs that feed on the crop without competition or predation. Farmers must handle soil leaching and bug plagues with fertilizer and pesticides, which create other problems. By mixing a variety of crops, permaculturists seek to keep soil nutrients high and bug populations low. The practice reduces the yield, but people still eat and the whole system is more sustainable over time.

Permaculture gardeners become adept at pattern recognition. All gardeners have this skill, but arguably the complexity of a permaculture garden heightens it. Each garden is almost like a small 'jungle', where the well-being of species is interdependent. Soil nutrients, bug populations, sunshine levels, and so on, are addressed by introducing something new to the garden, or by reducing something a little bit. The gardener can be quite articulate about some of these decisions. She bases others on hunches, derived from experience and 'tacit knowledge' that can be hard to articulate.

What has all this to do with ethics? I find it a helpful image to describe what goes on when we reflect and deliberate about what to do.

When permaculturists oppose monoculture (a fight I don't want to get into!), they oppose its reductionism. Of course, monoculture does something right, for it grows plants and people are fed. But it isn't a key to unlock every agricultural door. In the same way, the ethical reductions we've seen (ch. 1) may each articulate a truth and have a place; but when pressed into service alone, each can create problems. Also, these ethical reductions can fail to reckon with the other undertows of desire and social influence. Good ethical pattern recognition needs to consider these hidden forces.

Ethical complexity requires us to think more like a gardener than a solver of a mathematical problem. It's more like caring for a child than advancing a political cause. It's like keeping an overall eye on our health, or keeping a house and yard liveable, or promoting a healthy culture in a club or neighbourhood. Each case has many inputs, considerations and possible responses.

We describe the 'jungle-like' nature of each new scenario with a technical term, the *moral field*. The moral field is the particular space we're in while thinking through what's right or wrong. Scenarios include moral aspects that are not novel (hence the need for education and the wisdom of others). But the *particular combination* before us appears for the first time in history. A jungle botanist becomes ever more skilled in distinguishing what's recurring from what's new; so does a permaculturist in her garden; and so need we, in each moral field we encounter.

If the concept of a moral field helps us to see what about *our habitat* makes ethics complex, a German concept, *gestalt*, helps us to see what *within ourselves* adds to make ethics complex. *My gestalt is my inner interpretation of whatever is happening to me.* Gestalt refers to the way we each experience our world.

What goes on inside me interacts with whatever is around me, to form my gestalt. We each have a flow of emotions and thoughts that weave into our experiences of the external habitat, and with our responses. Various good things are on offer. We navigate social situations and influences. Threats need avoiding. On it goes, and our thoughts and emotions engage with this habitat in an interwoven *totality* – a gestalt. It's hard to analyse and explain because it *is* an interwoven totality, and because most of it lies beyond our immediate attention. The Oxford English Dictionary helpfully describes 'gestalt' as 'a "shape", "configuration", or "structure"' which 'forms a specific whole or unity incapable of expression simply in terms of its parts', much like a melody, as distinct from its individual notes.[1] Our gestalt is the music we make

---

1. *Oxford English Dictionary Second Edition on CD-ROM* (v. 4.0) (Oxford: Oxford University Press, 2009).

of our habitat. It's essential to our consciousness; we act in response to it; yet the bulk of it lies in our unawareness. We've already addressed a gestalt that operates primarily according to what I want and how I may belong – that is, according to the 'flesh' (ch. 9).

Some people never question their gestalt; they simply experience it, and proceed based on whatever then seems obvious. But ethics, I suggest, is about *learning to recognize more elements both of the moral field and of our gestalt awareness of it.* We can become better at navigating moral complexity when we enhance our moral pattern recognition skills. Our gestalt shifts as our moral imagination expands, giving us more to work with for sizing up situations and thinking about how we might handle them.

I'll also suggest that Christianity offers a rich and persuasive new gestalt for the moral fields around us. One biblical author describes Christians as those who have received 'a new birth into a living hope' (1 Pet. 1:3). Reflecting on this 'new birth', theologian Miroslav Volf notices that 'Christians don't come into their social world from outside' but 'are the *insiders* who have diverted from their culture by being born again'. As Christians inhabit their new birth within an existing culture, they ask, 'Which beliefs and practices of the culture that's ours must we reject now that our self has been reconstituted by new birth? Which can we retain? What must we reshape to better reflect the values of God's new creation?'[2] These questions interrogate both the moral field and the gestalt awareness we bring to it. Volf pictures a gradual process of pattern-discernment and response that cannot take place instantly, because the process of examining our culture, and if necessary differentiating ourselves from it, is complex.

The concept of 'new birth into a living hope' highlights the gestalt shift by which we see the whole package of our lives differently. 'New birth' distances us from the desire-based views of those who surround us (1 Pet. 1:14, 18). Instead of transitory lives governed by the onset of death, in the Christian gestalt, Jesus' resurrection (ch. 16) offers a new sort of life, and imports hope into our patterns of reaction to the here and now (1 Pet. 1:3). So a genuinely Christian ethic isn't reducible to a list of rules, rights, values or results. It gives a completely new way to participate in the patterns that surround us. (In Part 4, I'll call this new gestalt a 'unified field', arising from five biblical 'poles', that orients us to moral reality.)

I hope you'll not baulk at the complexity of ethics. I don't mean it's

---

2. Miroslav Volf, 'Soft Difference: Theological Reflections on the Relation Between Church and Culture in 1 Peter', *Ex Auditu* 10 (1994), pp. 18–19.

impenetrable, or only for clever people. I simply mean we travel well when we get real about the infuriatingly, mesmerizingly wonderful complexity of all that surrounds us – including God, who's at the centre of it all.

The biblical authors have a name for coming to terms with the complexity of each moral field we encounter. They call it 'discernment' (p. 312).

11. ARE THE PSYCHOPATHS RIGHT?

In Part 2 we've considered arenas of human experience we're often unaware of, but that have a dramatic effect on how we think ethics works and upon our practices. Although not strictly an aspect of our 'unawareness', there's a question we often fail to consider: how do we know that amoral people (like psychopaths) are not right all along?

In the history of human thought, some long-standing and widely held ideas turn out to be gigantic mistakes. Examples include the idea that human health consists in the balance of four 'humours', or that the human nervous system is powered by 'animal spirits', or that lights in the night sky are carried on a set of revolving, Russian-doll-like 'spheres' around the earth, or that light is carried on a mysterious invisible 'ether'. Christians and atheists think polytheism is another deeply mistaken yet tenacious idea, and atheists say the same of monotheism.

Perhaps it's like this for ethics. Is it just a bad idea? Ethics has been a seductive and long-standing idea – but what if the whole notion is a mistake? What if we've all been hoodwinked and ethics is not a notion that helps us?

Initially, the suggestion seems daft. But consider those we call *sociopaths* (also known as psychopaths). After what we see on television, we might think these people are all serial killers. But serial killers are just a small percentage of sociopaths. Sociopaths are people who, as far as psychologists can tell, experience no empathy toward others. For these people it is of no consequence to steal, hurt or use others as they see fit. They have effectively dismissed any ethical claims upon them. Yet they seem to function well enough. Perhaps sociopaths know something we don't: that ethics is an unnecessary and mistaken concept.

The nineteenth-century German philosopher Friedrich Nietzsche did not focus on sociopaths. But they illustrate some elements of his view. Ethical concepts such as virtue, duty or an impersonal universal good – these, thinks Nietzsche, are 'phantoms, expressions of decline, of the final exhaustion of life'.[1] Nietzsche celebrated *life fully lived*, and, as a romantic, thought emotions should be felt, exalted and unreservedly expressed. Our emotions energize and enhance our lives; but too often ethics stands in the way, straightjacketing us into conformity and repression.

So Nietzsche introduces the now widely held view that each of us should *choose for ourselves* whatever ethical values suit our temperament and enhance our lives. 'A virtue has to be *our* invention,' he declares. 'The profoundest laws of preservation and growth demand . . . that each one of us should devise *his own* virtue, *his own* categorical imperative.' (The *categorical imperative* was philosopher Immanuel Kant's name for a duty applicable to all.) We should no longer imagine ethics as a quest for what's universally true. We should see it as the pursuit of what's joyfully fulfilling. 'A people perishes if it mistakes *its own* duty for the concept of duty in general. An action compelled by the instinct of life has in the joy of performing it the proof it is a *right* action.'

Nietzsche's exultant vision of life's experiences fascinates many. He frees life from the junk and baggage that come with religion or morality, supposedly. This aspect of his writing has come into vogue. But another aspect of his view is less popular. He celebrates those ancient nobles who lived their lives to the limit. Very provocatively, he rejoices in those 'exultant monsters' who committed 'murder, arson, rape and torture', each a 'magnificent *blond beast*' of whom bards will sing of their exploits.[2] These people are not so different from the sociopaths we considered.

On hearing this aspect of his writing, most people recoil. People are quick to observe that society couldn't function if everyone lived like this. They also charge Nietzsche with the Nazi excesses that followed him four decades later. To be fair on Nietzsche, neither charge sticks. He did not want to see chaos

---

1. Friedrich Nietzsche, *The Anti-Christ*, tr. Reginald J. Hollingdale (London: Penguin, 1990), pp. 133–134 (§11), and for quotations following; emphases original.
2. Friedrich Nietzsche, *On the Genealogy of Morality*, ed. Keith Ansell-Pearson, tr. Carol Diethe (Cambridge: University Press, 1994), p. 25 (§1.11); emphasis original.

and anarchy, and would have had no time for the leadership of a failed artist (Hitler) and a myopic chicken farmer (Himmler).

Rather, Nietzsche's ideal society is the ultimate meritocracy. In this society, strength and skill ranks people. Strong warrior nobles rule everyone, the clever serve them and rule the weak and stupid, and the weak and stupid serve all. Notions of ethics, justice and democracy wouldn't dilute and confuse the strength of this society.[3] Its members would simply recognize power.

Humanity often seems to drift into such arrangements, where a powerful despot or dictator rules brutally and does what he or she wants. The weak are enslaved and exploited without compunction. Concepts such as rights, justice or ethics are ignored or mocked. In such societies, this is the obvious way to live. Might really is right – not that those at the top even concern themselves with the notion of right.

Now as you read these paragraphs you probably shake your head and object. But Nietzsche thinks you can do so *only* because somewhere along the line the puny people in the system invented ethical notions to curb the strong. In this way, all morality is a gigantic hoax: a powerful illusion that curbs the strong, invented by weak people who have no other real strength or skill or power.

Christian morality, thinks Nietzsche, is the leading example of this trickery. (Nietzsche was among the first to articulate a now common view that weak priests invented 'sin' in order to peddle 'redemption', all so as to have power over even weaker people.) He thinks Christianity is other-worldly and life denying, causing people to hate their bodies and their passions.[4] As he bitterly describes it, '*so* to live that there is no longer any *meaning* in living: *that* now becomes the "meaning" of life' for the religious person.[5] (Nietzsche is often correct to attack the power of priests and the way religion can suck the life out of people. For the reasons why, I commend the readings by Merold Westphal below.)

Most of us have two contrary responses to Nietzsche's thought.

1. We're deeply attracted to his yearning for vigorous, feelingful lives. We often feel that ethics stultifies the beautiful gift of our emotions. We want to live life to the full and like the thought that we can somehow be in charge of what matters to us, rather than labouring along under someone else's claims about what *should* matter to us.

---

3. Ibid., p. 121 (§3.25).

4. See Nietzsche, *Anti-Christ*, pp. 168, 187–192 (§43 and §§56–58).

5. Ibid., p. 168 (§43); emphasis original. See also pp. 187–192 (§§56–58).

2. But we reject Nietzsche's views about society. Even if Nazism was not Nietzsche's fault, 'How bound in time, how theoretical too, how inexperienced does Nietzsche's romanticizing about wickedness appear today! We've learnt to know it in all its miserableness,' wrote Thomas Mann in 1947, not long after the discovery of the death camps.[6] We hate despotism and tyranny, because we want no 'blond beast' enjoying his life at *our* expense. So our societies generate ever-increasing codes of justice and lists of rights to prevent us hurting each other.

Hence we hate and love ethics, agreeing with Nietzsche even while rejecting him. But what has all this to do with a Christian account of how ethics works? Nietzsche highlights a lot of what happens when Christians, and society, lose track of the Bible's teaching.

Biblical authors hate the way overbearing rules destroy life. For example, there are those who 'depart from the faith' and 'forbid marriage and demand abstinence from foods that God created'. But these were intended 'to be received with gratitude by those who believe and know the truth' (1 Tim. 4:3). Christianity, like Judaism before it, wholeheartedly enjoys the material world, for 'everything created by God is good, and nothing should be rejected if it is received with thanksgiving' (1 Tim. 4:4). 'Every generous act and every perfect gift is from above, coming down from the Father of lights' (Jas 1:17). These authors clearly love their lives, and oppose the meaningless use of morality to prevent joy. They respond to the world's goods with grateful thanks.

But they go beyond Nietzsche's simplistic affirmation of emotion. They perceive that life ceases to be enjoyable when our passions go sour, as when James observes:

> What is the source of the wars and the fights among you? Don't they come from
> the cravings that are at war within you? You desire and do not have. You murder and
> covet and cannot obtain. You fight and war. You do not have because you do not ask.
> You ask and don't receive because you ask wrongly, so that you may spend it on your
> desires for pleasure. (Jas 4:1–3)

We humans need somehow to make better sense of our emotional longings. They enrich our lives beyond measure, yet also threaten to destroy our best life together. The wrong kind of ethics only magnifies our problem:

---

6. Cited in Philippa Foot, 'Nietzsche's Immoralism', in *Nietzsche, Genealogy, Morality*, ed. Richard Schacht (Berkeley: University of California Press, 1994), p. 7.

'Do not handle, Do not taste, Do not touch' . . . All these regulations refer to things
that perish with use; they are simply human commands and teachings. These have
indeed an appearance of wisdom in promoting self-imposed piety, humility, and
severe treatment of the body, but they are of no value in checking self-indulgence.
(Col. 2:21–23, NRSV)

However, Nietzsche's account of the strong ruling the weak is an obvious
way of life quite hard to disprove. Sociopaths, despots, dictators and tyrants
all function quite well. They use what power they have to get whatever they
want. When it all boils down, we seem only to have a hunch and an almost
'blind faith' that they're wrong. Talk of rules, rights, compassion or justice
doesn't dissuade such people. Such talk is only persuasive when we're within
a large group of like-minded others. If we were to place ourselves in the
Somalia, Rwanda or Bosnia of the 1990s, Nietzsche's view would seem self-
evident and incontrovertible. Our 'large group of like-minded others' would
look like castaways on an iceberg in the sun.

It's quite frightening to think that perhaps the sociopaths are correct. Stop
reading for a moment, and pause to think – how would you argue against this
view? What strategy would you use?

A *scientific naturalist* might claim that sociopaths lack some ethically enabling
mental structure that the rest of us possess. A *utilitarian* or a *consequentialist*
might answer that society couldn't function if everyone acted as they do.
A *communitarian* might suggest that society has excluded these people, who
haven't therefore discovered the rewards inherent in sharing with others. A
deontologist might be content to point to the sociopath's flouting of ethical
'standards', 'God's law' or some other code. A *natural law* theorist might claim
that no human can cease to be a moral being in a morally ordered universe,
and that even the sociopath is a moral being of sorts when he lives by the code
of his own survival.

Even so, the existence of sociopathic people at the edge of any discussion
of ethics remains quite disconcerting. For *what if they're right?* No one can
absolutely disprove their way. Perhaps, in all its randomness, evolution has
thrown them up as the next stage of human adaptation, unfettered by the
bonds that hold back the rest of us. Perhaps the planet's destiny is for them
to succeed in enslaving society to their ends. Their survival code may simply
prove that there's no general morality, and that people are finally only wielders
of power.

Christians know just one antidote to the toxin that the strong should rule
the weak. It unfolds in the Bible's unexpected story. The tyrant's settled habit
of thought and action is upset when Jesus Christ, 'being in very nature God',

appears. He 'did not consider equality with God something to be grasped, but made himself nothing, taking the very nature of a servant' (Phil. 2:6–7, NIV). At a stroke, the most powerful Lord of the universe confirms that we're *power-ful* in order to *help* each other. Tyrants, says Jesus, 'lord it over' their subjects; but 'you are not to be like that. Instead, the greatest among you should be like the youngest, and the one who rules like the one who serves' (Luke 22:25–26, NIV).

Tyrant-thinking may seem true enough at first; but a day will come when everyone, including the most powerful, will bow before Jesus (Phil. 2:10–11). There's a marvellous paradox here, as tyrants are powerfully compelled to recognize that Jesus' humble way of life, not their own, is the ultimate truth.

The modern West has forgotten; but it once loved the sound of this alternate vision. Our rules, rights and values are a dim echo of Jesus' total demolition of the pretensions of power.

In Christianity's new gestalt (p. 72), we find the beginnings of joy, and challenge our emotions where they've gone sour. In response to Jesus' upset of human affairs, we begin to rebuild societies where people really do use their power to help others.

In Parts 3–4 we'll consider how Christians think of and act as if Jesus is the central element in reality, including ethical reality.

Further reading

** Banner, Michael C., *Christian Ethics: A Brief History* (Chichester: Wiley-Blackwell, 2009).

** Westphal, Merold, *Suspicion and Faith: The Religious Uses of Modern Atheism* (Grand Rapids: Eerdmans, 1993).

** Westphal, Merold, 'Taking Suspicion Seriously: The Religious Uses of Modern Atheism', *Faith and Philosophy* 4.1 (1987), pp. 26–42.

PART 3 JESUS VERSUS ETHICS

For a long time, scientists studying various forces in the universe (gravity, electromagnetism and various subatomic bonds) tried to do business with each other, but couldn't. It felt as though they should be able to, because forces are forces. But they couldn't get the various forces to 'talk' in the same 'language'. Therefore they sought after a *unified field theory* to explain all the forces in the same language. (I'm told they're getting close.)

Christianity has the same kind of effect for ethics. Rules, rights, values and results all try to contribute something to our moral knowledge, but don't join together very easily. Christianity helps us to interpret these various forms of moral language, and how they're interrelated. The purpose of Parts 3–4 is to outline the main concepts that underpin Christian ethics.

I'll not argue, though, that Christians have a monopoly on all answers. We remain flawed and limited creatures (pp. 52, 68, 151, 173) just like anyone else. But we've received some insights that may help others. (There isn't anything mysterious about how we 'received' them, either. They're on offer to everyone, and are accessible by everyday means.) Jesus Christ is essential to these insights, partly because he shows what a correctly functioning human looks like, and partly because he releases humanity from what's depressing about ethics. He knits things together, enabling us to participate in what surrounds us as we were meant to.

Jesus doesn't merely challenge some of our ethical thinking. He challenges abstract talk about ethics by his *person*, so that according to the Bible the main question becomes not 'Am I living ethically?', but 'How am I responding to Jesus Christ?' On this view ethics springs from Jesus Christ, and attempts to do ethics apart from Jesus become flawed. Part 3 unpacks how Jesus is the key to a unified understanding of our moral reality. They don't call it 'Christianity' for nothing.

12. A CHRIST-POWERED PLANET

In Part 3 we begin to consider how according to Christian thought, ethics springs from Jesus. This chapter shows how, according to the New Testament, Jesus Christ is the centre of all reality.

The authors of the New Testament don't approach reality in the same way we usually do, and don't approach ethics with our starting points.

- They don't state in a reductive formula how to live well (ch. 1).
- They don't reduce life to a series of decisions (ch. 2).
- They don't initially refer to or declare lists of rules (ch. 3).
- They don't begin with a list of rights (ch. 4).
- They don't start by identifying various values (ch. 5).
- They don't measure all actions by their results (ch. 6).

Anyone who's read the New Testament might remember moments where its authors *do* use some of these approaches; but for now, my main point is to observe that they accessed reality and ethics from *a different starting point* than ours. An excerpt shows what I mean, where Jesus is:

the image of the invisible God,
the firstborn over all creation;

because by Him everything was created,
>   in heaven and on earth,
>   the visible and the invisible,
>   whether thrones or dominions
>   or rulers or authorities –
all things have been created through Him and for Him.
He is before all things,
>   and by Him all things hold together.
He is also the head of the body, the church;
>   He is the beginning,
>   the firstborn from the dead,
>   so that He might come to have first place in everything.
For God was pleased to have all His fullness dwell in Him,
>   and through Him
>   to reconcile everything to Himself
>   by making peace through the blood of His cross –
>   whether things on earth or things in heaven.
(The 'Christ hymn' of Col. 1:15–20)

Christ makes God visible, Christ is responsible for creation, and somehow, Christ is making everything better. The words are clear enough. But if we're honest, their meaning is quite strange.

We've come to believe that in a diverse world no one should make such broad and sweeping claims about anyone. It also seems perilous to say that Christ is particularly interested in one particular group, called 'the church'. But a deeper kind of strangeness resides in these words. Imagine one human being doing everything listed:

- unveiling the invisible God
- making everything (including the world's powerful rulers)
- holding everything together, for all time
- mastering human death
- 'making peace' in a broken universe

Those convinced of this description of Christ find it breathtaking. It pictures a 'Christ-powered' planet, where 'everything' and 'all things' find a secure home in one who cares for everything and for all things – including *people like us*, who once were alienated and alone (Col. 1:21–22).

But others have a different reaction. They find the passage weirdly remote, even deserving of mockery. There are two broad reasons for their response.

First, there's our experience of human beings. Plainly, no human we know could match this picture. Therefore (critics conclude), it is ludicrous to imagine anyone matching it. Some therefore confine their attention to Jesus as presented in the Gospels. The best they can say of this passage is that it reflects some later mystical sentiment about Jesus.

Secondly, the 'Christ hymn' clashes with our conceptions of how the planet works:

- We might think of the earth as essentially 'sun-powered'. Orbiting the sun for billions of years, all of its processes (including us) result from the sun's energy. Life evolves and surges along in anarchy. No personal agency shapes anything much. In this story, humanity is just a blip tottering across the planet's surface.
- Or we might think human agency is a force to be reckoned with. The sun brought us this far, but we're now billions of the smartest (and potentially most destructive) animals the world has ever seen. Therefore humanity must now look to its practices, its actions and its leadership for the real story of how the planet runs. On this view the earth is 'human powered' – not in the sense that we supply its origins or its energy, but in the sense that we supply its destiny.

These two views emerge particularly when the 'Christ hymn' of Colossians 1 is raised in discussions of climate change (cf. ch. 40). On the face of it the best news the planet could have is that the one who made the earth continues to hold it together, and is committed to making peace between all its warring factions. He's above every 'throne or dominion or ruler or authority' – a relief to anyone trying to navigate the sectional interests of climate change: governments, scientists, energy lobbyists, green lobbyists, and Western or developing-world consumers. It doesn't follow that Christians necessarily think there's nothing to be done about climate change. As we'll see, whatever matters to Christ, Christians learn to act on; and in this case they do so in the optimistic hope that Christ hasn't abandoned his world.

Yet even so, for some people this 'Christ hymn' is an insult to the climate-change debate. 'This is serious,' they imply with a roll of their eyes. 'It's entirely up to us to fix it,' say those who believe in a human-powered planet. 'As if your Jesus story can make the slightest difference to climate processes,' say those who believe in a sun-powered planet. 'Take it away from here,' they all demand. My point isn't to blast such people for rejecting Christ. Rather, I've highlighted the way modern people access reality. *Our basic stories about reality tend to be human-centred or nature-centred, and in high-stakes discussions* (such as climate change), *these stories quickly emerge.*

In contrast, the New Testament authors thought that the history of Jesus Christ gave the most basic access to reality. That is also the case when they speak of ethics. How to live and what to do emerge as we participate in a 'Christ-powered' planet. I'll outline how this works for ethics in the rest of the book.

But before I do so, I need to say more for those who cannot yet board this train. I want to make some observations to those who find this 'Christ hymn' remote and other-worldly, or weirdly absurd.

The New Testament authors didn't begin as people who believed in a 'Christ-powered' universe. The evidence indicates that they were not under-educated, and could be sceptical and unbelieving. They journeyed through the usual human gestalt (p. 72) of living for pleasures of the moment and for group inclusion (chs. 7–8). They saw and knew brutality, and understood the reality of an oppressive political regime (the Roman Empire) better than anyone. They could easily have imagined the planet as 'sun-powered' or 'human powered'. They could have chosen any of several religious stories on offer.

But *something happened* to them. A particular man intersected their lives in a way that made 'Christ hymns' the thing to write. A 'Christ hymn' like the one in Colossians isn't even thinkable without this man. But once he appeared, and after the initial period of shock had passed, 'Christ hymns' needed to be written in response.

Christians know that claims about Christ, when stated in abstract, sound outlandish. But when we know Jesus' history, they don't. So much about the 'Christ hymn' *can* make sense for those who saw, touched and lived with Jesus. They realize it's hard for those who didn't encounter him, and urgently set about passing on what they saw, touched and heard (e.g. Luke 1:1–4; John 20:29–31; or 1 John 1:1–4).

If the Christ hymn sounds 'other-worldly', it turns out that participation in a 'Christ-powered' planet delivers some 'real-world' results that may appeal to someone who doesn't believe in Christ's lordship. Returning to the New Testament writers' approach to ethics:

- They never rely on a reductionist formula. Yet they regularly distil aspects of moral complexity into digestible principles, aphorisms and sayings.
- They recognize that we must make important decisions. A person's destiny can pivot on some decisions. But they know we're very poor

at making decisions well. They point to God's forgiveness, love and help as the safety net within which to make decisions.

- They don't immediately declare lists of rules, but offer some rules that promote harmony. They also evaluate what makes older rules good (e.g. the Ten Commandments) or bad (e.g. various religious rules).
- They don't list human rights, but emphasize how much each person matters, and speak of our various needs.
- Many of our values wouldn't impress them. But they commend life-affirming patterns and habits of action and feeling that build relationships and create safety (the New Testament's 'virtue lists', ch. 30).
- The results of actions are not their primary criteria of right and wrong. But they're helpfully future-oriented. They know the importance of the effects of our actions upon others. They also know that the *planet's* future should affect how we direct ourselves.

In each case, they're able to arrive at quite fine-grained conclusions about what matters, based on the logic of a 'Christ-powered' planet.

When an idea initially seems strange, *where it leads* becomes a good test for it. The 'Christ-powered' planet includes some very nice destinations.

13. 'FOLLOWING' JESUS

In Part 3 we consider how, according to Christian thought, ethics springs from Jesus. This chapter considers the most obvious way to access Jesus Christ: by 'following' his teachings. It arrives at a surprising conclusion: 'following' Jesus is an essential yet insufficient response to him.

'As he walked along, he saw Levi son of Alphaeus sitting at the tax collector's booth. "Follow me," Jesus told him, and Levi got up and followed him' (Mark 2:14, NIV). Here's the third moment in Mark's account when Jesus simply tells someone to follow, who then follows. These moments are initially quite bizarre.

Take the sheer randomness of the people Jesus asks. He seems simply to stroll along and pick on whomever he sees. He may have had something specific in mind about each of them; we don't really know. But these arbitrary calls seem to express his thinking that *everyone* needs to follow him (cf. Matt. 8:19–22; 16:24; 19:21).

Also, they respond instantly. They simply get up from whatever they're doing and follow. We cannot imagine ourselves doing that with anyone. To leave everything we know, for a stranger, is unthinkable. Apart from what we might lose, how could we trust them?

Around the same time as these episodes, Jesus' teaching was catching people's attention. People were amazed at his 'authority', in contrast to the local 'teachers of the law' (Mark 1:22, NIV). Perhaps that explains the instant response of those who followed. It was an impulse to spend more time with someone who amazed them, in contrast to the staleness of their religious leaders.

In some respects, little has changed. Even people whose lives have been puttering along quite nicely find that everything looks different when they stumble upon Jesus' teaching. People who've had a gutful of religion still 'follow' him today, and for many of them ethics consists in doing whatever he taught. The logic of their position is that since he makes sense about what they do understand, he can be trusted on what they don't. This isn't 'blind faith'; it's more like 'half-seeing faith', which is the kind of trust we always have in teachers whom we've good reason to trust. Since they make sense about what we do know, they probably make sense about what we don't.

But what made Jesus' teaching so 'authoritative', and why would that even be a good thing? We gain several impressions throughout the Gospels. The famous Sermon on the Mount is a good example. I'm reluctant to begin with it, since it's come to be treated as if it were all Jesus said, and is too easily plucked from the wider story of his life. But it was a major speech that many are familiar with, so I'll take the risk. (I'll touch on less than a third of it.)

Here Jesus engages with the Old Testament law (ch. 20), of which he's a huge fan. 'I tell you the truth,' he says with some gravity, 'until heaven and earth disappear, not the smallest letter, not the least stroke of a pen, will by any means disappear from the Law' (Matt. 5:18, NIV). Then he launches into a series of statements that upsets what was usually heard said about this law. In every case, he unveils something at the heart of each law:

- The law not to murder actually confronts our tendency to write each other off in contempt and anger. Not only does he oppose that tendency; incredibly, when we're on the receiving end of contempt, he wants us to overturn contempt by seeking for reconciliation (Matt. 5:21–24).
- The law against adultery unmasks the callous way men want sex as if it is only for their pleasure. Likewise, when the law permitting divorce degenerates into a pretext for serial marriage, men reveal their sexual self-obsession (Matt. 5:27–28; cf. 19:1–12).
- Rules against oath-breaking show how we play games with speech, fail to speak directly with one another and break our promises (Matt. 5:33–37).
- The law of retribution ('an eye for an eye') limited justice to no more than equivalent recompense. But it had become a licence for hate-fuelled vengeance. In stark contrast, Jesus shows us how to respond to those

who harm us as if they matter as much as we think of ourselves (Matt.
5:38–47).

Jesus has a special kind of awareness. He's uninterested in ethics as a superficial code (ch. 3). He could peer into the depths of the biggest code of his
day, and know what it was *for*. That's what gripped his hearers, and made him
seem authoritative. He stood way beyond mere repetition of the code. Nor
did he offer the kind of commentary on it that would elevate his standing in
a religious club.

He understood that the code promoted *quality relationships* between us. In
these relationships, people would move from contempt to reconciliation. A
man would use his sexual longings only to deepen his love for one woman.
We would seek for the kind of trustworthy, direct speech that bypassed the
need for elaborate oaths and contracts. We would do justice with such mercy
that even criminals would belong and receive love. In this highly unusual way
of being human, each person in the relationship is radically committed to the
good of the other.

As Jesus opposes our usual practices, we also hear a diagnosis that may be
new to us – that *many of our emotions are misplaced*:

- The angry person may have her good reasons. But something has gone
  wrong when anger energizes our quest to destroy another, rather than
  to solve the problem and find reconciliation.
- The would-be adulterer has not invented something new or novel when
  his sexual energy surges within him. But he moves in a gestalt (p. 72) that
  assumes his sexual longings are about himself. His moral imagination
  fails to notice that his sexuality is for *others*, to build a relationship and a
  family.
- Complicated oath-taking can appear nobly honourable. But it masks
  how we use speech to create distance and conceal ourselves from each
  other. Oaths may have begun as an attempt to rehabilitate speech in
  a difficult world where it's hard to establish trust. But when fear of
  each other controls us, our speech degenerates into an elaborate and
  meaningless game.
- Every society needs some kind of structure for justice. But when it
  degenerates into mere revenge that dehumanizes and marginalizes
  the offender, we corrode the *society* we set out to protect.

In other words, Jesus has a piercing knowledge of what we think we hide
– those attachments we would kill and die for in what Jesus calls our 'heart'

(p. 195). According to Jesus, 'where your treasure is, there your heart will be also' (Matt. 6:21). We've mangled all our attachments:

> From within, out of people's hearts, come evil thoughts, sexual immoralities, thefts, murders, adulteries, greed, evil actions, deceit, lewdness, stinginess, blasphemy, pride, and foolishness. All these evil things come from within and defile a person. (Mark 7:21–23)

The 'treasures' that we would kill for may be precious enough. But our attachments become so obsessive and blinkered that we fail to see other 'treasures' that may also be very precious.

To use Jesus' favourite term for himself, he's *the Son of Man*. There's some complexity to his self-chosen title. On the one hand, it was a typical Old Testament term for an insignificant, mortal, rank-and-file human being (e.g. Num. 23:19; Job 16:23; 25:6; Pss 8:4; 144:3; Jer. 49:18, 33; 50:40; 51:43; Dan. 8:17). As if to emphasize this point, the term becomes God's standard mode of address to the prophet Ezekiel. Yet it also subtly points to an Old Testament vision (Dan. 7:13–14), where a figure 'like a son of man' rises from earth to reign over it with God.[1]

Jesus therefore seems to refer to himself as *the representative human*. He isn't typical of what we usually drift into. He embodies what we were each *meant* to be. Since he embodies true humanity, Jesus' teaching does contain some 'universal' moral truths. He sometimes agrees with what other people and religions think about right and wrong. This agreement flows from our common humanity as inhabitants together in a moral order (ch. 22). To categorize Jesus as one of history's 'good moral teachers' has a grain of truth. But that label is insufficient without four further observations.

First, I've only reflected upon *a tiny fraction* of his teaching. Nothing can substitute for our reading and rereading the Gospels, allowing his teaching to wash over us in its full and unique force. Consider his statement to 'do to others as you would have them do to you' (Luke 6:31, NIV). Overuse has made

---

1. In this important vision a different Hebrew phrase (*bar 'enāš*) is used than for the references to everyday humanity (*ben 'ādām*). But the Greek translation used in Jesus' time (the Septuagint) employed the same Greek phrase (*huios anthrōpou*) for all these references. The Gospels use this Greek phrase for Jesus' self-address. It seems fair then to assume that the Gospels leverage the ambiguity of the term in the Hellenistic period. For a theological comment on this important title, see n. 3 on p. 97, below.

it a cliché for all that people know about Jesus. Similar statements were made elsewhere, so people like to conclude that Jesus simply taught moral common sense, and that he was one of many such teachers in the world's history. But the saying occurs as Jesus *attacks* moral common sense (in a discourse known as the Sermon on the Plain, Luke 6:17–49), even while using the proverbs, polemic and exaggeration common to wisdom teachers of his time. It doesn't really matter whether Jesus thought up the saying independently, or heard, liked and endorsed it because it fitted his view of empathic serving love. It functions as his test for a first approximation of what might be the right thing to do. It will not work on its own, apart from everything else he said.

Indeed as he goes on to say,

> I will show you what someone is like who comes to Me, hears My words, and acts on them: He is like a man building a house, who dug deep and laid the foundation on the rock. When the flood came, the river crashed against that house and couldn't shake it, because it was well built. (Luke 6:47–48)

'Following Jesus' is a life activity involving repeated scrutiny of and participation in his words. My lame gestures toward his ministry are about as adequate as a small brochure advertising Paris or Rome: there's no substitute for being there.

Secondly, there's a *centre of gravity in Jesus' teaching*. If we ignore this centre of gravity, we distort his teaching to become something he would neither endorse nor recognize. I was correct to observe that he seeks for a depth and quality of relationships between us that goes way beyond mere religious code keeping. But front and centre in Jesus' thinking is *the impossibility of disassembling these quality relationships from a relationship of quality with his God*, whom he regards as our Father in heaven (whether or not we care to think this way about God). The Gospels are laced with Jesus' fervent introduction to this Father, who 'causes His sun to rise on the evil and the good, and sends rain on the righteous and the unrighteous' (Matt. 5:45); who hears our prayers and gives generously (Matt. 6:9, 31–33; 7:11); and who shows what mercy and holiness are really like (Luke 6:51; Matt. 5:48). To imagine that Jesus merely rehashes some general ethical principles of benevolence or altruism is a fantasy. According to him, our 'hearts' (p. 195) are broken, and can only be renewed as we 'come to our senses' and find our Father again (Luke 15:11–32). He dreams of us entering a new 'kingdom', where all orbit joyfully around his Father. His life's work begins to make that dream a reality.

Thirdly, *the pattern of Jesus' life and practices* is every bit as important to watch as the content of his teaching. There's an extraordinary generosity and inclusiveness to the way Jesus conducts himself. His friendships were legendary. He would push aside his minders and detour to help insignificant children, marginalized women, immoral outcasts and diseased pariahs.

Fourthly, and harder to describe, is the way *Jesus' teaching is incomplete*. Given the honour Christians accord to Jesus' life and teaching, this claim may seem absurd – until we begin to see the overall drama of Jesus' time on earth and the subsequent exposition of it later in the New Testament. Jesus was not content merely to *teach* his followers how to live as members of the 'kingdom of God'. All four Gospels resoundingly agree that he was finally focused upon – even obsessed by – the pinnacle achievements of his life: his death and resurrection, and his return to the Father and gift of the Holy Spirit. In the nature of this case, it's up to others to expand upon the story that Jesus initiated. (Jesus expressly commits this task to his apostles.)

No one truly follows Jesus, then, merely by focusing upon the words he taught in first-century Palestine. That kind of focus is an essential response to Jesus, but not a sufficient response. Jesus doesn't merely sharpen our ethical awareness. He actually presents nothing less than a new way to be human. He upends, reshapes, reimagines and renovates everything we thought we knew about being a human. We glimpse this strange new truth about humanity in the next chapter. Furthermore, those final pinnacle achievements of his life affect how to become truly human. We consider how in chapters 15–16.

Further reading

* Dickson, John, *The Christ Files: How Historians Know what They Know about Jesus* (Sydney South, NSW: Blue Bottle, 2006). Online: <http://www.publicchristianity.org>.

* Dickson, John, *Life of Jesus: Who He Is and Why He Matters* (DVD and guidebook) (Grand Rapids: Zondervan, 2010). Online: <http://www.publicchristianity.org>.

14. TRUE 'IDENTITY'

In Part 3 we consider how, according to Christian thought, ethics springs from Jesus. This chapter addresses an unnerving possibility: that true humanity, and our real and true 'identity', can only be found as we participate 'in' the identity of Jesus Christ.

Modern Westerners mostly hate to picture themselves as following anything or anyone. I may follow 'my own way' or 'my heart', with my decisions finally pivoting on 'being true to myself'. I understand myself to have final say over myself, and I customize myself as I see fit. We can think and talk in these ways because we carry an intricately drawn and very extensive story of our personal 'identity'.

At its simplest, to have an identity simply means that we're not someone else, and that we retain many essential similarities from day to day. At its deepest, our identity describes the unique package of biology, desire, kinship, belonging and history that makes our 'self'.[1] These aspects combine to form the powerful stories we tell about what we like and hate, about what we will and won't do, about whom we'll be seen with, about what we avoid, and about what we hope and aim for.

---

1. For an example of how broad the concept has become, see Vernon White, *Identity* (London: SCM, 2002), p. 44.

In this chapter, I want to use this modern notion to show what Jesus thinks he does for us. In short, he thinks we find how to be truly human – the human we were meant to be – when we *share* (somehow!) in *his* 'identity'.

I've already hinted that we're not really masters of our identity. Those thoughts, feelings and habits that comprise our identity and make us who we are haven't come from nowhere. Our self is largely a gestalt (p. 72) of our inner loves interacting with the social influences that surround us (chs. 7–9). Whether or not we realize or care to admit it, we already follow something.

Some people are happy to picture themselves as following someone. If I said I follow Jesus, the Buddha, the Dalai Lama, or the Qur'an, you'd think I meant that, in some way and at some level, I allow one of these to alter what I think and do. A follower's identity isn't fixed. 'Who I am' changes because of whom I'm following.

In the previous chapter, I pointed to Jesus' followers in the Gospels, and to the way people still follow his teaching. But I also suggested that *Jesus' teaching is incomplete*. No one truly follows Jesus merely by focusing upon the words he taught in first-century Palestine, because the pinnacle achievements of his life that come *after* his teaching (chs. 15–16) also help us discover a new way to be human.

Although people follow Jesus throughout the Gospels, the apostles writing the New Testament letters never talk of 'following' him. Perhaps the letter writers simply wanted to avoid any confusion. Gospel followers physically walked with Jesus, a practice that became impossible after his departure. If first-century people had been encouraged to follow Jesus, they might have left their homes for Palestine in search of him. (The New Testament letters in English Bibles can now afford to deploy the metaphorical term 'follow' without any such confusion. It sometimes translates concepts such as imitating Jesus, or identifying with his people or siding with his cause. However, the Greek word for 'following' doesn't appear in these letters.)

But the lack of 'following' in the letters goes much deeper: it's an *insufficient* metaphor to describe Christ's impact upon our identity. The apostles prefer to describe people as being 'in Christ'. This and similar turns of phrase occur well over a hundred times in the New Testament letters.

I may be wrong, but I don't think anyone would ever describe herself as being '*in*' the Buddha, the Dalai Lama or the Qur'an.[2] Likewise, it would have

---

2. I realize it sounds odd to use the Qur'an as my third example rather than the person of 'The Prophet'. But I'm told that many Muslims *follow* the Qur'an in the way Christians follow Jesus, whereas 'The Prophet' *reveals* truth analogously to how Christians construe the Bible.

sounded quite bizarre for any of Jesus' contemporary followers to say they
were 'in' him. Only after the pinnacle achievements of his life can it make
sense to be 'in' Christ.

No one finds it easy at first to grasp what's going on here, for there are
several angles to being 'in Christ'. This unique concept diffracts into a rainbow
of related ideas. The first (and easiest) describes *a way of belonging together*.
Churches exist 'in Christ' (e.g. 1 Cor. 1:2; Phil. 4:21; 1 Thess. 1:1; 1 Pet. 5:14),
and there are bonds of affection between co-workers 'in Christ' (e.g. Rom.
16:3, 9). Perhaps they're simply 'in Christ' in the same way a military person
might refer to a colleague 'in the service', or in the same way that Communists
are 'in' the same movement.

But it seems to go deeper: 'in Christ we who are many form one body, and
each member belongs to all the others' (Rom. 12:15, NIV). Only an exception-
ally close-knit military unit, or an extremely idealistic political party, would
speak in this way. Yet in this second angle on being 'in Christ', people who
don't necessarily know each other well still regard one other with a quite powerful sense of care, because each has become *a participant with Christ's very own
self*. (Clearly, such an extraordinary idea can only succeed if Jesus is unique in
human affairs.)

Belonging and participation 'in Christ' occurs as individuals undergo *a
fundamental shift in their identity*. According to this third angle, 'if anyone is in
Christ, there is a new creation; old things have passed away, and look, new
things have come' (2 Cor. 5:17). A new 'someone', who's somewhat unknown
to us, arises from whomever we thought we were.

This creation of someone 'new' sounds intriguing at first, and perhaps
even appealing on our worst days. But for modern Western people, troubling
issues are at stake. For this third angle on being 'in Christ' seriously contends
that one's identity can somehow be formed by *another*, rather than by myself
and my experiences. If we've become used to conceiving ourselves and our
identity as a unique and particular story – one that deserves the respect of all
who encounter us – then it becomes strange and troubling for this *other* to step
in and take over.

Not only that, but we find an alarming fourth angle, where whatever identity we currently conceive for ourselves is *alienated from true humanity* if not
measured against Christ's identity. One famous 'in Christ' passage pictures
people doing what humans normally do: living by the immediate recommendations of our 'flesh' (ch. 9), 'following the desires of flesh and senses'
(Eph. 2:3, NRSV). The problem isn't with the body and its desires, but with our
tendency to fixate upon these at the expense of all else (ch. 7). This form of
life seems natural enough – until compared to the way of Jesus Christ, against

whom we appear so tragically petty that our normal way is described as a form of living death (Eph. 2:1).

Against this backdrop of normal human life the fundamental shift in identity begins as people are 'created' – recreated, that is – 'in Christ Jesus' (Eph. 2:10, NRSV). Just as humanity was created in God's 'image' (Gen. 1:26–27), so also is the Father at work to recreate humanity into his Son's 'image' (Rom. 8:29; 1 Cor. 15:49; 2 Cor. 3:18).

> Not many of you were wise by human standards; not many were influential; not many were of noble birth. But . . . you are in Christ Jesus, who has become for us wisdom from God – that is, our righteousness, holiness and redemption. (1 Cor. 1:26–30, NIV)

Romans and Jews fiercely held their ethno-religious identity claims. But Paul rejected his as 'filth', to 'gain Christ and be found in Him' (Phil. 3:8–9). He thinks that Jesus' way of being human is universal for all humanity.[3] Whoever we think ourselves to be, Jesus' humanity encompasses and 'decodes' everyone's diversity, all journeys and every vocation. To be truly human involves knowing him and participating with him.

To participate in Christ is to begin a new voyage of discovery. We don't lose our past stories, yet increasingly we understand ourselves in reference to

---

3. It is worth pausing to observe an important Christological point. It concerns the significance we attribute to Jesus' twin aspects as 'Son of God' and 'Son of Man'. 'Son of God' and 'Son of Man' do not align with Jesus' divinity and humanity respectively. Both titles have divinity and humanity in view. Rather, they respectively emphasize how Jesus is *particular* yet also *universal*. Oliver O'Donovan sums it up neatly: 'As the one whom God has sent he is irreplaceable; as the new man he is the pattern to which we may conform ourselves' (*Resurrection and Moral Order: An Outline for Evangelical Ethics*, 2nd ed. [Leicester: Apollos, 1994], p. 143). The title 'Son of God' highlights Jesus' unique achievements, such as his death for sin (Gal. 2:20), his resurrection (Rom. 1:4), his destruction of the devil (1 John 3:8), and his passing 'through the heavens' (Heb. 4:14) to be with the Father. The title 'Son of Man' highlights the universality of Jesus' representation, such as his 'lordship' over the Sabbath to reinstate its restfulness for humankind (Mark 2:27–28), and his rule of humanity that fulfils human destiny (Dan. 7:13–14; Acts 7:56; Heb. 2:6–9; Rev. 14:14; see further above, p. 91). The title emphasizes how his way of being human truly 'images' God, and so becomes the pattern for all humanity. His particularity and universality combined make him suitable to mediate between us and the Father.

Jesus Christ. I cannot predict or sum up that lifelong project, because to do so would tempt you to orient yourself to my template of it, rather than to Jesus himself. But even though the twists and turns of this journey cannot be predicted or summarized, its outcome is the disclosure of *a Jesus-shaped version of our 'self'*. As C. S. Lewis once put it:

> Christ will in fact give you a real personality; but you mustn't go to Him for the sake of that. As long as your own personality is what you are bothering about you are not going to Him at all . . . Your real, new self won't come as long as you're looking for it. It will come when you are looking for Him.[4]

In one of the Bible's most evocative depictions of this disclosure, the risen Jesus promises to give those who participate with him 'a white stone, and on the stone a new name is inscribed that no one knows except the one who receives it' (Rev. 2:17).

Yet the claim that each person's identity needs recreating 'in Christ' appals modern people. It seems 'hegemonic' – a term once used to describe the reach of empires, but now used to describe pernicious ideas that obliterate everything precious and particular about a person. The hegemony *would* be pernicious if we were talking of any person, nation, ideology, family or group other than Christ. There's no neat argument to defend Christianity at this point other than by pointing to the person of Jesus, who is uniquely able to make beautiful and liveable the claim that his humanity is the best pattern for everyone's. It will turn out that his humanity has what it takes to restore the best of freedom (ch. 31), diversity (ch. 46) and the cultures of communities (chs. 18, 25, 34).

However, people in Christ do take a long time to 'catch up' on their new identity. Our identity stories can function as a kind of prison; and although he flings open the door, it can take us quite a while to inhabit freedom. In a moment of exasperation, the apostle Paul writes to some that 'I was not able to speak to you as spiritual people but as people of the flesh, as babies in Christ' (1 Cor. 3:1). These people retained their usual habit of living for bodily desires, and particularly for social status. When it came to appropriating their new identity in Christ, they had the unformed awareness of infants.

There's good news in this 'catch-up' problem: Christ willingly regards people as 'in him' even when we're poor at remembering ourselves that way. Participation in Christ doesn't hinge on how good we are at remembering that

---

4. C. S. Lewis, *Beyond Personality: The Christian Idea of God* (London: Centenary, 1944), p. 64. (I am indebted to Anthony Chung for this quotation.)

we belong to him. But there's also bad news: like all humans, people who bear the name 'Christian' also fixate on 'the desires of flesh and senses' from time to time. Their failure to grasp their new identity in Christ drives many of the horrific hypocrisies littering Christian history.

The language of being 'in Christ' appears later in the New Testament, but Jesus introduced the concept. 'Remain in me,' he said, 'and I will remain in you' (John 15:4, NIV). He used the metaphor of a grapevine to signal the fundamental change of identity involved:

> Just as a branch is unable to produce fruit by itself unless it remains on the vine, so neither can you unless you remain in Me. I am the vine; you are the branches. The one who remains in Me and I in him produces much fruit, because you can do nothing without Me. (John 15:4–5)

Like us, it may have been normal for them to see themselves as individuals who prospered by seeking whatever goals seemed self-evident to them. Unlike us, it was probably normal for them to see themselves as bound to a collective, 'Israel', and prospering or languishing according to Israel's fortunes.

But Jesus powerfully challenges his followers' self-identity at this point. Jesus thinks they (and we) can only prosper ('produce fruit') when they see themselves as participants with each other via participation with him, and that *this* identity unlocks their truest humanity. Two stunning conclusions follow.

First, to participate in Christ is to begin to love as he loved. That will touch our passions and affections – all of our existing desires, hates, reactions and wants (ch. 7). *What we love may change.*

Secondly, *there's the power of a new inclusion* in Christ. He meets our need for belonging, and offers the antidote to the pressures that surround us (ch. 8).

Jesus enters into all of our human loves and hates, and all our histories, traditions, camaraderies and rivalries, *to change them.* Later New Testament authors continued this thinking, incorporating the pinnacle achievements that followed Jesus' initial declaration that 'branches' need their 'vine'.

Further reading

* Jensen, Michael, *You: An Introduction* (Sydney: Matthias Media, 2008).

** Stewart, James S., *A Man in Christ: The Vital Elements of St Paul's Religion* (London: Hodder & Stoughton, 1935).

*** Campbell, Constantine R., *Pauline Participation* (Grand Rapids: Zondervan, forthcoming).

15. HOW THE CROSS CHANGES US

In Part 3 we consider how, according to Christian thought, ethics springs from Jesus. This longer chapter explores six implications for ethics arising from Jesus' death – a pinnacle achievement of his life.

People like to imagine the implications for the human race if some alien entity suddenly appeared to all. Movies such as *2001: A Space Odyssey*, *Independence Day*, *War of the Worlds*, *The Hitchhiker's Guide to the Galaxy*, *The Day the Earth Stood Still* and *V* all play out this scenario in different ways.

According to the logic of the Bible, the death of Jesus Christ (often simply alluded to as 'the cross') constitutes just such a momentous intervention into human affairs. 'The grace of God has appeared' (Titus 2:11, ESV) and is 'bringing salvation for all people'. The death of Christ was not only another death among billions; it altered human affairs irrevocably.

My purpose in this chapter is to outline what inferences the New Testament authors drew about our lives from Jesus' death. For, according to Titus 2:12, the 'grace' that appeared also 'trains' people to become like God (ch. 21) and to experience reordered desires (ch. 7). But how could such training possibly proceed?

In what follows, I'll assume that the New Testament authors hold to a 'penal substitutionary' view of the atonement. The jargon sounds ugly, but refers to an act many Christians regard as entirely beautiful. (For a more extensive account of it, see the readings below.)

At the point of his death Jesus undergoes a dreadful separation from his Father. ('My God, my God, why have you forsaken me?', Mark 15:34, NIV.) He experiences God's wrath against human wickedness in this moment, *even though nothing in his own relationship with the Father called for it.* But out of great love for an otherwise condemned humanity, Jesus freely chose to endure this horror. Amazingly, it turns out that in fact God took back his judgment against *us* upon *himself* (since Jesus was the incarnate Second Person of the three-personed Godhead). Once expressed against the man Jesus, you and I need face no terrible judgment of God (unless we try to face God on our own terms, uninterested in Jesus). In this way, Jesus made it possible for people to experience God's fatherly friendship, no matter what evils we carry.

What, then, do the biblical authors deduce from Jesus' death about *how to live?* The alien incursion of God's grace manifests in several directions, so the material is hard to summarize. But I'll attempt to do so under these six statements about the death of Christ:

1. *Christ's death undoes our fixations on performance*
2. *Christ's death shows an enmity to sin that rejects our regular way of being human*
3. *The heroism of Christ's death unveils a new human purpose*
4. *The peace won by Christ's death commences our new, true inclusion*
5. *The suffering of Christ's death explains our adversity*
6. *The style of Christ's death inducts us into new habits*

Christ's death undoes our fixations on performance

Christ's death makes possible a new, free and clear relationship with his Father: we're freed from the need to 'be good' to impress God.

We've already seen a centre of gravity in Jesus' teaching (p. 92), that each of us needs a relationship of quality with our Father in heaven. But no such relationship is possible while there's any chance of our being condemned by God. Divine condemnation, both in its possibility and our misunderstandings of it, distorts and dogs human life and confuses ethics. Ritual guesswork to appease God then preoccupies religious people. Self-referential obsession about how God thinks of them distracts from their ethical activity, and distorts it. Meanwhile, non-religious ethicists feel compelled to assert that people can act well without fear of God. In fact, the prospect of God's judgment is not the main Christian motive for doing good. I understand these non-religious attacks though, because a lot of religion does orbit around such motives.

But, to put it bluntly, Christ's death smashes through all that by destroying the nexus between our performance and our acceptability to God. As Paul puts it in Romans, Jesus Christ's obedient and graceful 'act of righteousness' brings 'righteousness' and 'eternal life' to the many (5:18–21), so that 'there is now no condemnation for those who are in Christ Jesus' (8:1, NIV). No matter *who* we are, no matter *how bad we are* at things, Christ's death opens the way for a relationship of trusting intimacy with the Father. 'In him and through faith in him we may approach God with freedom and confidence' (Eph. 3:12, NIV). In Christ, 'religion' becomes a relieved celebration of peace with God. We're free to discover how ethics works without the constant distraction of having to deflect God's judgment. We learn to act well to uphold whatever is good, rather than as a continual activity of self-justification.

Christ's death shows an enmity to sin that rejects our regular way of being human

The immensity of Christ's death also discloses that our normal, casual, self-enclosed and self-absorbed ways of operating according to our 'flesh' (ch. 9) are actually horrendous.

In Romans 6 Paul uses a curious phrase to describe Christ's death: those in Christ have 'died to sin'.[1] At first this phrase sounds as if Christians live perfectly – as if their capacity to sin has 'died'. If that were what it meant, Christians would be successful only in self-deception, and onlookers would rightly marvel at our pathetic rationalizations when we claimed to do no wrong.

But it turns out that 'dying to sin' refers to the way Christ's death defuses God's judgment against sin, with those in Christ being the beneficiaries. Paul then responds to the natural enough (if raucous) response of those who, like all of us, have grown used to fixating on our own pleasures and interests: 'Should we continue in sin in order that grace may multiply?' (Rom. 6:1). In other words, if Christ's death has destroyed the nexus between our performance and our acceptability to God, isn't it business as usual? Wouldn't that simply highlight how kind and forgiving God is?

The question is a typical example of the way one's identity may take some

---

1. I suppose I should pause to define *sin* here; but I'll assume we agree it has something to do with badness. The passage doesn't define sin, because biblical authors weave a cumulative profile of it (as they do with other large concepts such as *love* or *goodness*). Sin is 'lawlessness' (1 John 3:4) and 'unrighteousness' (1 John 5:17). It is the opposite of trust in God (Rom. 14:23). It is a short-lived pleasure (Heb. 11:25) that entangles us (Heb. 12:1) with the worst kind of desire-fulfilment (Jas 1:14–15). It is also a betrayal of our connection to others (e.g. Num. 5:6; 2 Sam. 12:1–13; 1 Cor. 8:12; 11:27).

time to catch up (p. 98) to a new identity 'in Christ' (ch. 14). A quadruple-bypass patient may continue to smoke; a compulsive gambler may keep at it, even after someone pays his debts for him; and someone freed from God's condemnation may like her new 'opportunity' to sin. But each has failed to notice the dedication of his or her rescuer, *and their rescuer's bitter enmity toward whatever destroys those in need of rescue.* The rescuer dreams of a future far more worth loving than the rescued person's previous self-obsessed fixations and addictions – if only the rescued would give it a chance.

Usually, we see sin as a seductive opportunity to advance ourselves in some way. But the gigantic opposition hurled against it – the death of God's very Son, in fact – alerts us to some blind spots. It begins to dawn on us that perhaps our sin had a few problems we hadn't quite noticed.

The death of Christ rejects our regular way of being human. In 1 Corinthians 6:9–11 Paul lists settled habits of life that all seem normal and natural to the participants. Greed, drunkenness, trickery and slander would sum up the practices of many modern workplaces. The worship of objects and images sums up much modern religious practice. The sexual practices he describes are now commonly accepted lifestyles. Therefore modern Westerners routinely reject his view that such ways of being disqualify us from life with God. But in contrast to these regular ways of being, 'you were washed, you were sanctified, you were justified' he says to his readers, in a direct allusion to the death of Christ (v. 11, NIV). I may view these practices as routine; but the immensity of Christ's action against them alerts me that in fact, all is not well.

Peter, using the metaphor of 'blood' (1 Pet. 1:14–19), considers Christ's death. In an allusion to the Old Testament system of animal sacrifice, Christ was 'a lamb without blemish or defect' (NIV). Hence his 'blood' is more precious than gold; and at the price of his ultimate excellence, Christ bought or 'redeemed' people from 'empty' ways of life mediated to us through our false inclusions with others, and from our standard uses of desire that are expressed in ignorance, yet have become evil. For Peter, the death of Christ explicitly alerts us that our usual ways of being human have gone haywire. In the absence of Christ, they would directly attract God's wrath. It just doesn't matter if we judge our ways to be conventional, normal or no big deal. The death of Christ states the contrary.

The heroism of Christ's death unveils a new human purpose

Once my friend Steve rescued me from a vicious ocean current. I can truthfully say I owe him my life. In reality, I've not given him my life. Nor would he expect me to, or know what to do with it if I did. Yet the biblical authors believe, with utter seriousness, that we do owe Christ our life in precisely the sense that I've not given it to Steve.

When Paul continues his line of thought about being 'washed', 'sanctified' and 'justified', he concludes an argument against sexual immorality by saying that the body is 'for the Lord' (1 Cor. 6:13, NIV) and that 'You are not your own; you were bought at a price. Therefore honour God with your body' (1 Cor. 6:19–20, NIV). Christ died 'so that those who live' (those who no longer face God's wrath) 'should no longer live for themselves, but for the One who died for them and was raised' (2 Cor. 5:15).

Is this reasonable? When a hero saves, we respond with affection and love.[2] But does it follow that the hero should expect our continued and total allegiance? Not usually. But here the biblical authors blend our response of affection to Christ's heroism with a second point: that just as Christ's death rejects an old way of being human, so also it unveils that there's a new way. Our allegiance to his heroism discloses *entire new purposes* to being human.

Paul's full sentence reads, 'The body is not meant for sexual immorality, but for the Lord, and the Lord for the body' (1 Cor. 6:13, NIV). Apparently, we don't even know what our body is *for* until we find it to be *for* the Lord, and him *for* it. (In contrast, many regularly imagine it to exist for sex.) It takes Christ's heroism to unveil our real purpose. Elsewhere Paul uses a startling image to make the same point: after the death of Christ, people 'have been set free from sin and have become slaves to righteousness' (Rom. 6:18, NIV). Paul knows that this language of slavery, drawn from human affairs, is risky. The mysterious reality is that 'anyone joined to the Lord is one spirit with Him' (1 Cor. 6:17). (The language of 'resurrection' also unveils our new purpose, ch. 16.)

In its rejection of standard humanity and its unveiling of a new purpose, we begin to see how Christ's death functions to reveal and form our new identity (ch. 14). We begin to find that our true self is Jesus-shaped – a version of ourselves we couldn't possibly have anticipated, engineered or conjured without him.

---

2. Not even this claim is always true. A man I know – call him Dave – rescued a stranger from certain death at sea. Dave later visited the victim to check on his progress. The victim and his family casually ignored him. This episode of indifference is a perverse example of disordered desire. It echoes our casual dismissals of Christ's heroic death.

The peace won by Christ's death commences our new, true inclusion

The power of new inclusion in Christ meets our deepest need for belonging, and offers the real antidote to the social pressures that surround us (ch. 8). Christ's death initiates this new inclusion, and several New Testament passages amplify this theme. Perhaps the most famous of these is Ephesians 2:14–17, where the death of Christ destroys hostility between Jew and Gentile. These groups had a special significance in the Bible's story arc (ch. 19). Yet the hostility between them typifies corrupted human sociality (ch. 8). Christ set out to 'create in himself one new humanity in place of the two, thus making peace,' and to 'reconcile both groups to God in one body through the cross, thus putting to death that hostility through it' (Eph. 2:15–16, NRSV). There could be no more corporate language of inclusion than this 'one new humanity'. (The original striking metaphor is literally of 'one new human'.) The new Christian identity brings *corporate* peace with it.

So Paul insists that factionalism and personality cults have no place in any Christian grouping (1 Cor. 1:10–13). Christians enable the weak, don't merely serve their own interests, and seek the kinds of agreements with one another that accord with Jesus Christ. 'Accept one another, then,' Paul concludes, 'just as Christ accepted you' (Rom. 15:7, NIV), alluding to his death. The death of Christ rectifies our failed attempts at inclusion, and initiates a new, true inclusion.

The suffering of Christ's death explains our adversity

The New Testament suggests that to be in Christ entails participation in his sufferings. For modern people, the whole New Testament discussion of suffering is most odd, and it wouldn't even occur to us to visit it in our deliberations about right and wrong. We tend to think that ethics mainly focuses on what to do in various decisions (ch. 2), and that right and wrong revolves around our choices. No one chooses adversity, so we think that suffering isn't particularly relevant to ethics except where it distracts us from being or doing or finding good.

Yet the New Testament authors include our sufferings among all our other actions and responses. Their school of moral formation shapes our experience of suffering. It isn't incidental guidance, either, as if the main game is to be good or happy while suffering snaps at our heels. Rather, they think suffering exists on the same continuum as any other lived outcome of participating in Christ. So Paul wants 'to know Christ and the power of his resurrection and the fellowship of sharing in his sufferings, becoming like him in his death' (Phil. 3:10, NIV). Out of context, the comment sounds masochistic. But understanding his new identity as being formed in Christ, Paul simply aligns himself with the pinnacle achievements of Jesus' life (ch. 16) and expects to participate in all of them (cf. 1 Cor. 4:9–13, suffering that Paul later calls his 'ways in Christ', v. 17; also Col. 1:24; 2 Tim. 2:3).

So it's usual in the New Testament to parallel our encounters with various external hostile forces to Jesus' experiences of those who unjustly sought to destroy him (2 Cor. 1:5–8; 4:7–11; 12:9–10; Phil. 1:27–30; 2 Tim. 3:10–12; Heb. 12:3; 1 Pet. 2:19–23; 3:13–18; 4:12–19; 5:9). This interpretation of suffering simply extends Jesus' own teachings and predictions on the matter (e.g. Matt. 5:10–12; Mark 8:34–38; Luke 16:22–23; John 15:18–24; 16:33).

Today, of course, postmodernism has taught us to suspect persecution claims as the kind of victim-talk that merely masks and justifies our self-interest. This talk becomes all the more powerful when we can align ourselves in it with Jesus Christ himself. Sadly, we can find Christians who too quickly claim persecution when other explanations for their suffering can be found. Hence Peter's neat qualification becomes most helpful: those who suffer for crime or folly may not self-deceptively construe this suffering as participation in Christ's sufferings (1 Pet. 2:20; 4:15). This distinction teaches us to discern between mere self-interested victim-talk, and suffering that occurs while we trust and follow Christ.

The New Testament authors also go beyond the hostile forces external to our will to consider those *internal* struggles we experience as a weakness. Even these struggles are paralleled to those of the 'One who has been tested in every way as we are, yet without sin' (Heb. 4:15). This author parallels Jesus' endurance of persecution (Heb. 12:3) to our struggle against sin that 'ensnares' us (Heb. 12:1). 'Since Christ suffered in the flesh,' argues Peter, 'arm yourselves also with the same resolve – because the One who suffered in the flesh has finished with sin – in order to live the remaining time in the flesh, no longer for human desires, but for God's will' (1 Pet. 4:1–2). The middle clause about the sufferer being done with sin is ambiguous. It either refers to Christ himself (as in the HCSB translation quoted), and so reminds us again of Christ's enmity against sin in his suffering and death. Or it refers to each Christian's endurance of temptation, serving notice that sinful responses are no longer our norm.

Either way, Christ's cosmic attack on sin parallels the moments when we interrogate and challenge our desires. The 'human desires' mentioned here are not inherently evil. Christ's suffering extends our imaginations beyond them, to show that we play for much higher stakes than a quest for personal happiness. As we participate with him, many of our desires *will* be met; but meeting our desires is no longer the controlling consideration of our lives.

Jesus and his followers describe external adversaries and inner temptations using the same Greek word (*peirasmos*), and quite casually blend the two concepts together. They don't think, as we often do, that external pressures are more noble than inner temptation. Rather, *all* such trials are on a continuum with Christ's own life and death. By putting suffering in this context, they make it more intelligible and regard it with an interesting optimism. Of course, they're human enough to wish to avoid trials. As Jesus taught them, they pray against suffering (Matt. 6:13; cf. Luke 22:42). Yet since the perfect Jesus suffered and was made even 'more perfect' through suffering (Heb. 2:9–10; 5:8–9), they become optimistic about the effect of suffering upon our 'character' – the sum total of our settled patterns and habits of action and feeling that others use to summarize us. They can speak of trials as growing and enabling maturity, hope and trust in God (Rom. 5:3–5; Heb. 12:7–11; 1 Pet. 1:6–7; Jas 1:2–4). The author to the Hebrews uses this concept as a prelude to an extended and imaginative discovery of several new ways of living (Heb. 12:12 – 13:17).

We usually salve our suffering by meeting our immediate desires with those regular shortcuts ('sin') that often cause suffering for others. But Christ's suffering normalizes and demystifies suffering. Those in Christ learn that suffering is a regular occurrence. 'It is necessary to pass through many troubles on our way into the kingdom of God' (Acts 14:22). In Christ, we begin to receive, construe and respond to suffering differently.

The style of Christ's death inducts us into new habits
The death of Christ has already yielded enough data for us to imagine many different ways of being. But there's more. The *style* of Christ's death also unveils a new way of being.

I don't mean to imply that his crucifixion was 'chic' or somehow 'stylish'. It was the most demeaning, brutal and ignoble form of torture and execution devised by the Romans. Yet Jesus' death had the stamp of greatness upon it:

> Do nothing out of selfish ambition or vain conceit, but in humility consider others better than yourselves. Each of you should look not only to your own interests, but also to the interests of others.

> Your attitude should be the same as that of Christ Jesus:
> Who, being in very nature God,
>   did not consider equality with God something to be grasped,
> but made himself nothing,
>   taking the very nature of a servant,
>   being made in human likeness.

And being found in appearance as a man,
> he humbled himself
> and became obedient to death
>> – even death on a cross!

(Phil. 2:3–8, NIV)

The unparalleled Jesus Christ spiralled ever downwards for us, ultimately to his death. Those who've responded to this death bear the imprint of his Way. Jesus exhibits a settled pattern and habit of action and feeling toward others (a virtue) called *humility*. (Biblical authors often tease out his greatness using the language of virtue, ch. 30.) The Romans despised and mocked humility. Increasingly so will the post-Christian West. But the style of Christ's death upstages this mockery, showing humility to be the best expression of sociality.

Humility overlaps with the way of *service* (Phil. 2:7). Before his death, Jesus explicitly rejected the usual modes of human domineering and instructed his disciples always to understand themselves as servants, never masters (Matt. 20:25–28). His expectation of death was the linchpin of his argument, and the New Testament authors never forget it. 'We who are strong ought to put up with the failings of the weak, and not to please ourselves,' as Paul puts it. 'Each of us must please our neighbour for the good purpose of building up the neighbour. For Christ did not please himself' (Rom. 15:1–3, NRSV).

Kindness, compassion and *love* also emerge as habits springing from Christ's death. 'Be kind and compassionate to one another, forgiving each other, just as in Christ God forgave you' (Eph. 4:32, NIV), a verse heightened by its contrast to our standard modes of desire and inclusion (bitterness, rage, anger, brawling, slander and malice, v. 31). 'Live a life of love,' Paul concludes, 'just as Christ loved us and gave himself up for us as a fragrant offering and sacrifice to God' (Eph. 5:1, NIV). Such love shapes the way a husband approaches his wife (Eph. 5:25–33). The gender roles pictured there are unnerving to us (ch. 42), but the Jesus-shaped habit of masculine service commended here gives a woman less to fear.

Jesus' death makes him the cosmic ambassador of forgiveness; therefore a deep logic of *forgiveness and reconciliation* (ch. 29) arises from his work. Jesus had already telegraphed that the practice of forgiveness between humans is elementary to relationship with the Father (e.g. Matt. 6:12–15; 18:21–35; Mark 11:25; Luke 6:37; 17:3–4), and he practised forgiveness with majestic poignancy as he died (Luke 23:34). The followers did likewise: 'Bear with each other and forgive whatever grievances you may have against one another. Forgive as the Lord forgave you' (Col. 3:13). Although reconciliation can proceed only when the other signals a willingness to repent (cf. Matt. 18:15–17), this practice becomes the only known way to move broken relationships into a healthy future.

Similarly, Christ's death is our universe's central instance of *grace*. Grace describes God's extension to us of goodness, kindness and mercy. Grace is fundamentally undeserved, and God's gift of it defies all analysis. Yet seen finally in Christ's death, grace is definite, trustworthy and *real*.

In the middle of a long and fascinating argument exhorting generosity to the poor, Paul avoids commanding his readers and alludes to the death of Christ. 'For you know the grace of our Lord Jesus Christ, that though he was rich, yet for your sakes he became poor, so that you through his poverty might become rich' (2 Cor. 8:9, NIV). These fascinating chapters (2 Cor. 8 – 9) have a strange effect on readers: as we read, our generosity grows as grace 'rubs off' on us.[3]

I began the chapter with Titus 2:11–12, where grace appears, brings salvation and instructs or trains. I asked how such training could possibly proceed, and now we have some clue.

In Christ's death, God exhibits unbounded merciful grace. Those who experience grace then find their own gracelessness unmasked. Our selves are revealed as captive to 'various passions and pleasures' as we live 'in malice and envy, hateful, detesting one another' (Titus 3:3). We often think of all that as interesting, even good. Passion and pleasure, envy and ambition, competition and hate can energize us. They get us out of bed. They drive us to act powerfully in the world. They're addictive. But *after* Christ exhibits God's grace, this kind of everyday humanity looks foolish, deceptive and simply wrong (Titus 3:3). A gestalt shift (p. 72) occurs: in comparison to grace, passions that once seemed interesting and good become boring and sad. So in the words of the NIV translation, grace 'teaches us to say "No" to ungodliness and worldly passions, and to live self-controlled, upright and godly lives' (Titus 2:12). As the author to the Hebrews observes, 'it is good for the heart to be established by grace' rather than by rules (Heb. 13:9). God's grace toward us in Christ stabilizes and reorders our 'heart' (p. 195) in a way that no external moral code can match.

So the death of Jesus is a pinnacle achievement of his life, and represents an unparalleled intervention into human affairs. It frees us from our distracting fixations on impressing God. It highlights and rejects our regular ways of

---

3. For an extended reflection on this effect, see Andrew J. B. Cameron, 'A Theological Approach to Social Reform, Advocacy and Engagement', in *Another Way to Love*, ed. Tim Costello and Rod Yule (Brunswick East, Vic.: Acorn, 2009), pp. 37–56.

being human, and it unveils new purposes for us. It commences the best kind of inclusion we can have. It creates a meaningful, hopeful context for our suffering. It pioneers a 'style' of being that includes humility, service, kindness, compassion, love, forgiveness, reconciliation and grace.

But the pinnacle achievements are not over, and there's yet more to Jesus that shapes who we are. 'For if while we were enemies we were reconciled to God through the death of his Son, how much more, since we have been reconciled, will we be saved by his life?' (Rom. 5:10, NET)

Further reading

** Jeffery, Steve, Michael Ovey and Andrew Sach, *Pierced for our Transgressions: Rediscovering the Glory of Penal Substitution* (Nottingham: IVP, 2007).

** Stott, John R. W., *The Cross of Christ*, 20th anniversary ed. (Nottingham: IVP, 2006).

16. HOW RESURRECTION CHANGES US

In Part 3 we consider how, according to Christian thought, ethics springs from Jesus. This chapter explores the implications arising from the other pinnacle achievement of Jesus' life: his resurrection.

To be 'in Christ' (ch. 14) brings a fundamental change to our identity. But what changes in action and behaviour would result from this change of identity? As Jesus himself put it, remaining 'in him' and then 'producing fruit' has a lot to do with trusting and inhabiting his directives on love (John 15:10–17). 'By this all people will know that you are My disciples, if you have love for one another,' he states (John 13:35). Jesus is content to summarize hundreds of pages of Scripture as building a deep love for God and for each other (Matt. 27:37–40; Mark 12:30–31; Luke 10:27–28). Later New Testament authors repeat this summation (Gal. 5:14; Rom. 13:9; Jas 2:8). In over five hundred references to love, they wholeheartedly agree that it's at the core of Christian identity.

We could almost leave it at that. Love is spectacularly easy to imagine. We love the sound of 'love'. When it comes to whom we love, how to love them, and whether we're loved, we work with our hunches. For this reason, people grow impatient when thinkers examine love in more detail and when they try to define 'what are loving actions' and 'what makes them so'.

Yet it turns out that *analysing and describing* love is spectacularly difficult.

I don't propose to try it here. The Bible mentions love quite a lot, but offers no sweeping discourses on it. An exception might be 1 Corinthians 13:4–8 (the passage people cannot resist at their weddings), where love refracts into a series of virtues – patience, kindness, the absence of envy, and so on. Yet each of these virtues is also a rich and complex aggregate. Each is a distinct and settled pattern of action and feeling that in turn requires further reflection and analysis (ch. 30).

Oddly, then, we may be none the wiser about what actually to *do* in various situations if we simply say that our new identity in Christ is expressed through love. But that statement isn't as serious as it sounds. It only shows that the New Testament authors enjoy exploring the fine-grained detail of love from a variety of angles. If we take the time to join them, we begin also to discover the detail. Love is like the compass heading when we use Google Earth or Google Maps zoomed right out. Just as a spin of the mouse wheel zooms us into the detail, so also some roving around the deeper logic of the Bible zooms us into some detail on the ways of love.

That, in a sense, is the task of this entire book, and of every other decent book giving a Christian account of ethics. But for the purpose of this chapter, we'll consider how the pinnacle achievements of Jesus' life place us in Christ to create a new *and loving* way to be human.

By the pinnacle achievements of Jesus' life, I mean his death and resurrection, his return to the Father and his gift of the Holy Spirit (chs. 15–17). We saw (ch. 13) that following Jesus is incomplete without reference to them, and to be in Christ requires them. But how do these achievements offer a new way to be human?

Jesus' death both reveals and begins to form the Christ-shaped version of ourselves that I've been calling new identity (ch. 14). I examined Jesus' death in ch. 15, and will repeat the main conclusions:

1. *Christ's death undoes our fixations on performance.*
2. *Christ's death shows an enmity to sin that rejects our regular way of being human.*
3. *The heroism of Christ's death unveils a new human purpose.*
4. *The peace won by Christ's death commences our new, true inclusion.*
5. *The suffering of Christ's death explains our adversity.*
6. *The style of Christ's death inducts us into new habits.*

But to be in Christ is also to share in *Jesus' resurrection*. Christians are confident of life after death because of it. But another conclusion is less well known: that 'just as Christ was raised from the dead through the glory of the Father, we too may live a new life' (Rom. 6:4, NIV). In other words, the Father instigated this enormous divine project to provide us *a better way to be human*. Just as Jesus rose from death, so may we be 'resurrected' from the bleak ways of life we thought were normal. *We need a kind of resurrection* to bring about the gestalt shift (p. 72) from the old self to the new. In Christ, we participate in Christ's own resurrection to undergo this resurrection and gestalt shift.

An extended discussion of sexual practices in one Christian community pivots on Jesus' resurrection. 'God raised up the Lord and will also raise us up by His power' (1 Cor. 6:14). Why this comment? Because the quest for sexual pleasure comes as second nature to many of us. It's a straightforward expression of our 'flesh' (ch. 9). Yet without our realizing it or caring, many of our sexual practices are a direct attack on *justice*, where the pleasure seeker refuses to recognize that his or her simple sexual pleasure powerfully steals from another (1 Cor. 6:8–10; cf. ch. 43). For Paul, nothing short of a newly 'resurrected' way of being human can break humans out of these patterns.

He expounds a similar line of thought when he describes people as 'hidden with Christ in God' (Col. 3:3, NIV). Pause for a moment and picture the best-looking actor or model you can think of. (To help you, I'll throw in Anne Hathaway or Benicio del Toro.) Now imagine having to accompany him or her to a red-carpet ball. Obviously, we would prefer to be seen at our slimmest and best next to them. At a much more profound level, something similar is at work here: 'When Christ, who is your life, appears, then you also will appear with him in glory' (Col. 3:4, NIV). We realize with a jolt how good it would be, if found in that company, at least to seem a *little* like Christ.

For example, we're generally hazy about what exactly might be wrong with lust, greed, sexual immorality, anger, rage, malice, slander, filthy language and lying (Col. 3:5–9). But we begin to sense that next to Christ's way of being human, they look bad and smell worse. 'You used to walk in these ways, in the life you once lived' (Col. 3:7, NIV); but the way of being human that sits better alongside (or 'in') Jesus Christ includes compassion, kindness, humility, gentleness, patience, forgiveness, peace – and love, 'which binds them all together in perfect unity' (Col. 3:14, 12–15, NIV). Virtues like these often transmit Jesus' new way to be human, in contrast to typical human vices. (I examine these highly compressed forms of moral language in ch. 30.) Paul pictures us 'clothing' ourselves in these virtues.

The clothing metaphor continues. 'You have taken off your old self with its practices and have put on the new self, which is being renewed in knowledge in the image of its Creator' (Col. 3:9–10, NIV). As the true human, Jesus both offers the clearest access for how to be human; as the Son of God, he brings us into contact with the 'image' intended for humanity.

To live 'in Christ' is like being invited by a brilliant footballer – say, a Beckham or a Ronaldo – to join his team. I'm actually a fat slob, and so possibly are you. Next to us are a bunch of other wheezers, geezers, whingers and the attention-deficit disordered. He scores all the goals and wins all the matches. Meanwhile, we, his team, zigzag around him gibbering in circles, or just lie listlessly on the ground. Yet he allows us all to share his glory.

As a member of this team, your body and its ingrained habits are against you; some days, you just want to eat and watch telly again. Yet, over time, his way rubs off. You eventually learn to run the ball in his direction. His tactics and moves start to interest you. Bit by bit, you move as he moves. And although everyone knows you're still you, *you start to look like a footballer*. According to the Bible, 'Christian ethics' is only the response of that team of misfits to its awesome captain – the responses of those who really don't have a clue, participating alongside someone *who really, really does*.

But this isn't the film cliché where a team of misfits 'follows their heart' and 'finds the hero within'. There's a final, hidden secret to joining in his moves. 'If the Spirit of Him who raised Jesus from the dead lives in you, then He who raised Christ from the dead will also bring your mortal bodies to life through His Spirit who lives in you' (Rom. 8:11). We need now to examine Jesus' final pinnacle achievement: the gift to us of his Spirit (ch. 17).

Further reading

** Harris, Murray J., *Raised Immortal: Resurrection and Immortality in the New Testament* (London: Marshall, Morgan & Scott, 1983).

* Morison, Frank, *Who Moved the Stone?* (London: Faber & Faber, 1930).

** Peterson, Eugene H., *Practice Resurrection: A Conversation on Growing up in Christ* (Grand Rapids: Eerdmans, 2010).

* Strobel, Lee, *The Case for the Resurrection* (Grand Rapids: Zondervan, 2009).

*** Wright, N. T., *The Resurrection of the Son of God* (London: SPCK, 2003).

17. WORKING WITH THE SPIRIT

In Part 3 we consider how, according to Christian thought, ethics springs from Jesus. This chapter examines how we participate with humanity's truest human, Jesus Christ, through the work of that Person of the Godhead who was integral to Jesus' humanity: the Holy Spirit.

People function well enough 'according to the flesh' (ch. 9) People like their desires (ch. 7) and need their inclusions (ch. 8). We have anguished, angry or frightening episodes along the way, but muddle along. Such a life works, in its own way. We can go a long time without questioning what we do and how we do it.

Then Christianity comes our way, and we hear that Christ's death rejects these regular ways of being human (p. 102). We become aware of an enormous gap between our existing gestalt (p. 72) in the 'flesh', and a new way of being 'in Christ' (ch. 14). We think about what Jesus opposed in his death (ch. 15), and about his 'resurrected' new way of living (ch. 16). We begin to 'play the game' in Jesus' own way, watching, learning and trying out choices like his (p. 114 and ch. 32).

But, before long, we may find ourselves trying to close the gap between the old and the new by using sheer will power. We hear biblical commands (ch. 23) and simply try to bend our wills and change, as if we can reprogramme our bodies once we've received the proper programming in our minds. So we begin to believe, and even teach, that life simply boils down to our choices. We're culpable for bad choices, and so we should make good choices as 'people of integrity!' (as a preacher once yelled at me).

But this way of seeing humanity short-circuits what the Bible takes to be the miserable depths of our conundrum: that while we're culpable for the evil results of various actions, *we really are truly trapped* in desires and inclusions that are effectively beyond our power to fix. The living death from which we were rescued is far reaching. Our habitual tendency to fixate upon the wants of our body and on our social standing (chs. 7–8) cannot be touched solely by shifting our fragile mental processes. Smokers, alcoholics and other addicts are no different from the rest of us: we *all* face endless fixations and warped loves we can never properly master.

I think of Sean Penn's magnificent portrayal of this conundrum in the 1995 film *Dead Man Walking*. Utterly trapped by his desire for inclusion, Matthew Poncelet participates in a brutal rape and double murder. His journey with Susan Sarandon's Sister Prejean consists in accepting what she called his 'responsibility': that although he was trapped and felt helpless, he was also entirely culpable for his actions. He was a creature dominated by his 'flesh'. The biblical authors insist that all of us, whether Christian or not, remain something like Poncelet.

This conundrum is a serious problem, and the Holy Spirit is its antidote. Another pinnacle achievement of Jesus' life is *his return to the Father and his gift of the Holy Spirit*. This Spirit ensures that the results of being 'in Christ' begin to materialize in our lives. Our future-oriented hopes are right and proper; but the best of futures eludes us. It eventually occurs *through the Spirit*, and doesn't hinge upon the power of our imagination or will. Just as the Spirit raised Christ from death (Rom. 1:4), so also does he move us from the state of living death (Eph. 2:1) to the best kinds of result (Rom. 8:11). Faith includes the quiet and hopeful expectation that the Spirit will work everything out.

The Holy Spirit is 'the Spirit of Jesus' (Rom. 8:9; Phil. 1:19; 1 Pet. 1:11), whom the resurrected Jesus 'pours out' on people (Acts 2:33). The Spirit is deeply allied to Christ, and we receive him because of his connection to Jesus. The Gospels present Jesus as a person whose entire life and destiny are threaded with the Spirit. He is, effectively, human society's first 'Spirit-powered' man. Humans to date have gone with the thoughts and instincts of their body-based brains (their 'flesh', ch. 9); but this man's body and mind were, somehow, perfectly harmonized with the Spirit (and so with the Father). His appearance, mission and action are Spirit-driven (Luke 2:25–35; 3:22; 4:1, 14, 18; 10:21). The Spirit was integrally present in the 'offering' made by his death (Heb. 9:14). He was resurrected – which is also to say, vindicated and proven to be good – by the Spirit (Rom. 1:4; 1 Tim. 3:16; 1 Pet. 3:18).

Such a man is so unprecedented that it might sound as though he was 'possessed' by the Spirit as in some sort of horror scenario. A few minutes of Gospel reading shows precisely the opposite. Jesus was completely possessed of his own faculties: spontaneously good in his loving, vibrantly quick-witted in his thinking, unerringly clear in his choosing. We see at once the truest being a human could have. To be 'Spirit-powered' is to be finally, truly human. So when the New Testament pictures *us* as 'Spirit-powered', the parallels with Jesus' own life are most striking:

- We're rescued and changed by the Spirit (Titus 3:5; 2 Thess. 2:13), just as the Spirit 'offered' and raised Jesus (references above).
- The Spirit enables a new mission in people (cf. 1 Thess. 1:5–6), just as he enabled Jesus' mission (above).
- The Spirit supports our approach and prayer to the Father (Rom. 8:26–27; Eph. 2:18; 6:18; Gal. 4:6; Jude 20), just as Jesus communicated with the Father in a relationship made one by this Spirit.
- Just as Jesus endured, his Spirit enables us to retain hope, despite physical adversities (Phil. 1:19; Rom. 8:9; 1 Pet. 1:11).

In other words, we're no longer *inwardly alone*: 'he lives with you and will be in you', says Jesus (John 14:17, NIV). Jesus almost risks blurring the boundaries of identity between Father, Son, Spirit and humanity: 'I will not leave you as orphans; I will come to you. . . . I am in my Father, and you are in me, and I am in you' (John 14:18, 20, NIV). In words originally directed to the Twelve, Jesus seeks to drive home the deep communion now possible between us all. So the Spirit also reshapes how we respond to others. He enables a new kind of 'oneness' or 'unity' between people, which they work to protect (Eph. 4:2–3). Cooperation with the Spirit can be as simple as loving others (Col. 1:8).

We can therefore participate alongside the Spirit's work, which Paul asks God to promote (Eph. 3:16) and urges people not to resist (1 Thess. 5:19). No matter how much I lack in will power or imagination, I may 'keep in step with the Spirit' (Gal. 5:25, NIV). Paul also uses some interesting language of dual agency, where 'by the Spirit you put to death' acts that don't match Jesus (Rom. 8:13, NIV). This kind of 'fellowship with the Spirit' (Phil. 2:1) is our participation in the resurrected life of Jesus. It's great news for anyone who has ever wanted to become a little more like Jesus Christ, but doesn't have a clue how to. By the Spirit, Jesus' activities *now extend to our daily activities and experiences.*

It all adds up to a *second* way to view humanity: 'according to the Spirit'. At its best humanity is, like Jesus, 'Spirit-powered'. I've already touched on the two ways of seeing us (ch. 9; cf. Rom. 8:1–38; Gal. 5:15 – 6:10). Jesus introduced the clash between these two ways of viewing true humanity (e.g. John 3:6), which his followers continued to use as a diagnostic to account for two differently motivated sets of people (e.g. Jude 19). When humanity is viewed 'according to the Spirit', we regain insight into our natures as beings created for a *kind of community* (chs. 18, 25) of which we cannot be aware when we casually attempt to justify our vices (ch. 30). Our vices are not life affirming or community building; but this second way of regarding humanity gives us options. 'So then, brothers, we are not obligated to the flesh to live according to the flesh' (Rom. 8:12): we're no longer forced to view ourselves as powered by the immediate demands of bodies, brains and social collectives.

'Spirits' of any sort are notoriously hard for modern Westerners to think about. But I'm struck by how hard we've made it for ourselves. Our continual narratives of self-discovery, self-improvement, self-realization, self-fulfilment and self-identity can fill us with a heady sense of power. We actually exult in our created human architecture and in our amazing ability to affect our environment; but converting this exultation into narratives of the self becomes a kind of mental stimulant. Like many stimulants, the more we take, the less effective it becomes. These narratives eventually format our minds so that we think it unbelievable that we may have inward company with the Godhead through the Spirit. Bitter loneliness is the dark underbelly and unadvertised price of these stories: those moments when 'no one understands' 'how hard it's been for me', 'what I've achieved', 'how it feels for me', 'who I am', and so on.

In jubilant contrast, 'fellowship with the Spirit' is a participation with One who is unseen yet revealed in the life, resurrection and promise of Jesus. The 'problem' of the unseen Spirit is no different to conceiving how God the Father creates and sustains a world by the Spirit (Gen. 1:2) *and* by using natural processes (e.g. Acts 14:17). It's no different to the way the resurrected body of Jesus was both physical *and* spiritual, fit both to commune with humans (e.g. Luke 24:36–43) *and* to reside in heaven (1 Cor. 15:3–49). To 'walk not according to the flesh but according to the Spirit' (Rom. 8:4, ESV), while people around me are often controlled by the terms of the physical, is the practice of seeing *more* to true humanity now that Jesus has 'walked by the Spirit'. It's also a kind of dawning joy: that my 'flesh' no longer has to walk alone.

Do we experience a direct awareness of the Spirit? Christians debate about that. On the one hand, some too quickly assert that their 'good' emotions (e.g. joy, courage, exultation, triumph) are direct manifestations of the Spirit.

But these emotions are a part of our created being, and it doesn't treat God properly to equate the Person of his Spirit with any created thing. Yet, on the other hand, people are regularly surprised by joy in a difficult situation, or by courage against some group, or in amazement at prayerful relationship with God, or by their newfound boredom with some old addiction. We may have helpful dreams, visions or intensely 'convicting' thoughts. Each of these is also part of our created life. But when they don't contravene the elements of the Bible's story arc (chs. 19, 26), we can be delighted that the Spirit is at work to form the Jesus-shaped version of ourselves.

Further reading

** Cary, Phillip, *Good News for Anxious Christians: 10 Practical Things You Don't Have to Do* (Grand Rapids: Brazos, 2010).

** Deenick, Karl, 'Who Is the "I" in Romans 7:14–25?', *Reformed Theological Review* 69.2 (2010), pp. 119–130.

*** Hohne, David A., *Spirit and Sonship* (Farnham: Ashgate, 2010).

18. COMMUNITIES IN CHRIST

In Part 3 we consider how, according to Christian thought, ethics springs from Jesus. The first major outcome of Jesus' life and work is a shock to our 'flesh': that others really do matter. They're not the backdrop for the drama that's 'me'. When the early Christian communities lived their identity in Christ, they also disclosed true humanity, including that humanity is meant to act with and for one another.

In the iconic Australian film *The Castle*, battler Darryl Kerrigan is about to lose his low-priced bungalow to an airport expansion masterminded by a corporate conglomerate. Kerrigan seeks advice from a dusty small-time solicitor, Dennis Denuto, who insists the matter is way out of his league. But Darryl's boundless optimism puts them before the bench of Australia's Federal Court. The best argument Dennis can muster is that to take Darryl's house is against 'the vibe' of Australia's Constitution. Dennis's inability to argue the matter in legal detail is comically lame – but his claim turns out to be deeply true. What would be 'the vibe' of someone whose identity is now 'in Christ' (ch. 14)?

The first major shock for someone in Christ is that other people are not just a necessary ingredient through which I may enact the standard responses of my 'flesh' (ch. 9). They're not merely the backdrop for the drama that's 'me'. In Christ, a gestalt shift occurs (p. 72). I participate in *a community of others* who really do matter, and who are equally as precious as my precious self. This new way of being human began to emerge when we saw how Jesus' death and resurrection shape human life (chs. 15–16). In this chapter we'll begin to get at the 'vibe' of a *community* who lives this new gestalt. (This 'vibe' is so important in Christian thought that we'll return to it in chs. 25 and 34.)

I'll look at what the twenty-one letters of the New Testament say about this new group life. At the end of this chapter an appendix lists the relevant biblical references, and something about my method. Now I mainly want us to have some sense of the ethical 'ballpark', or moral vision, of these communities and of their leadership. It isn't possible to list this material in order of importance, since they are all important. So let's just plunge in, almost at random.

Endurance through trials is frequently emphasized. We wouldn't normally class this subject as a matter of ethics; but for these authors, patient persistence in the face of internal temptation and external hostility is central to living well (see p. 105).

Submission, obedience and *honour* to God, to one another, to church leaders, to ruling authorities, by children to parents, by slaves to masters and by wives to husbands all appear regularly. Modern people are quite suspicious of and hostile to such ideas (cf. ch. 42). But these authors consistently emphasized them, believing them to enable peaceful relationships.

Sexual self-restraint, by contrast, is infrequently mentioned, although when it's mentioned the matter is quite clear. The home of sex is marriage, and any other use of sex represents a form of injustice or disordered desire (chs. 36–37).

Care for wives, slaves and children is expected of powerful men who are in Christ. Our tendency is to attack their position and to mock such care. But in this literature, power is an accepted reality; yet in Christ it is consistently bent toward the service of the less powerful (chs. 11, 42).

The exercise of *mercy* is consistently opposed to vengeance. *Humility* is often contrasted to criticism. *Grace* is sometimes opposed to bitterness. Likewise, those in Christ train themselves toward *empathy* and against mere self-interest (with 'empathy' our modern word for various biblical expressions of the concept).

A constantly recurring theme is for *equity and inclusion.* In Christ, people are given back to each other in a new way, where we're enabled to see all as treasured by God. All are welcomed to this community regardless of their race or status, and whatever their struggle with sin. (However, this inclusion doesn't and cannot extend to those who overtly and consistently oppose Christ or his new way of being human.) Equity may seem to contradict the theme of submission (above), but these authors were able to see submission and equity as complementary.

Hospitality and sharing appear with a frequency that can be confronting to modern urban people. Interestingly, there are clear limits on hospitality for these early Christian communities: it was emphatically to be withheld from wandering preachers who reinvented Christ in the image of their distorted desires. However, hospitality was the default position for those in Christ.

Several famous passages commend *mutual service* through use of each individual's specific *gifts and skills* (which overlap with instructions relating to the conduct of church meetings that I won't examine here). These authors also repeatedly exhort their readers to persistent *prayer, praise and worship*. These practices are integral to their conception of a life lived well in Christ, and we seriously distort their view if we think that human-to-human and human-to-planet activity can be separated from our response to God. So we find several statements of what we may call *theological ethics*, where the best of human action is pictured as a response to the prior acts of God in Christ.

The 'vibe' of these letters also emerges from more abstract concepts such as 'good' and 'evil', and from metaphors such as 'light' and 'darkness'; although we don't really know what these signify until we look at the more substantive practices that are commended and opposed. Similarly, New Testament communities were constantly called to pursue *peace* and to discover and enact an affection of *love*, both within and beyond their community. These are *unitive* concepts – umbrella terms that give an overall intention and trajectory to the life of a person in a community.

Also, everything listed so far has a parallel set of 'speech acts' – the disciplined usage of words to express the 'vibe' we're seeing. For example *agreement* is pursued, and pointless quarrels avoided. *Patterns of speech* are explicitly synchronized with practices of submission, sexual purity, care, mercy, humility, grace, empathy, equity, inclusion, hospitality, prayer, praise and worship, peace and love.

There also follows a parallel set of 'money acts'. Discussions of money are not quite as extensive as discussions of speech. Money is never rejected as such, but New Testament authors regularly highlight how it elicits disordered desires (ch. 7) by itself becoming a false object of love and by enabling the powerful to grasp more power. In contrast, money, economic activity and *work* (ch. 41) are presented as having a proper goal: the *care of family* and of near neighbours. In this respect money is accepted, along with markets, as a means by which to organize *sharing*.

We have at least seen the profile of groups worth belonging to. But more is at stake here: the commands and instructions to these groups have disclosed something about *humans and human community in general*. That is, the life of these communities makes implicit claims about true humanity, and point to the way humanity is meant to operate together. A few elements are disclosed.

First, we find a style of life that bears the imprint of the *character of God* (ch. 21). Explicitly and implicitly, many of these instructions pivot on what's known of God through the appearance and achievements of Jesus Christ. In these communities, people enact a way of being that parallels God's own way of being to the extent possible for humans. These communities seek after whatever it may look like to live in God's 'image'.

Secondly, we find the created 'hard-wired' element of humanity. The care practices of Christian community presume and affirm *a created moral order* (ch. 22): human bodies have basic needs and limits, and basic dependencies upon the natural environment. Also, their practices in relation to speech, sex and inclusion show that human bodies are 'wired' to thrive with some kinds of speech, sex and inclusion, while other kinds of speech, sex and exclusion are toxic. In these communities, we find that humanity cannot pretend away this 'wiring' in the name of other 'values' we might invent.

Thirdly, we find a purposive, future-oriented *teleological* element (ch. 24) deriving from the discovery of *a new future*. These communities assist to reorder human desires toward humanity's real purpose, which is finally to enjoy God and each other. The community discloses that true humanity isn't meant to be apart from one another, against one another or in competition with one another. True humanity exists to be with and for each other.[1]

So fourthly, we find a reciprocal relational element (chs. 25, 39). In a world surrounded by obsessive desires and false inclusions (chs. 7–8), these communities in Christ retrieve a way of relating based on God's character, on our created nature and on our true purpose. They show how a new, true inclusion can replace the false inclusions and negative social influences around us. We also see that relationships are repaired and enabled by mercy and forgiveness (ch. 29). When the community thrives on 'continual' praise and prayer, we discover how God has been the central member of human community all along. When authority, gifts and skills serve others, we learn that power isn't always a threat. It can sometimes be celebrated as good (cf. ch. 42).

Finally, we notice that *commands reveal* more about reality itself (ch. 23). They're not merely arbitrary diktats to prove the power of the commander or to supress those commanded. In Part 4 we'll revisit both this insight and the way identity in Jesus Christ is enacted in communities ('churches') to give access to the created order, to a new future and to the character of God.

But for the moment let us observe what these disclosures mean for

---

1. Michael C. Banner, *Christian Ethics: A Brief History* (Chichester: Wiley-Blackwell, 2009), p. 105.

onlookers. Christian communities send ripples into surrounding communities who don't identify with Christ. Of course, some who watch these communities may hate what they see, because their desires run in a different direction (cf. Rom. 1:32; 1 Pet. 4:4). But not all: many will be attracted by these practices (Matt. 5:16; 1 Pet. 2:12) and may even seek to emulate them.

You don't have to be an expert on the Roman Empire to realize that this was the situation for Christians living there. Some Christian practices seemed evil or insane to Roman neighbours (such as equity and inclusion, sexual purity, mercy, grace and humility or praise to Jesus). Others elicited deep respect and agreement (e.g. submission, work and family care). Neighbours were simultaneously attracted and repelled by Christians.

Two thousand years later we find ourselves in a similar situation, although the details differ. Many Christian practices remain deeply counter-cultural. Those who are not in Christ find some practices to be evil or insane (e.g. submission or sexual self-restraint). Other practices elicit deep respect and agreement (e.g. equity and inclusion). But the disclosures and practices of Christian community have been let loose in the West for so long as to be part of the air we breathe (ch. 27) and people who don't identify with Christ now sometimes call Christians to remember what they're meant to be (e.g. the forceful expectation of absolute sexual self-restraint when caring for children).

In any given culture, you can never quite tell what aspects of life in Christ will arouse fear and suspicion, or respect and agreement, from those around. And you can never quite tell which practices will be picked up by others.

Appendix to this chapter: sources and method

In focusing upon the New Testament letters, I've not taken into account several other sources for the 'vibe' of the New Testament communities, such as the teachings of Jesus, the Revelation to John, the Bible's general vision of the future, or the foundations laid in the Old Testament concerning the natural order and character of God. All of these have a unique position in the Bible's overall 'story arc' (ch. 19), and all contribute significantly to the moral imagination of a Jesus-shaped community (ch. 25). The moral vision of the letters emerges in several ways:

- *Narrative.* The way each author gives accounts, tells stories and makes claims all add together to convey an impression of how to live well. Christians immerse themselves in this narrative throughout their lives. (Parts 3–5 of this book attempt to get at some of this narrative.)

- *Virtue and vice lists.* At several key points the New Testament authors list various virtues and vices. This highly compressed language describes *settled habits and patterns of action and feeling.* These goldmines of ethical instruction are often overlooked; I'll have a go at assessing them later (ch. 30).
- *'One another' sayings.* This outstanding set of sayings is found across all the New Testament authors and woven throughout the other categories. They continually enable people to construe themselves as *inhabiting reciprocal relationships* (rather than just as lone atoms, who wander detached through a crowd).
- *Specific instructions.* Exhortations and commands (ch. 23) appear frequently, often as a conclusion to a letter. We modern people rarely risk such direct advice to one another, but these authors had no such reservations.

My account of the 'vibe' drew mainly on the virtues and vices, the 'one another' sayings and the specific instructions. I did not attempt to incorporate narrative material. Nor did I look at the very important and recurring language of imitation (ch. 32), food-related freedoms (e.g. Rom. 14; 1 Cor. 8 – 10; Col. 2; Heb. 13; see ch. 31), duties specific to elders and to running church meetings (e.g. 1 Cor. 11:2–16, 14), or the important discussion on marriage and singleness in 1 Corinthians 7 (because none of my categories adequately summarizes it; see chs. 36–37). I've deliberately blended together the authors' differing emphases, and my organizing categories could be contested. My discussion was based on the following biblical references.

Specific instructions
Endurance through trials: Romans 12:12; 1 Corinthians 16:13; 2 Timothy 2:3–5; Hebrews 12:1–13; James 1:2–4, 12–15; 5:7–8, 10–11; 1 Peter 3:13–18; 4:1, 12–19.
   Submission, obedience, honour:

- to God: James 4:7
- *to one another*: Romans 12:10; Ephesians 5:21
- *to church leaders*: Galatians 6:6; 1 Corinthians 16:1; 1 Thessalonians 5:12–13; 1 Timothy 2:11–12; 5:17–19; Hebrews 13:7, 17; 1 Peter 5:5
- *to ruling authorities*: Romans 13:1–7; Titus 3:1; 1 Peter 2:13–17
- *to masters*: Ephesians 6:5–8; Colossians 3:22; 1 Timothy 6:1–2; Titus 2:9–10; 1 Peter 2:18–25
- *to husbands*: Ephesians 5:22–24; Colossians 3:18; Titus 2:4–5; 1 Peter 3:1–6
- *to parents*: Ephesians 6:1–3; Colossians 3:20

Sexual purity: 1 Corinthians 5:1 – 7:9; Ephesians 5:3–5; 1 Thessalonians 4:3–8; Hebrews 13:4; Jude 7.

Care for wives, children and slaves: Ephesians 5:25–33; 6:4, 9; Colossians 3:19, 21; 4:1; 1 Peter 3:7.

Work and family care: Romans 12:11; Galatians 6:5; Ephesians 4:28; 1 Thessalonians 4:11; 5:14a; 2 Thessalonians 3:6–13; 1 Timothy 5:3–8.

Mercy (not vengeance): Romans 12:14, 17, 19–20; Ephesians 4:26, 32; Colossians 3:13; 1 Thessalonians 5:15; James 2:12–13; 1 Peter 3:9; Jude 22–23.

Humility (not criticism): Romans 12:3, 16; 1 Corinthians 3:18–23; Galatians 6:3–4; Philippians 2:3–4, 14; 1 Timothy 6:17; James 1:9–11; 4:6–16; 5:9; 1 Peter 5:5–7.

Grace (not bitterness): Philippians 4:5; Hebrews 12:15.

Empathy: Romans 12:15; Galatians 6:4–5; Philippians 2:4.

Equity and inclusion: 1 Corinthians 4:6b; 11:17–34; 1 Thessalonians 5:14; 1 Timothy 5:22; Hebrews 13:3; James 1:9–11, 27; 2:1–9, 15–16; 1 John 3:17–18.

Hospitality and sharing: Romans 12:12; Ephesians 4:28; Hebrews 13:2, 16; 1 Peter 4:9; 1 John 3:16–17; 3 John 6–8.

Service of gifts:1 Corinthians 12:1–31; Romans 12:4–8; Ephesians 4:11–12; 1 Peter 4:10–11.

Use of money: 1 Timothy 6:6–10, 17–19; Hebrews 13:5; James 5:1–6.

Prayer, praise, worship: Romans 12:12; 2 Corinthians 13:11; Ephesians 5:18; Philippians 4:4, 6; Colossians 4:2; 1 Thessalonians 5:16–18; 1 Timothy 2:1–2, 8; Hebrews 13:15; James 5:13–18; 1 Peter 4:7; Jude 20–21.

Overall unitive concepts

Peace: Romans 12:18; 14:19; 2 Corinthians 13:11; Ephesians 4:3; 5:19–20; Colossians 3:15; 1 Thessalonians 5:13b; Hebrews 12:14; James 3:18; 1 Peter 3:11.

Love: 1 Corinthians 13:1–7; 16:14; Romans 12:9–10; 13:8–10; Galatians 5:6, 13–14; 6:2; Ephesians 4:2; 5:2; Colossians 3:14; 1 Thessalonians 3:12; 4:9; Hebrews 13:1; James 2:8; 1 Peter 1:22; 4:8; 2 Peter 1:7; 1 John 2:9–11; 3:11–15, 18, 23; 4:7–21; 2 John 5–6.

Speech-acts (paralleling other norms)

Agreement without quarrelling: 1 Corinthians 1:10–13; 2 Corinthians 13:11; Philippians 1:27; 4:2.

Speech in general: Ephesians 4:25, 29; 5:4; Colossians 4:6; 1 Timothy 1:3–6; 4:7; 6:3–5; 2 Timothy 2:14–16, 23; Titus 3:2, 9; James 1:19–20, 26; 3:3–12; 4:11–12; 5:12; 1 Peter 3:9–10; Jude 16.

Theological ethics (where the action of God is explicitly or implicitly linked to human action)

2 Corinthians 4:11; 9:13; Galatians 2:19–20; 5:5–6; Ephesians 2:8–10; Philippians 2:12–13; Colossians 1:9–11, 14; 1 Thessalonians 1:2–6; 1 Timothy 1:5; 4:4–5; 2 Timothy 1:7–10; 3:14–17; Titus 2:11–14; 3:3–8; Hebrews 13:20–21; James 1:21–25; 1 Peter 1:13–16; 2 Peter 1:3–11.

Virtue and vice lists

See chapter 30 in this book.

'One another' sayings

Romans 1:12; 12:5, 10, 16; 13:8; 14:13, 19; 15:5, 7, 14; 16:16; 1 Corinthians 11:33; 12:25; 16:20; 2 Cor. 13:12; Galatians 5:13, 15, 26; 6:2; Ephesians 4:2, 25, 32; 5:21; Philippians 2:3; Col. 3:9, 13; 1 Thessalonians 3:12; 4:9, 18; 5:11, 15; 2 Thessalonians 1:3; Hebrews 10:24; James 4:11; 5:9, 16; 1 Peter 1:22; 4:9; 5:5, 14; 1 John 1:7; 3:11, 23; 4:7, 11–12. A quick summary:

- Greet, accept, forgive, submit, instruct, serve, agree with, build up, pursue good for, accept some responsibility for, confess to, pray for and love one another, showing humility kindness and hospitality.
- Avoid provoking, envying, 'biting and devouring', criticizing, lying to and complaining about one another.

19. THE 'STORY ARC' OF THE BIBLE

In Part 3 we've considered how ethics springs from Jesus. We're therefore in a better position to see how the Bible has an overall direction and trajectory – a 'story arc' that culminates in Jesus Christ.

The previous chapters have concentrated on Jesus Christ. Not only does he challenge many conceptions of ethics; it turns out that his own person is prior to and more important than abstract ethical conceptions. On a Christ-powered planet (ch. 12), ethics can really only spring from Jesus Christ, and all attempts to do ethics apart from Jesus Christ become severely flawed. The main question of our lives becomes not 'am I living ethically', but 'how am I responding to Jesus Christ'. They don't call it 'Christianity' for nothing.

Claims about Jesus will continue dividing people until either the sun explodes or Jesus returns, depending on who's right. Can the grand claim that ethics springs from Jesus really stand? Someone could attempt to discredit it by attempting to discredit Jesus himself. However that approach never quite succeeds, if only because Jesus attracts millions on his merits. He continues to trump his opponents by the evident excellence and by the pinnacle achievements of his life (chs. 12–18).

But the more clever rebuttals don't try to discredit Jesus directly. They simply observe that Christians apparently draw their morality from everywhere, including from all over the Bible, and not only from Jesus. How can ethics spring from Jesus if not even Christians proceed on this basis?

In an early episode of the US presidential television drama *The West Wing*, President Josiah Bartlett meets Dr Jenna Jacobs, who asserts that homosexual practice is an 'abomination', based on the Bible's Old Testament prohibition of it. Bartlett reduces this assertion to absurdity by pointing to parts of Old Testament law considered untenable or ridiculous today. (The writers based the scene on the Internet-circulated *Letter to Dr Laura*, a sarcastic polemic directed against conservative US radio talkback host Dr Laura Schlessinger.)

The *West Wing* scene (and the letter) intends to attack Old Testament practices in general and conservative Christian opposition to homosexuality in particular. But these opponents also attack the *method* of those who think ethics springs directly from the pages of the Bible. Like Jenna Jacobs, many Christians assume that the whole Bible is 'God's word'. Yet Christians also consider Jesus to be 'God's Word'. How then should we live, if both are true? How can ethics spring from Jesus, if parts of the Bible that predate him also contribute?

Although I agree that the Bible is 'God's word', I respectfully disagree with the way many (like Jacobs) draw morality from it. I believe they fail to take into account the overall 'story arc' of the Bible. President Bartlett and the author of the *Letter to Dr Laura* seem also not to know how many Christians regard this 'story arc'.

Without getting into too much detail, I want to explain this turn of phrase. I've stolen the term 'story arc' from scriptwriters of television series, who in addition to the plots of each individual episode like to develop an overall plot as the season unfolds. They also like to add depth and texture to their characters so that, over time, we get to know and love or hate them with increasing depth.

The Bible has this kind of story arc. Each book of the Bible is like an individual episode, with its own intricacies, characters, plots and themes. But they add together to become more than the sum of their parts as we begin to discern an overall plot. We also begin to discern the main recurring character – God – with increasing depth.

You won't find the term 'story arc' in learned theological tomes; they prefer to speak of *salvation history, progressive revelation, biblical theology* or various forms of *dispensationalism*. The differences between these ways of putting it are the details I don't want to get into. Nothing substitutes for reading and experiencing this 'story arc' for ourselves, but here's my rough summary:

1. God prepares a magnificent world, and populates it with human beings who live interdependently with its land, its animals and each other. In

God's vision for this world, people accept it joyfully and collaborate with God to develop and care for it well.

2. Individually and collectively, humans desert God's vision, giving themselves over to whatever desirable objects and group inclusions suit them. We distort society and ravage the planet in the process.

3. God commits to rescuing the world from this human folly, beginning with the man Abraham. The network of his descendants – old Israel – becomes the first community to rediscover life as God imagined it, in part through their participation in a series of fatherly instructions contained in the Bible's first five books, the Pentateuch (ch. 20). These form a kind of constitution for their life together, ordering and guiding their relationship to the land, each other and God.

4. But they strain and test the relationship with God almost to breaking point. There's a roller-coaster sequence: Egyptian slavery, then liberation; a meeting with God at Sinai, the reception of his law, then a betrayal; wanderings in the wilderness, then the military conquest of their 'Promised Land' (ancient Palestine); a ramshackle federation led by a series of judges; a golden age of monarchy led by the kings David and Solomon; then civil war and a nation divided north–south; and a succession of generally failed kings (both north and south). Throughout it all, the people keep reverting to the usual ways of being human around them. Through his law and prophets God opposes these practices; yet, with godlike loyalty and faithfulness, continues to love them.

5. The penultimate tragedy occurs in the eighth century before Christ, when the Assyrians annihilate the northern kingdom (Israel). The last great tragedy of the Old Testament period comes in the sixth century before Christ, when the Babylonians devastate the southern Kingdom (Judah) and forcibly resettle the populace in Babylon. The prophets declare this morale sapping exile to be a terrible judgment by God. It triggers a profound new consideration of the nature of God's relationship with these people. Some eventually return to Judah, but melancholy prevails. They await a majestic divine intervention – a return to the original dream.

6. The true solution to this exile is Jesus. But his intervention doesn't establish a new dominion of Israel, which everyone had grown to expect as the story unfolded. He begins a different kind of 'kingdom' – for Israelites *and* others. His teaching shows a new way of life for its citizens, where the weak are included, the proud learn humility and the powerful serve.

7. His death opens this way, finally repairing the cosmic rift between

humanity and God. Accepting God's retribution for the failures both of Israel and the world, Jesus' death (ch. 15) secures the forgiveness of God toward all humanity, as given to those 'in Christ' (ch. 14). Jesus' resurrection (ch. 16) and gift of the Spirit (ch. 17) pioneer the start of a new world where there's harmony again, an end to corruption and distortion, and a new way of being human. All are called and commanded to participate in this new way of being human in Christ.

8. New Testament authors expand on how communities in Christ live (ch. 18). At their worst, they highlight humanity's failed old way of life, and our need for God's forgiveness and restoration. But those in Christ seek to retrieve the best of the new world from the worst of the old. At their best, each person and community in Christ offers a glimpse of his new, 'resurrected' way of being human.

9. As the Bible closes, it looks forward to the end of history (ch. 24). Christ finally acts against the horrors of human wickedness, and the restoration of God's original dream for the world becomes complete. In this new cosmos, Jesus' way of upholding and powering it (ch. 12) becomes obvious to all, and those who rejoice in this lordship participate alongside him.

Like all summaries, my summary of this story arc could be disputed. But my purpose in this chapter is to show what it means for ethics. For example, I mentioned the military conquest of a 'Promised Land', when the Israelites violently expelled the previous inhabitants at God's command, as a judgment against them. The biblical authors present this activity as right and proper for the people of the time.[1] But it doesn't follow that 'holy war' remains a proper activity. For, as the Bible's story arc unfolds:

---

1. I recognize that many struggle to accept how this activity could be proper for people of any time. Modern readers find it terrible, especially after the genocides that littered the twentieth century. Some think the notion that God commanded it was merely an excuse to legitimate the attack. For others, if God did command it, then he was wrong to do so. But these parts of the Bible seem intended to show God's absolute mastery over life and death, and his sternness toward those whom he opposes – aspects of God that modern people also deeply resent, and which also drive our opposition to these texts. But none of the 'back story' between God and the defeated people is given. Perhaps the basis of God's hostility is not our business. Even if we remain disturbed by these events, the death of Christ (ch. 15) ends this kind of judgment. Arguably, we've become people horrified by holy war partly *because* of God's merciful salvation through Christ.

- *God's judgment is complete*: Jesus' death and a future final judgment complete God's objection to humanity's evils. It's no longer the task of any human agency to enact this kind of judgment against a group.
- *The home of God's people is no longer a political dominion or a physical land,* for Jesus' kingdom is 'not of this world' (John 18:36), and the truest 'citizenship' of those in Christ is 'in heaven' (Phil. 3:20). Therefore the proper 'home' of God's own will not be some specific patch of land.[2]
- *Belief in God is a response to his Word,* brought about by the mysterious work of his Spirit (ch. 17). Physical coercion cannot force belief in God.

So proper attention to the Bible's story arc makes clear that Christians are not to engage in 'holy war'. If there can ever be a justification for war, it cannot be to effect God's judgment, or to win a land for God's own, or to force belief in God; and so although 'holy war' appears in the Bible, its story arc shows that it's no longer permitted.

The effect of the Bible's story arc on the moral logic of 'holy war' is only one example among many. It turns out that the story arc affects thinking about ethics in many ways. Here are some more examples:

- The forgiveness and mercy shown toward humanity by Jesus' death has made it proper for human judges to show mercy in their judgments.[3]
- The inclusivity of communities in Christ (ch. 18) means that flawed and broken people of *every* race are now joyfully welcomed – even including extreme 'sinners' (but not those who openly and consistently continue to oppose Christ's new way of being human). There were hints of this inclusivity in the Old Testament, but it becomes overt in the New.
- The Old Testament law – the fatherly instruction that guided old Israel's life together – isn't automatically binding upon people today. This matter was a source of immense contention and discussion in the later New Testament. Its authors realized that Jesus' death and resurrection somewhat changed our relationship to this law. This matter is so important that I'll consider it further in the next chapter (ch. 20).

---

2. Modern Zionists disagree, but I find their account of the Bible's story arc unconvincing.

3. See Oliver M. T. O'Donovan, *The Desire of the Nations* (Cambridge: Cambridge University Press, 1996), pp. 256–261, 276–278.

The last of these points is what makes me think that Jacobs was wrong. We would need more information from across the Bible's story arc to evaluate homosexual practice. (See further ch. 44.)

The same comment applies to all and every matter in ethics. A Christian account of ethics, when doing its job well, has to do business with this 'story arc'. As Oliver O'Donovan puts it:

> Each area [of ethics] has to be given, as it were, a salvation-history of its own. Marriage is a gift of creation; it is taken into the reconciling fellowship of Christ; it is confronted with the challenge of the eschatological kingdom. Telling the truth is a task entrusted to Adam as he names the animals; it is a responsibility of redeemed humankind which has been told the truth about itself in Jesus; and the full disclosure of the truth is the content of God's future judgment. Work is a gift of creation; it is ennobled into mutual service in the fellowship of Christ; it gives place to a final Sabbath rest. And so on.[4]

By giving each area 'a salvation-history of its own', O'Donovan means that Christians seek to discern the moral logic of each area as it emerges from the Bible's story arc. But the Bible is a big book, and that task takes time.

In fact, the Bible is effectively *Jesus' own story arc*. Hence it's quite coherent for Christians to regard the Bible as 'God's word' even though ethics springs from Jesus. Part 4 sets out what this story arc, culminating in Jesus, means for ethics. A Christian account of ethics emerges from what I call five 'poles':

Ch. 21: The character of God
Ch. 22: Creation and 'moral order'
Ch. 23: Commands that reveal
Ch. 24: A new future
Ch. 25: Jesus-shaped community

I then show how these poles are each a part of a 'unified field' of moral reality (ch. 26). But before proceeding to these poles and to the account of how they work together, I'll pause to consider in more detail what Christians make of the Old Testament and its laws, now that we're in Christ.

---

4. Oliver M. T. O'Donovan, *Resurrection and Moral Order: An Outline for Evangelical Ethics*, 2nd ed. (Leicester: Apollos, 1994), p. xvii.

Further reading

** Goldsworthy, Graeme, *The Goldsworthy Trilogy* (Carlisle: Paternoster, 2000).

** Goldsworthy, Graeme, and Brian Rosner (eds.), *New Dictionary of Biblical Theology* (Leicester: IVP, 2000).

** 'Introduction to the Bible' (a course unit in Moore Theological College's *Preliminary Theological Certificate*); Australia: <http://external.moore.edu.au>; UK: <http://open-bible-institute.org/moore>.

20. OLD TESTAMENT LAWS

In Part 3 we've considered how ethics springs from Jesus. We've begun to see how the Bible has an overall story arc – a direction and trajectory culminating in Jesus Christ. But if ethics springs from Jesus, what are we to make of the laws and rules in the Bible's largest section, the Old Testament? Some Christians base their entire ethic on it. Other Christians ignore it entirely. A third approach is proposed.

As this book has unfolded, I've only briefly touched the thickest section of the Christian Bible – the thirty-nine books of the Old Testament. Written over several centuries, this material contains much morally oriented data:

- *The Pentateuch* (Genesis–Deuteronomy) sets out a law code for the budding nation of Israel.
- *The Histories* (Joshua–Esther) recount many characters who act well and badly as the overall drama unfolds. (So also does the Pentateuch.)
- *The Wisdom literature* (Job–Song of Songs) collects insights that many ancient Near Easterners would regard as self-evident. It dialogues with these insights, accepting or modifying them according to Israel's understanding of reality under God.
- *The Prophets* (Isaiah–Malachi) act as prosecutors, amplifying the Pentateuchal law to show where Israelites are living for false desires and inclusions. Often they attack the exclusion and exploitation of

the vulnerable, and condemn the corrupt governance of Israel's leadership. They also act as visionaries, recasting God's dream for how Israel may live well as a community under God.

But this literature isn't primarily a set of moral treatises. Its moral dimension springs from other aspects of it: the character of God (ch. 21), his promissory 'covenants' with Israel, the longing for a dependable and true leader. And throughout, the moralities and world views of neighbouring cultures appear and impinge upon the Israelite story. (So also do their armies.)

So far I've mainly looked to the New Testament literature for moral data, partly as a kind of short cut in view of our place in the Bible's story arc (ch. 19). Those in Christ are like the elves of Tolkien's Lothlórien forest, or like the Pandoran Na'vi of James Cameron's *Avatar*, who dwell among the spreading branches of an enormous tree. Jesus himself even sees it that way: 'Remain in Me . . . I am the vine; you are the branches' (John 15:4–5). This 'vine' has deep roots in the Old Testament.

But I want to visit two disputes that continually reappear in Christian discussions of ethics. I'll introduce them as strongly stated opposing positions, with labels:

1. 'The Pentateuchal law is God's eternal Word. Christian thought about right and wrong must be based upon it' (the *theonomist* view).
2. 'Ethics is properly understood to spring from Jesus Christ. No Old Testament literature has any bearing on Christian thought about right and wrong' (the *antinomian* view).

I've overstated these positions: in both cases, only a few would put it like that. But they map the ends of a spectrum of Christian views about the moral relevance of the Old Testament. I'll say why I disagree with both.

The first followers of Jesus had a long-running discussion about their relationship to the Pentateuchal law. At first, it obviously seemed to apply to them. Jesus had stated his appreciation of it (see p. 89); who were they to disagree? But it gradually dawned on them that he had said this prior to the pinnacle achievements of his life (chs. 15–17), which turned out to eclipse even God's Old Testament law. The implications unfold at first around *the old food laws* (see p. 159).

At around the same time, the Jewish Saul of Tarsus radically changes his allegiance from old Judaism to Christ (Acts 9:1–31) and becomes 'Paul', Christ's ambassador toward those who know nothing about Israel's history or laws (Acts 13:46; Rom. 11:13). This task causes him to extend the early discus-

sion about the law to its logical conclusion. He states it bluntly, and provocatively for many at the time: 'you are not under law' (Rom. 6:14). Several of
Paul's discussions are woven around this phrase 'under law' (1 Cor. 9:20–21;
Gal. 3:23; 4:4–5, 21; 5:18) or some equivalent. Paul consistently asserts that
this code doesn't bind Christians, since 'Christ is the end' (perhaps meaning
'goal') 'of the law' (Rom. 10:4). Christians are now under 'the law of Christ' (1
Cor. 9:21; Gal. 6:2), to use an equally provocative phrase.

In other words, the law for the nation of Israel doesn't bear down as law
upon those in Christ. Some scholars dispute this conclusion (either that Paul
thought it, or that it is so), but I cannot ever see how. The message is simple:
God has so arranged human affairs that his instructions to ancient Israel no
more directly accuse us than do, say, the laws of ancient Rome.

Yet Christians have consistently baulked at such a conclusion. What about
the clarion excellence of the Ten Commandments? What about the Old
Testament's clear lines of demarcation for sexual morality? What about the
prophets' reapplication of the law to address social injustice? Under various
names (e.g. *theonomy* or *reconstructionism*), some Christians have argued that
these laws govern Christians at least, or even everyone. But I repeat, with Paul:
they no longer have any formal legal relevance to us.

The position I'm now putting attracts a theological swear word. I'm called
antinomian, someone who's anti-law. Confusingly, this swear word is used in
two ways. It can refer specifically to those (like me) who think Old Testament
law no longer binds us as law. It can also refer to those (unlike me) who think
we should not bother ourselves with right and wrong at all.

My kind of antinomianism can give rise to the view that 'no Old Testament
literature has any bearing on Christian thought about right and wrong'. For if
I think that not even the hard-core legal aspects of the Old Testament have
any relevance to thought about right and wrong, then it surely follows that I'll
allow no place for the more morally ambiguous sections of the Old Testament.
Surely I'll argue that prophetic calls to include the poor in Israel were just that
– calls to a nation long gone. Surely I couldn't possibly draw any moral conclusions from narratives of Israelites acting well or badly. I'll probably even have
to argue that the wisdom literature has no particular claim upon me, since it's
only an Israelite dialogue with ancient Near Eastern neighbours. I'll end up
only taking notice of the Old Testament's yearnings for a dependable and true
leader (who finally appeared as Jesus Christ). Yet I don't make all these conclusions. I'll explore a later development in Christian thought to explain why not.

After the New Testament period, Christian readers of the Old Testament
tried to make sense of two things. They wanted to take Paul's view seriously.
They also wanted to understand why various utterances in the Old Testament

law seemed to retain such deep truth – such as 'You must not steal. You must not act deceptively or lie to one another' (Lev. 19:11), or Jesus' favourite, 'love your neighbour as yourself' (Lev. 19:18). They reasoned that Old Testament laws could be sorted into one of three categories:

1. *Civil laws* that define how to run the new nation.
2. *Ceremonial laws* that govern the new nation's worship.
3. *Moral laws* that retain enduring relevance to all people everywhere.

They concluded that while the first and second categories were no longer binding, the third was. The Ten Commandments (or at least the first nine of them) were taken as moral laws. In the period of the sixteenth-century Reformation, another debate arose about the uses of this moral law. The disputants agreed that moral law could show people how God was opposed to them (unless he rescued them). They agreed it might shape modern civil laws. But they disagreed about a so-called 'third use': whether or not these moral laws should guide Christian behaviour.

Now this is all very interesting, but unfortunately a key step has been lost (for me, at least) somewhere in the mists of time. For how do you decide in which 'hopper' an Old Testament law belongs? How could you know whether to discard it as an old civil or ceremonial law, or to keep it as a moral law? Each generation would have to consider each, law by law. But people didn't do that, and simply asserted sections as 'moral' or not. We then have to trust the asserter without knowing his reasoning. We're effectively still 'under the law' (and someone's interpretation of it).

Yet the original hunch, that various utterances in the Old Testament law retain deep truth, should not be lost. Here's a section that stirs my heart and expands my horizons:

> You must not oppress your neighbour or rob him. The wages due a hired hand must not remain with you until morning. You must not curse the deaf or put a stumbling block in front of the blind, but you are to fear your God; I am the LORD.
>
> You must not act unjustly when rendering judgment. Do not be partial to the poor or give preference to the rich; judge your neighbour fairly. You must not go about spreading slander among your people; you must not jeopardize your neighbour's life; I am the LORD.
>
> You must not hate your brother in your heart. Rebuke your neighbour directly, and you will not incur guilt because of him. Do not take revenge or bear a grudge against members of your community, but love your neighbour as yourself; I am the LORD.
> (Lev. 19:13–18)

These words cause me to see differently. Why? How? I take it that they express

- the nature of a life that bears the imprint of God's own character
- the preciousness of others who are made and loved by God
- the good of a community dwelling together in reconciled harmony
- a vision of how the future could be, lived together under God
- all expressed in a way that interrogates the loves and inclusions I currently think are important

In other words, they express, in a particular time and place, the contours of a 'unified field' of moral reality that we'll see in chapter 26. I don't pretend to be able to access this Old Testament material other than as a Christian reader. But my task becomes to see how it expresses and reflects moral truths that are at one with a life in Christ. I may not be under this law; but as I read it with interest, it expands my moral imagination. Thinking how Christ relates to it then expands my moral imagination further. (As Luther once memorably put it, 'If you wish to fulfil the law and not covet, as the law demands, come, believe in Christ in whom grace, righteousness, peace, liberty, and all things are promised you.'[1])

The same kind of reasoning applies to the prophetic material, the wisdom material and the stories about characters. Each in its own way expands my understanding of creation, community, the future and God's character (Part 4). This material is not for brandishing as a set of rules. As I 'wear' this material like a set of 'glasses' (to borrow a wonderful metaphor from John Calvin), it shifts my gestalt (p. 72). It enables me to better decode my complex world (ch. 10).

This way of looking at it means I don't really consider myself an antinomian, for I consider all parts of the Old Testament to have some bearing on Christian thought about right and wrong. But it isn't a rule-based kind of bearing. Rather, it promotes and expands Christian wisdom. For want of a better label, I take a 'Christian wisdom' approach to the Old Testament and its laws.

A small example may illustrate where we've come. One area of debate among Christians concerns how we're to receive those parts of the Old

---

1. Martin Luther, 'The Freedom of a Christian', in *Luther's Works*, vol. 31, ed. H. Grimm (Philadelphia: Fortress, 1957), p. 348. Online (in an older version): <http://www.fordham.edu/halsall/mod/luther-freedomchristian.html> (accessed 15 July 2010).

Testament that protect the interests of the excluded or vulnerable (glimpsed in the quotation above from Leviticus, and amplified several times over throughout the Old Testament).

- A theonomist approach might say, 'These laws are clear: we must care for the vulnerable.'
- An antinomian approach might say, 'These laws are for the people of their time; in no way do they prove that Christian people are tasked to care for the world's vulnerable.'
- A 'Christian wisdom' approach might say, 'These laws reveal the "shape" of God's world, and show that those who have responsibility need to help set conditions under which the vulnerable are protected and included.'

Further reading

** Brock, Brian, *Singing the Ethos of God: On the Place of Christian Ethics in Scripture* (Grand Rapids: Eerdmans, 2007).

*** Cameron, Andrew J. B., 'How "Ethics" Works: An Engagement with John Calvin', in *Engaging with Calvin: Aspects of the Reformer's Legacy for Today*, ed. Mark D. Thompson (Nottingham: Apollos, 2009), pp. 230–253.

** Cameron, Andrew J. B., 'Liberation and Desire: The Logic of Law in Exodus and Beyond', in *Exploring Exodus: Literary, Theological and Contemporary Approaches*, ed. Brian S. Rosner and Paul R. Williamson (Nottingham: Apollos, 2008), pp. 123–153.

** Sloane, Andrew, *At Home in a Strange Land: Using the Old Testament in Christian Ethics* (Peabody, Mass.: Hendrickson, 2008).

** Wright, Christopher J. H., *Old Testament Ethics for the People of God* (Leicester: IVP, 2004).

PART 4 FIVE THINGS THAT MATTER

What stays the same, and what changes?

You may be very impressed by the *flux* seen across time and space. If you're into astronomy and cosmology, you picture a universe seething with matter and energy, with stars and planets forming and reforming, our own earth a bit player in that passing parade. You may be convinced that life and our species surged forth from this flux, has changed radically through time and will change just as much again. Cultures have come and will go, and their values with them. Our own personalities, our wants and needs, will change just as dramatically, right up until we die. The sun may twinkle now but it will blow out fat and red, burning the earth, then to shrink and die until the universe goes cold. On this view nothing much is permanent.

Or you may think differently. Whether or not all that cosmic stuff is true, there remain constantly recurring patterns on the human historical scale. Humans have needed food, families, love and friendship since long before they wrote about it, and will continue to have such needs far into the future. Enfolding us all, our planet sustains life and breath, and has done so from the distant past and will do so into the future. The *stability* seen across the part of space and time relevant to humans impresses you.

Each view has an impact on how you think about ethics. If you're into stability, you'll tend to think that ethical 'norms' (standards of right and wrong) are similar from one age to the next. If you're into flux, you'll prefer to think that ethical norms are temporary, coming and going with different times and cultures. Each view is quite compelling, and it can be difficult to decide between them. Indeed, we're each too limited to have the necessary perspective to determine which is correct.

This is why Christians rejoice in the news that the voice of an uncreated One has entered our limited frame, giving a perspective on it that we cannot achieve alone. My purpose in this section is simply to introduce five 'things that matter', which appear and recur across the Bible's story arc (see p. 133).

During this section, you may wonder what has happened to everything about Jesus covered in chapters 12–17. Chapter 25, on 'Jesus-shaped community', summarizes this material. This kind of community opens our way to the first four things that matter, which is why I think it comprises the fifth thing that matters.

Sometimes I refer to these things that matter as 'poles'. I don't mean 'poles' like Maypoles, or as in pole-vaulting. Rather, just as I can walk no farther than the North or South Pole, so also here: moral reality doesn't extend beyond these five things that matter. There are no human-invented improvements, replacements or extensions to these 'poles'. They're the boundaries, if you like, of moral reality.

A Christian account of ethics emerges from these five biblical 'poles', because in Christian thought they retain the same enduring relevance now as when the Bible was written. They're how the voice of the uncreated One orients us in the tussle between flux and permanence. Chapter 10 outlines how they combine to form a 'unified field', the new 'gestalt' (p. 72) in which to regard moral reality. Some conclusions follow about how we might then interpret the language of rules, rights, values and results (ch. 27).

In Part 4 we're examining how ethics emerges from five 'things that matter', which recur throughout the Bible's story arc and remain relevant. This chapter examines the first of these: the settled, good and knowable character of God.

'Be perfect', says Jesus, 'as your heavenly Father is perfect' (Matt. 5:48). This is a rather large thought. A second (by Paul) is like it: 'Be imitators of God' (Eph. 5:1). The followers of Jesus agree. 'Just as he who called you is holy, so be holy in all you do' (1 Pet. 1:15, NIV), for God intends 'that we may share in his holiness' (Heb. 12:10, NIV). 'The one who does what is right is righteous, just as He is righteous' (1 John 3:7).

These urgings to copy God may not yet convince you. You may think humans cannot be like God: perhaps you think we're too flawed (after all, most of us seem unable to become like Mother Theresa, let alone God); or perhaps you think we're too different (no one would urge a human to copy the sun or a volcano: how would you even go about it?). Or, you may even doubt that humans *should* be like God, either because you don't see what makes the connection necessary, or because you simply don't like him.

Here I aim simply for us to begin to grasp what Jesus and his followers meant. I want to show that Christians think God has a well-defined good character, and to introduce a little of that character. Later I'll claim that the relevance of his character isn't only that it can be 'copied'. For it turns out that this character is *so* enduring, *so* good, and its possessor unique, so that it affects the very substructure of ethics itself (ch. 22.)

For Jesus and his followers to urge us in this way they must have had what philosophers call a 'thick' conception of God. This is as opposed to a 'thin' conception, such as if you only think of God as a 'force behind nature', or as the 'spark within all life'. If those were all you had to work with, there would be nothing to imitate and no real substance to being 'perfect'. So it seems they have in mind something richer. To get our heads around what they may mean, we could take a small step and then a much bigger step.

The small step is easy enough. We would begin with the immediate context of each comment. Paul speaks of being 'kind and compassionate to one another, forgiving one another, just as God also forgave you in Christ. Therefore, be imitators of God, as dearly loved children' (Eph. 4:32 – 5:1), just as awestruck little ones copy their fathers. Those who've experienced God's forgiveness do a small version of it on others. It's the best kind of transference, where his personality 'rubs off' on us. Being in Christ involves taking on a 'new self, created according to the likeness of God' (Eph. 4:24, NRSV). This new way of being human involves truth-telling (not lies), honest labour (not theft), speech that builds up others (not bitchiness and insult), and compassion and forgiveness (not vengeful rage). Each of these, it seems, is Godlike.

The immediate context of Jesus' call to 'be perfect' was his famous 'Sermon on the Mount' (which I touched on in ch. 13). Here Jesus pictures a quite unusual way of being human, one radically committed to the good of the other. It includes extreme generosity, even toward enemies (such as when God sends the sun and the rain on everyone whether or not they respect him).

So even with just a small step we've begun to discover the deep conception of God held by Jesus and Paul. Evidently, they do not think of God as capricious. They assume God has a stable character. They draw from a sum of God's actions and affections known over time, and commend them to us.

The second and much bigger step we could take would look at where they discovered this character. But that's a daunting task, since Jesus professes to have found it primarily in the Old Testament, and the New Testament authors profess to have found it both in the Old Testament and through Jesus' life and pinnacle achievements (chs. 12–18). Our big step would therefore be to delve into the entire Bible to discover this character of God.

The problem is that God is the first person to appear in the first verse of the Bible, and the central figure of its final chapter. The entire collection of biblical books is preoccupied with God. Like many Christians, I've been dipping in and out of the Bible for some years, from which I have a well-formed series of impressions about God's character. But now that the heat is on to convey some of this, I find it quite difficult.

It's a bit like that moment at a party when someone says, 'So tell me about you.' Don't you find it difficult to sum up in a few sentences what makes you tick, the experiences you've had, the nuances to your personality, and all the years of your history? Likewise, I swallow hard when someone at a party says, 'So tell me about Mary-Anne,' my wife of twenty-four years. I know what makes her laugh (joyous reunions, pompous ministers, puns). I know what engages her affections (fiction books, marginalized people, breakers in the surf) and what make her bored or angry (clichés, self-righteousness, duplicity). I've seen how glad she makes children feel, how she can warm up a room full of anxious and shy people, and I've seen what makes her angry. But ask me to tell you all about her? 'Well . . .' I begin – then I start to sound like some self-absorbed idiot, as if I haven't even noticed the colour of her eyes.

Anyway, I'll have a stab at telling you about God's character. But it will be a lame substitute for getting to know him through the pages of Scripture, as Jesus and Paul did. It will be as lame as my few sentences on Mary-Anne compared to twenty-four years of living with her.

In the Bible's grand story arc (ch. 19), God's character emerges gradually. The God of the Old Testament gradually refracts into the Father, Son and Spirit of the New Testament; and in the New Testament, it's safe to say, the name 'God' is synonymous with 'Father'.[1]

At his first appearance, where he creates and provisions an entire cosmos, God's extreme liberality is quite unnerving. He's also unnervingly stern. His punishment of Adam and Eve is decisive, although not excessive. But later,

---

1. I recognize that for some women and feminists this fact has become a threat. Unfortunately, this book is not about responding to that important problem. I'm only outlining the way the scriptural texts present God, so I don't shy away from using the pronoun 'he' for God. But to someone with these concerns I make two suggestions. First, Scripture presents God's 'patriarchy' as good. The character of God, although worryingly fierce at some points, resolves into a character that can be trusted and enjoyed. Unless we've decided that all patriarchy is bad by definition, these texts offer to show how patriarchy may be good, and what makes bad patriarchy bad. (Ch. 42 is relevant to this point.) Hence my second suggestion: consider how generations of women have been able, with very many still able, to receive and enjoy this scriptural account of God. They have not all been hoodwinked or coerced by male oppressors. Some genuinely love and adore the Father (and Son) of whom they read in the Bible.

seeing that 'the wickedness of humankind was great in the earth, and that every inclination of the thoughts of their hearts was only evil continually', God 'was sorry that he had made humankind on the earth, and it grieved him to his heart' (Gen. 6:5–6, NRSV). So he determines to 'blot out from the earth the human beings I have created' (Gen. 6:7, NRSV) in the famous flood. Clearly, this person has extremely powerful sensibilities about right and wrong, although at this stage they're not entirely clear.

A favourite stratagem by the recent round of atheists is to mock God's fierceness as capricious and extreme. (The intensity of this mockery is striking, since, after all, these people think God doesn't exist. I'm unclear how a non-person can engender such hatred.) But the way the Bible paints it, you may as well attack the burdensome oppressiveness of gravity – which is, after all, very mean. It won't let us fly, it makes us climb stairs and it squashes us with falling walls. According to the biblical authors, you can attack God all you like, or just work with him as he is – which turns out to be far easier than we first suspect.

His sensibilities do begin to emerge, and I'll jump to an astounding moment when God himself explains them. In a moment of extraordinary intimacy, Moses witnesses God describing the way he sees himself:

> The LORD[2] passed before him and proclaimed, 'The LORD, the LORD, a God merciful and gracious, slow to anger, and abounding in steadfast love and faithfulness, keeping steadfast love for thousands, forgiving iniquity and transgression and sin, but who will by no means clear the guilty, visiting the iniquity of the fathers on the children and the children's children, to the third and the fourth generation.' (Exod. 34:6–7, ESV)

If you feel cross about 'the third and the fourth generation', perhaps something has gone wrong with you as a reader, or with your habits of response to God. We may wonder whether children should wear a parent's sin (that odd

---

2. Biblical translators respectfully use 'LORD' to parallel the practice of ancient Jews. They used a polite substitute for God's personal name, which for centuries they never spoke aloud. They did so in deference to God's astounding power and majesty. Hence we're amazed when Jesus himself goes to the opposite extreme and addresses God intimately as *Abba*. Those in Christ are encouraged to do the same (Mark 14:36; Rom. 8:15; Gal. 4:6). Against the backdrop of God's fierceness, this intimacy is a monumental leap forward, made possible by our participation in Christ's perfect Sonship (chs. 12–17).

word 'iniquity'). But do consider the rest: that here's a merciful and gracious person, who loves to forgive.

Mercy, grace and forgiveness are only a big deal if you think someone has done something very bad. God estimates that humanity acts really badly very often, and he forcefully resists these acts (as seen e.g. in the flood narrative I mentioned above). He will 'by no means clear the guilty'. The line about fathers' sins being 'visited upon' successive generations of children could simply be an evocative phrase to describe how seriously extensive is God's justice. It could also depict the way the results of a father's sin reverberate down through the generations. (In either case, the misunderstanding that children pay for parental sin is corrected by the prophet Ezekiel, who asserts that God insists 'the son will not share the guilt of the father, nor will the father share the guilt of the son,' Ezek. 18:20, NIV.)

This strong desire for justice almost contradicts God's strong desire to give mercy. (According to Ezekiel, God insists that 'the soul who sins is the one who will die,' 18:20; yet 'I take no pleasure in the death of anyone . . . Repent and live!' 18:32, NIV.) But God's settled character is to uphold justice *and* to give great mercy. This dual aspect of God's character is deeply mysterious. It's quite hard for us to fathom how God doesn't privilege one over the other. But this character translates into an ardent commitment to humanity, called *steadfast love*. Steadfast love is an inexorable, unimaginable determination to care for people both by holding to account those who do evil, and by reconciling with those who do evil.

This triad – God's justice, mercy and steadfast love – is the backbone of God's character as it emerges. The Bible's story arc describes how God lives out this triad in his relationship with humanity.

But it also turns out that God himself makes a distinct imprint upon how ethics works. That is, the relevance of God's character to a Christian account of how ethics works even goes beyond how well we do to copy God. It turns out that God may even have *structured* aspects of himself *into the way things work*. I'll turn to this concept in the next chapter.

22. CREATION AND 'MORAL ORDER'

In Part 4 we're examining how ethics emerges from five 'things that matter', which recur throughout the Bible's story arc and remain relevant. This chapter examines the second of these: the order of a good creation, shaped by the good God.

Where does an ethic come from? Is it as the nineteenth-century German philosopher Friedrich Nietzsche said (summarized by John D. Caputo)?

> Once upon a time, on a little star in a distant corner of the universe, clever little animals invented for themselves proud words, like truth and goodness. But soon enough the little star cooled, and the little animals had to die and with them their proud words.[1]

Is ethics simply the invention of beings who impose their will upon what they see? Do we construct values as an activity of the mind? Is it that people simply like to talk up useful concepts like goodness, rights, values, and so on? Christians recoil, for this idea ignores the role of God. But some people think that, according to Christianity, God simply does the same thing: *he* constructs values as an activity of *his* mind, imposing the result upon humanity because

---

1. John D. Caputo, *Philosophy and Theology* (Nashville: Abingdon, 2006), p. 1.

he's powerful and able to do so, using a system of command, expectation and judgment.

In both these cases, *voluntarism* is at the base of ethics. Voluntarism is the view that someone's will – either God's or humanity's – projects right or wrong upon the neutral canvas of reality. The ancient Greek philosopher Plato once posed the famous *Euthyphro dilemma* about how ethics works: does God make something good by commanding it, or does God command what's already good? The theological voluntarist shrugs and replies, 'It's good because God commands it.' The non-theological voluntarist (like Nietzsche) says, 'I'm not interested in God; but if something is good, it's only because someone somewhere has declared and demanded that it be so.' Is voluntarism really how ethics works?

Voluntarism has a natural enemy and I've spent a moment outlining voluntarism to bring its enemy into focus. According to this enemy, the answer is *no*, voluntarism isn't really how ethics works. The substrate for right and wrong lies beyond human will. Reality around us somehow contains the substructure of right and wrong. (I'll return to God's will shortly.)

Consider a simple example. Oxygen is good because it serves another good – it keeps us alive. Hence it's bad to suffocate, strangle or smother someone. According to voluntarists, each of those moral terms ('good' and 'bad') is a mere definition: we *choose* to define life and therefore oxygen as good, and murder by suffocation as bad. In this case, 'goodness' is just a handy word the little animals thought up to emphasize how much they need oxygen. There's nothing intrinsically great about oxygen; it's just another neutral element in a morally neutral cosmos.

The natural enemy of voluntarism is *moral realism*. According to the moral realist, that murder is bad, that life is good and that whatever enables life (e.g. oxygen) is good are not merely statements of human preference. These statements describe *how things really are*, whether or not people believe it. Moral realists generally hold that we inhabit a *moral order* – a kind of moral 'ecology' that sets the conditions for what we know as goodness and badness.

For what we inhabit is orderly in many other ways. Gravity always attracts, and doesn't randomly repel. Iron and oxygen stay stable, and don't randomly transmute into lithium or argon. People don't shape-shift or wink out of existence. Forests and oceans don't swap places overnight. Although we can imagine other universes, planets or times that don't exhibit this order, they're quite irrelevant to our human time and place, which does have it.

The phrase 'moral order' depicts the way right and wrong are somehow woven into this general order.[2] If we think that this order is the basis for claims about right and wrong and that they're well beyond the desires and decisions of our will, then we're moral realists.[3]

Voluntarists may argue to drain a wetland we don't like or cannot use, or to kill a baby no one wants. For the moral realist, the wrongness of these acts lies beyond our desires. Biodiversity and human life are good; hence we're to care for both. When a human-rights activist declares that the right not to be murdered is independent of local cultures where people might quite like to kill others, the activist is morally realist in mood.

In voluntary euthanasia, people respond to pain and suffering by hating their life, and we kill them. The fight over this practice shows the basic commitments in play. The voluntarist believes in the sufferer's estimate of his or her life as a worthless evil. The moral realist claims that the good of human life is bigger than our perceptions of it.

---

2. For what I take to be the definitive discussion of the concept of order and its relation to moral order, see Oliver M. T. O'Donovan, *Resurrection and Moral Order: An Outline for Evangelical Ethics*, 2nd ed. (Leicester: IVP, 1986), pp. 31–38, and *passim* chs. 3–4. O'Donovan makes key distinctions, which I have sidestepped in the interests of brevity. For example, he thinks that the moral order in creation is constituted both in its *generic order*, the relationships of things next to each other (which science can observe) and in its *telic* order, the purposive relationship of things *for* other entities (which does not fall within the domain of science).

3. Actually, the labels *voluntarism* and *moral realism* pass over many discussions in moral theology and philosophy. Among theologians, *natural law* approaches to ethics most strongly represent moral realism. They notice the moral relevance of the natural order, but can be naively optimistic about our capacity to decode its relationships and significance. Among philosophers, moral realism divides into *naturalist* and *non-naturalist* versions. Voluntarism overlaps a cluster of views. Some voluntarists are *constructivist*. Other constructivists are a hybrid of realism and voluntarism, holding that a perceiving agent is essential to morality, but that there are objective constraints on what and how they perceive. Some views hold both moral realism and constructivism to be in error (e.g. moral *non-cognitivism* and *expressivism*; moral *nihilism* and *scepticism*; and *error theory*), and some of these could even be called voluntarist. (I thank Emma Wood for her guidance around this field.) However, I think voluntarism versus moral realism remains a useful broad distinction. For an introduction to voluntarism in the senses used here, see Oliver M. T. O'Donovan, 'The Natural Ethic', in David F. Wright, *Essays in Evangelical Social Ethics* (Exeter: Paternoster, 1981), p. 22; and O'Donovan, *Resurrection and Moral Order*, pp. 16–17.

So for moral realists we're deluding ourselves if we don't *receive* oxygen, life and many other elements of material existence as good. Since these all exist together in a moral order (or moral 'ecology', as I put it earlier), the moral realist also sets about discerning, receiving and then defending or promoting various *relationships* between things,[4] which also constitute goodness. It's the *relationship* between oxygen and life that makes oxygen good. We do no harm to moral order by selling or discarding a bottle of oxygen, except if to do so deprives some human or animal life of oxygen.

But the discernment of relationships between things is much more complex than this simple example suggests, for the moral ecology is complex (ch. 10). Therefore, moral realists argue among themselves about the relationships between things, and how best to defend or promote these relationships. Those arguments don't mean that moral realism is wrong – just that it's harder to do than some reductionist approaches to ethics (ch. 1).[5]

I take the position in this book that Christian thought about ethics is morally realist, but that decoding moral ecology is almost beyond each *individual*. Our difficulty begins in our limitations as finite creatures with a tiny perspective. It's complicated by our fixations on various desires (ch. 7) and by our need to be included in social groups and their schools of moral formation (ch. 8). According to Christian thought, we need God to decode moral order because moral knowledge best occurs in partnership (like just about all knowledge, actually).

The ancient biblical depiction of humanity's 'Fall' consists partly in the fight about how good and evil will be known – whether in partnership with God, or as humanity strikes out alone (Gen. 2:9, 17; 3:5–6, 22). In this literature, to

---

4. This sentence uses the term 'relationships' non-personally to describe how various aspects of the material order interact. I risk confusion when later in the book 'relationships' means 'personal relationships' – those 'connections' with another person where we advance each other's good, or our own good at each other's expense, or some combination.

5. People who know a bit about ethics will complain that I have ignored the so-called *naturalistic fallacy*, which claims we cannot derive an 'ought' from an 'is' – that we cannot simply observe how things are, then say what to do. The English philosopher David Hume alerted us to the issue (*Treatise of Human Nature*, 3.1.1). With his usual scepticism, he challenged ethical thinkers to explain better how their morality connects with the material order. It is an interesting and hard challenge. But it doesn't follow from it that there is *no* connection between 'is' and 'ought', or that a moral realist bent in ethics is 'fallacious'.

'know' connotes experiential knowledge. Therefore, the act of eating from 'the tree of the knowledge of good and evil' cleverly enacts, embodies and constitutes humanity's attempts to know morality by decision and experimentation. When humanity is later described as 'in Adam' (1 Cor. 15:22; cf. Rom. 5:12–19), this solidarity is due in part to humanity's persistent refusal to know good and evil in partnership with God. We act according to the recommendations of our 'flesh' (ch. 9). Not only do we choose and practise values of our own devising, but as members of a herd, we 'even applaud others who practise them' in calculated opposition to whatever God is said to prefer (Rom. 1:32). (The conflict is so primal that even this paragraph may raise your hackles. This book offers several ways to begin exploring and interrogating that response; ch. 33 may be a helpful waypoint.) Throughout the Bible's story arc (ch. 19), God continues to decode moral order for humanity, culminating in the life, teaching and pinnacle achievements of Jesus Christ (Part 3 and ch. 25).

But what I've said addresses only an *epistemological* problem (a 'how things are known' problem). That is, I've only said something about how Christianity might approach the complexity of knowing moral order. However, if moral realism is true, there's a deeper *ontological* problem (a 'how things are built' problem) that Christianity must address. For if 'goodness' inheres in the material order, can Christians seriously believe that God remains supreme?

That is, how would the moral realist, if she believed in God, reply to Plato's Euthyphro dilemma? Surely she must be asserting that 'God commands what's already good', an answer that would imply that good is supreme over God, which no Christian believes. Therefore, the Christian moral realist has a more subtle reply.

God 'saw' that every aspect of the planet was *good* (Gen. 1:4, 10, 12, 18, 21, 25), culminating in his forceful observation (v. 31) that everything – including humanity – is *exceedingly good*. Theological voluntarists must hold that the creation was 'declared' good, as an act of definition. But the text puts it differently: even though God has made everything and remains supreme over it, he 'saw' that it was all good. The phrasing seems to be a form of *recognition* by God of the goodness of his handiwork.

However, God too is good. According to the prophet Habakkuk, the 'eyes' of the one who 'saw it was very good' are also 'too pure to look on evil' (Hab. 1:13, NIV). God describes himself as just, merciful and steadfastly loving (ch. 21). We find that goodness is intrinsic to the Godhead when Jesus reveals how Father, Son and Spirit faithfully give 'glory' to one another where glory is due (John 16 – 17). Elsewhere John simply summarizes the goodness of God: 'God is love' (1 John 4:8, NIV), and 'God is light; in him there is no darkness at all' (1 John 1:5, NIV).

What, then, could 'connect' all the following statements?

1. God is good.
2. The creation is good.
3. Nothing is greater than God (including 'good').
4. God observes and proclaims a good creation.
5. God isn't a part of creation.
6. Creation isn't a part of God.

For the Christian moral realist, the connection is that *the world has some imprints of God's goodness*. God has somehow structured aspects of his own good character into the way things work. Proverbs 8 contains the simplest demonstration of this claim, where a woman called 'Wisdom' sings about herself. The authors of the Proverbs don't speak of ethics as such. Wisdom is their name for that package of experience, discernment and knowledgeable love of God that enables a good life.

So a woman called Wisdom stands next to the foot-traffic of a town, calling out to the passers-by and urging to take her seriously whoever will listen. At first she appears as an outsider – the kind of person that may be worth listening to but whom we often ignore (like our mothers). But as the chapter proceeds, she emerges more and more majestically, culminating in these astounding words:

> The LORD made [or 'possessed'] me
> at the beginning of His creation,
> before His works of long ago.
> I was formed before ancient times,
> from the beginning, before the earth began.
> I was brought forth
> when there were no watery depths
> and no springs filled with water.
> I was brought forth
> before the mountains and hills were established,
> before He made the land, the fields,
> or the first soil on earth.
> I was there when He established the heavens,
> when He laid out the horizon on the surface of the ocean,
> when He placed the skies above,
> when the fountains of the ocean gushed forth,
> when He set a limit for the sea

so that the waters would not violate His command,

when He laid out the foundations of the earth.

I was a skilled craftsman beside Him.

I was His delight every day,

always rejoicing before Him.

I was rejoicing in His inhabited world,

delighting in the human race.

(Prov. 8:22–31)

God builds with Wisdom alongside him. Christians have long been impressed by the resonances between Wisdom and Jesus, both of whom are pictured as 'with God' from the beginning (John 1:1–2, in the case of Jesus). The apostle Paul even calls Christ 'God's power and God's wisdom' (1 Cor. 1:24); hence the conclusion that the planet is 'Christ powered' (ch. 12). But for the moment, notice how in this poem Wisdom is herself *involved in shaping the cosmos*. The Old Testament authors would never have taken Wisdom to be a separate god from God: rather, we have here a poetic description of *how God's own good character*, personified as Wisdom, governs and shapes the world he's made.[6]

This imprint of God accounts for some familiar patterns in our social experience. The God who made us loves truth, just as relationships seem to require truth. The persons of the Godhead steadfastly love one another, just as our closest relationships (such as marriage, ch. 37) are constituted in steadfast love. God enacts justice, and the necessity of justice is structured into the marrow of group life. God reconciles and includes wayward people, and the need for inclusion resides deep within us all. Our sociality bears the imprint of his character.

We begin to see, then, that because of who God is in himself (ch. 21), we have the basis for a moral order embedded in the very stuff of our world. By imitating God (cf. ch. 32), it turns out we enter into an experience of the way we're meant to inhabit our bodies, our relationships and the entire order that surrounds us.

---

6. See further Tremper Longman III, *How To Read Proverbs* (Downers Grove: IVP, 2002), pp. 33, 110, 143.

Further reading

*** Cromartie, Michael (ed.), *A Preserving Grace: Protestants, Catholics, and Natural Law* (Grand Rapids: Eerdmans, 1997).
** Longman III, Tremper, *How to Read Proverbs* (Downers Grove: IVP, 2002).

23. COMMANDS THAT REVEAL

In Part 4 we're examining how ethics emerges from five 'things that matter', which recur throughout the Bible's story arc and remain relevant. This chapter examines the third of these: the biblical commands and imperatives that continually reveal something about God's cosmos and interrogate our responses to it.

Most people are aware that the Bible includes hundreds of rules, but remain unaware of the helpful discussions in Christianity about how to regard them. This discussion occurs within the pages of the Bible itself, and throughout Christian history. Here are some examples of biblical rules:

- The most famous law code of the Old Testament, which we call the *Ten Commandments* (originally God's 'Ten Words'), is listed twice (Exod. 20:1–17; Deut. 5:6–21). In each case, they headline a series of other laws and instructions to the ancient Israelites.
- These other laws and instructions are a major part of the first five books of the Bible (the *Pentateuch*). They have a broad range of focus – from (e.g.) 'You must not go up to My altar on steps, so that your nakedness is not exposed on it' (Exod. 20:26) to 'At the end of every three years, bring a tenth of all your produce for that year . . . [Then] the foreign resident, fatherless, and widow within your gates may come, eat, and be satisfied' (Deut. 14:28–29).

- Biblical *wisdom literature* is often phrased as what looks to us like rules. It sometimes adds reasons: 'Do not answer a fool according to his foolishness, or you will be like him yourself' (Prov. 26:4). However, this literature can throw us off-balance by also stating an opposite 'rule': 'Answer a fool according to his foolishness, or he will become wise in his own eyes' (Prov. 26:5).
- Old Testament *prophets* did not issue new rules so much as reiterate old ones: 'Repent! Turn from your idols and renounce all your detestable practices!' (Ezek. 14:6, NIV).
- *Jesus* sometimes phrases *his instructions* as rules: 'If your brother sins against you, go and rebuke him in private. If he listens to you, you have won your brother' (Matt. 18:15). 'This is what I command you: love one another' (John 15:17).
- Letters from the apostles often include imperatives: 'Just as the Lord has forgiven you, so also you must forgive' (Col. 3:13). 'Greet one another with a kiss of love' (1 Pet. 5:14). 'Rejoice! Let your graciousness be known to everyone' (Phil. 4:4–5).

We can pluck bugs and insects from their forest habitat and pin them starkly to a board, as if that's all there is to them. Similarly, we can caricature biblical rules out of their context. Each of the examples I have listed originally appears in a context that makes it intelligible. We saw in chapter 3 the way Matilda trusted her father's rules, and Eric could see his mother's reasoning behind her rules. Similarly, biblical rules appear in relational and rational contexts. Each has a home that gives it meaning and enables readers to trust it as good.

In contrast, many people have come to believe that Christian ethics merely consists of an abstract and arbitrary rule code. They think Christians generate this code by trawling through the Bible and listing all the imperatives. I need to make five comments in response.

First, many old biblical rules are no longer binding upon Christians. They have an important place where they appear in the Bible's story arc (ch. 19); but as the story unfolds, our relationship to them changes. Not everyone agrees with this conclusion, and in ch. 20, I touched on a long-running dispute between Christians over their relationship to the legal material of the Old Testament.

Secondly, some Christians follow a New Testament (or post-Resurrection) based rule code. They generate this moral code by finding every New Testament imperative that has general applicability. I think this practice is a Christian version of reductionism (ch. 1). These New Testament imperatives are necessary within, but not sufficient for, a Christian account of morality.

Thirdly, some 'rules' are not even rule-like. They're excited invitations to participation (they're *exhortations*). When I say, 'Play football with me,' it appears on the page as a command. But in the context of a close relationship where we both love football, those words elicit excited and happy participation. 'Rejoice!' and 'Let your graciousness be known to everyone' (Phil. 4:4–5) are like that. After full immersion throughout Philippians in the logic of Jesus (somewhat like Part 3), these words articulate the joy and grace already rising up within readers as they respond to Jesus. It would be unfair to accuse these exhortations of somehow oppressing Christians.

Fourthly, biblical rules often state their logic, initiating us into the rationality that makes the rule good. When Jesus expects his followers to 'go and rebuke' someone 'in private' (Matt. 18:15), his vision is for quality relationships where we listen to each other's concern and win each other over. In other words, Jesus' rule comes from a moral vision of reconciled relationships. Therefore, we read each biblical rule carefully in context, to discern the moral vision it expresses.

Fifthly, followers of Jesus can be intensely negative about rules. Bare rules are often pointless: '"Do not handle, do not taste, do not touch"? All these regulations . . . have a reputation of wisdom by promoting ascetic practices, humility, and severe treatment of the body' but 'are not of any value against fleshly indulgence' (Col. 2:21–23). Indeed, they often have exactly the reverse of their intended effect: 'I would not have known what it is to covet if the law had not said, You shall not covet. And sin, seizing an opportunity through the commandment, produced in me coveting of every kind' (Rom. 7:7–8).

But despite these five caveats, I seek here to show that the commands of God are one of the five 'things that matter' from which ethics emerges. Yet how can this be so, when I've spent so much time observing the contextuality of biblical rules, and have gone as far as to claim that our relationship to many biblical rules has changed as the Bible's story arc unfolds? I base my contention that God's commands retain enduring relevance on two observations.

First, many of God's commands seem obviously to retain enduring relevance. For example, Old Testament authors continually repeat that those with any kind of power or responsibility cannot neglect, oppress, exploit or discriminate against a poor or marginal person (e.g. Exod. 22:1–4; 23:3, 9; Lev. 19:15; Deut. 24:14; 27:19; Prov. 22:22–23; Isa. 1:17; Jer. 22:16; Zech. 7:10). The same concern for such people is retained in the New Testament (e.g. Gal. 2:10; Jas 2:6–9; 1 John 3:17). Most people can see that this cluster of rules retains enduring relevance (except if they like to create exclusive groups, ch. 8, while dehumanizing others). When these rules appear in the Bible, they often explicitly arise from God's character (ch. 21), since he loves all who are poor or marginal. We've also seen how the moral order of his creation somehow reflects his character (ch. 22). So it's no surprise when modern readers, whether Christian or not, can appreciate the enduring relevance of this cluster of rules.

Secondly, then, it seems obvious to several of the biblical authors that God's 'word' lasts for ever (1 Chr. 15:16; Pss 105:8; 119:89; Isa. 40:8; Matt. 5:18; 1 Pet. 1:25). Now in many cases, this 'word' refers to his promise to care for those who trust him; but the biblical authors don't distinguish too sharply between his words of promise and his words of fatherly instruction.

Again we may ask, though – how can this 'word' be said to endure when our relationship to some moral instructions seems to change? The classic example would be Old Testament food laws. This list of instructions marked ancient Israel as God's own (e.g. Lev. 17:10–16; Deut. 14:3–21). But Jesus himself reveals that 'unclean' foods stand for a deeper truth about the 'unclean' desires of our inner world (Mark 7:15; cf. ch. 7). In a series of subsequent episodes and discussions, these old laws are gently set aside by Jesus' followers, always with great consideration toward those who still think them to be binding (Acts 10:9–29; 11:1–9; 15:1–29; Rom. 14:1–12; 1 Cor. 8:1–13; 10:23–33; Col. 2:16). Similarly, the Bible's story arc alters our relationship to several other ancient commands relating (e.g.) to male circumcision, temple sacrifices, priestly practice and structures of social organization.

We could traverse the Bible examining each imperative to see in what respects it endures, and how our relationship to it has changed. That task is too large for me to pursue here, and it would be too hard for you to read my results. (Serious readers of the Bible continue this task for life.)

We've seen (ch. 20) how previous generations of Bible readers did something like this by distinguishing between *cultic laws* (such as those relating to food laws), *civil laws* (those relating to structures of social organization) and *moral laws* (rules that remain relevant to all humans everywhere). But people who use this distinction rarely show their working, and the conclusions of previous generations of Bible readers became the assumptions of later generations. So this method of distinction doesn't really help those who want to know *what makes* a given biblical imperative have enduring relevance, or not.

Jesus had a way to determine the respect in which biblical imperatives endure. He thought that Old Testament commands showed how we may better love God and others (e.g. Matt. 22:37–40). Jesus thought that ancient biblical commands offered guidance in love to the people of his day. 'Love' is an umbrella term, and I've observed above that analysing and describing love is spectacularly difficult (p. 111). But the biblical commands begin this analysis and description, unpacking discrete aspects of how to love. Jesus' followers continue his practice of understanding Old Testament commands through the lens of love.

Love also guides their *practice of commanding*, as seen in Paul's curious description of his train of thought about how to handle one situation. Paul wanted Philemon to be reconciled with Philemon's former slave, Onesimus. He says to Philemon that 'although I have great boldness in Christ to command you to do what is right, I appeal, instead, on the basis of love' (v. 8). This could simply mean that he loves Philemon enough to spare him the unpleasantness of a command. But I suspect the thought is bigger. I suspect he wants Philemon to act from love toward Onesimus, not merely in response to a command. A command would have been appropriate, and could have achieved the same result. But Paul wants more: for Philemon to *know* the love that the command would only have *pointed* toward. We tend to fixate on commands, and forget the love that drives them. This episode highlights the way commands, when properly understood, enhance love. It also highlights the way we experience commands as unpleasant at first.

C. S. Lewis offers a powerfully helpful comment on this unpleasant aspect of commands.[1] Psalm 19:8–10 perplexes him. The psalmist celebrates the entire Pentateuchal law as being more desirable than gold or honey. How could these rules be 'delicious'? It's a strange idea at any time, thinks Lewis; but all the more when a rule contradicts a seemingly innocent desire. How can the prohibition of theft be at all like honey for 'a hungry man left alone, without money, in a shop filled with the smell and sight of new bread, roasting coffee, or fresh strawberries'? The man may obey or even respect the rule. 'But surely it could be more aptly compared to the dentist's forceps or the front line than to anything enjoyable and sweet.'

But Lewis, an expert in literary criticism, finds a clue to unlock this puzzle when he looks at Psalm 119, which also celebrates the law. It's a cleverly structured, intricate piece of literature. Lewis thinks it reflects the way the psalmist sees the whole Old Testament law – as a cleverly structured, intricate guide to moral life for ancient Israel.

Someone who has taken the time to 'see into' this structure, if caught starving in a coffee shop, would be able to care for the shop's owner. Initially, the rule cuts across him like a knife, challenging and interrogating his desires. But he's able to love the owner as well as the food. In this moment, the rule leads him to discern something deeper about our world's moral ecology (ch. 22). By

---

1. C. S. Lewis, *Reflections on the Psalms* (London: HarperCollins, 1958), p. 47.

knowing the goodness both of the food and of its owner, he might even have his moral imagination expanded to the point where, despite his immediate desires, he's able to *ask* the owner for help, and perhaps *offer* whatever he can to share with the owner in return. He doesn't presume to pre-judge, like a consequentialist (ch. 6), that those courses of action are unlikely to succeed, and so theft is more likely to give him what he wants. He has genuinely come to believe that the universe, and his own corner of it, doesn't work that way. Nor does he presume, like the consequentialist, simply to exclude the preciousness of the owner from his current train of thought. His universe includes reconciled relationships, based on sharing and love (ch. 18). He enacts what the rules defend and promote.

Given these considerations, here are some suggestions for how to think about and approach imperatives in the Bible:

1. Anything originally presented as deriving ultimately from the mind or voice of God remains, in principle, very precious to us.
2. We search each command for what it originally *revealed* about the lived-result of the character of God (ch. 21), about the nature of the created moral order (ch. 22), about God's future dream for his world (ch. 24) and/or about being a Jesus-shaped community (ch. 25).
3. We search each command for what it originally revealed about how to *love*. That is, we look for the guidance each command offers about how to respond with proper affection toward God, the created order and each other. (Perhaps this is just another way of putting the previous point.)
4. We evaluate each command for whether the Bible's story arc (ch. 19) alters our reception of it. Is it later taken to symbolize or refer to something deeper? Would the social context, structures and concerns inherent in it remain in some form for a later society? Does the story of Jesus (Part 3) mean that we view the rule differently?
5. We allow it to interrogate our desires as we experience them (ch. 7), and to challenge the false inclusions we regularly give ourselves to (ch. 8). What do *our reactions against it* say about *the way we are at this time*?

The biblical commands endure not in the sense that their original meaning stands unchanged for all time. Rather, they continue to guide us in the deep structures of how God has made us to inhabit his world. They also challenge our desires in ways we usually don't like or appreciate at first. But if we're willing to work with their grain, at first seeing and then loving what they defend, our moral imagination expands to where *we* may say, 'His commands are not a burden' (1 John 5:3).

24. A NEW FUTURE

In Part 4 we're examining how ethics emerges from five 'things that matter', which recur throughout the Bible's story arc and remain relevant. This chapter examines the fourth of these: a new future. As the real trajectory of the world is unveiled, it formats our trajectory in the present.

You've probably seen a few 'end of the world' films in your time: *Terminator 2: Judgment Day, The War of the Worlds, Cloverfield, Children of Men, I Am Legend, The Day the Earth Stood Still, 2012, Knowing, The Book of Eli, The Road* . . . I'm something of a connoisseur of such films, which have recurring themes.

They preview what we'd feel in these scenarios. We catch a glimpse of *dread*, that sure expectation of certain doom, the evil twin of hope. Admittedly, we don't feel it while absorbed in the handful of beautiful on-camera people who survive. We only catch this glimpse when we place ourselves among the tens of millions who die horribly, out of the frame, where most of us would probably be!

For what would we do if our death and that of everyone we knew were a few hours away? These films highlight the way human beings thrive on the expectation of a good future. As far as we can tell, no other animal is like this. We seem to need the knowledge that we, our family and the human race can look forward to something. We call that *hope*.

Such films usually include fanatical bit players who dress strangely and yell 'Repent!' a lot. Christians have always been an 'apocalyptic' lot, but such depictions are about as close as many modern Westerners ever get to Christian apocalypticism. These stories often flirt with the possibility that maybe the Christians are onto something, although they usually reject Christian ideas (especially repentance).

I have to admit to some embarrassment when I see these portrayals of Christian belief. I've stopped caring about the Hollywood staple of Christians as unbalanced and dangerous nutters. Rather, it all reminds me of the long and embarrassingly fruitless history of Christian future-prediction. Despite Jesus' express injunction not to bother (Matt. 24:36), the Christian future-prediction industry and the internecine disputes it generates has trivialized the Bible's message and robbed us of its intended effect.

For the biblical authors said a lot about the future. (This kind of biblical talk is *apocalyptic*. It builds to tell the plot of the end of the Bible's story arc, ch. 19. Theologians call this endgame *eschatology*.) They don't talk about it to titillate our penchant for guessing future events. They seek to replace bleakness and dread with *hope*. They seek to describe the sure basis of hope, and to explore all the ways that hope affects our *present*. We'll now examine how they think of the future as a time when we'll *see things as they really are*, and how we're inhabitants of *a trajectory engineered by God*. They show how we can *participate in this new trajectory*, because it has the capacity to create a new trajectory for our own desires, thoughts and actions. We'll examine the *linchpin of their hope* – what makes it more than a mere projection of imagination. I'll also add why the kind of hope on view doesn't finally result in arduous labour, but in *a new kind of restfulness*.

Seeing things as they really are. One New Testament passage (2 Pet. 3:5–13) speaks of a 'day' when 'the heavens will pass away with a roar, and the heavenly bodies will be burned up and dissolved, and the earth and the works that are done on it will be exposed' (v. 10, ESV). This is often taken to refer to the annihilation of everything, but that isn't what it describes. In its colourful language of the 'heavens' disappearing, it refers to the 'lid being lifted' off human affairs (cf. Isa. 34:4; Rev. 6:13) so every human activity becomes evaluated from God's perspective, and every human eye sees how God intends life to be lived. Once this trajectory to human affairs becomes clear, Peter thinks 'holiness and godliness' are the obvious response, since 'we are waiting for new heavens and a new earth in which righteousness dwells' (v. 13, ESV).

We do find the logic of his appeal a little hard at first. How does such a life follow from this unveiled future? After all, we regularly enter new situations: we start new jobs, get married, go to Venezuela, and so on; yet we don't particularly think our basic identity should alter. We expect to take 'who we are' into that future. We expect to be able to 'do what we want' and to 'be ourselves' there.

But, according to Peter's logic, to enter God's future is to enter the very 'home of righteousness' (v. 13, NIV), a new habitat that *does* require a new way of being fit for it. (Indeed, perhaps his logic even challenges the casual assumptions of the previous paragraph. Maybe starting a new job, getting married and going to Venezuela *do* each entail, in their own way, the kinds of changes to our 'self' that make us fitting for those arenas.) 'Since you are waiting,' concludes Peter, 'be diligent to be found by him without spot or blemish, and at peace' (v. 14, ESV).

Paul's way of making the same point is that people will need a 'spiritual body' – a kind of Spirit-powered body, in fact – to inhabit the same place as Christ himself (1 Cor. 15: 44–50; cf. ch. 17). This logic of the future, where we'll see things as they really are and can grow toward a fitness for it, is also seen in an extended metaphor involving night and day (1 Thess. 5:1–10). People get drunk and sleep at night, as seems fitting at the time. Similarly, we're often content to orient our lives around our desires and existing systems of inclusion, as seems fitting to our 'flesh' (ch. 9) in the moment. But a few remember that everything will look different in daytime; and 'day' comes to represent the clarity we receive when every human activity is evaluated from the God's-eye perspective and when every human eye sees how God intends life to be lived. People armed with foreknowledge of that clarity will therefore navigate the 'night' differently (1 Thess. 5:11–22).

In more technical language, there's a concept of *natural teleology* at work here. God inducts us into the proper end, goal or *telos* originally envisaged for humanity. This true human identity, originally and finally seen in Christ (Part 3), entails practices proper to this *telos* such as worship of God rather than ignorant rebellion, and loving care of others rather than callous unconcern or self-interested engagement.

For any of us may resist. Activities we innocently refer to as 'defining my own identity', 'being who I am', 'choosing my values' or 'following my heart' can add up to a refusal to participate in the trajectory God has for us. Hence some of the Bible's descriptions of hell (e.g. Matt. 25:30; 2 Thess. 1:9) focus on its inherent isolation, alienation and separation. It makes sense to leave alone people whose lives have been spent defining themselves. Of course, descriptions of painful fire also depict hell. Jesus is the most extreme exponent of these (e.g. Matt. 3:12; Luke 16:23–24; John 15:6), even pioneering in the use of the fiery, sulphurous rubbish dump south of Jerusalem as his favourite image of hell (Matt. 5:22, 29–30; 10:28; 18:9; 23:33; Mark 9:42–49; Luke 12:4–5). Opponents of Christianity wilfully misrepresent these images to slur God as a cosmic sadist, a response that ignores the intention to warn us (which no sadist would offer). Pain metaphors alert us that the narratives of supreme independence and domineering voluntarism (see p. 149) we invent for ourselves are contrary to our design: we become our own worst enemies. We consign ourselves to hell's alienation and self-aggrandizing loneliness. That way of putting it doesn't mean we cleverly plan our destination, for *God* finally reaches a point where he wants no part of those who actively resist his goodness, and his judgment of hell simply gives to us what most befits our character.

A trajectory engineered by God. However, once we relent through 'repentance' and participation with God in Christ, God enables and directs our growth in our proper trajectory. We've seen (ch. 15) how the grace made apparent in the death of Christ then formats our trajectory as we await 'our blessed hope, the appearing of the glory of our great God and Saviour Jesus Christ' (Titus 2:11–13, ESV). An opening paragraph to one New Testament letter (1 Cor. 1:4–8) also marks the way God's grace was first given in Christ, and continues as God makes people 'rich in everything' (v. 5). Paul anticipates that 'he will also confirm you to the end, blameless in the day of our Lord Jesus Christ' (v. 8). From the beginning to the end of their participation with him, God consistently 'formats' a person to match the trajectory of the cosmos. Paul puts the same thought more briefly elsewhere: 'he who began a good work in you will bring it to completion at the day of Jesus Christ' (Phil. 1:6, ESV).

Participating in the new trajectory. When Paul observes that God 'works in you, both to will and to work for his good pleasure' (Phil. 2:13, NIV), there's an initially frightening correlative instruction: 'work out your own salvation with fear and trembling' (Phil. 2:12, NIV). But the corollary supposes that we *participate in the implications* of 'our own salvation' – not that we're in the monumentally difficult business of constructing it. We 'fear and tremble' simply because the stakes are high (and not due to fear of final failure and rejection by God). Once God sweeps us into his trajectory, we *enact* the seriousness of it.

Hence Paul's group praises God for the way Christians in Colossae love 'all the saints because of the hope reserved for you in heaven' (Col. 1:4–5). Their present performance of Christian community (ch. 18) matches the biblical picture of the final heavenly community, which will consist, as the theologian Augustine once put it, in 'the enjoyment of God and of one another in God'.[1]

---

1. Or is a near equivalent: twice in *City of God* §19.13 and once in §19.17. Augustine, *The City of God against the Pagans*, tr. R. W. Dyson (Cambridge: Cambridge University Press, 1998), pp. 938, 940, 947.

They inhabit their future in their present. Its implications have become straightforward to them.

Likewise, Peter speaks of 'minds ready for action' and of a new kind of self-discipline resultant upon '[setting] your hope completely on the grace to be brought to you at the revelation of Jesus Christ' (1 Pet. 1:13), in contrast to being 'conformed to the desires of your former ignorance' (v. 14), a neat allusion both to our standard false construals of the purposes of our desires, and to our usual systems of false inclusion (chs. 7–8). Even the rich, then, can look past false systems of inclusion and the false lure of wealth:

> Instruct those who are rich in the present age not to be arrogant or to set their hope on the uncertainty of wealth, but on God, who richly provides us with all things to enjoy. Instruct them to do good, to be rich in good works, to be generous, willing to share, storing up for themselves a good foundation for the age to come, so that they may take hold of life that is real. (1 Tim. 6:17–19)

All the logic of the new future comes together in this passage. The 'good foundation' that they 'store up' is, again, not so much a *construction* of their own future as *a proper alignment with their true future* in Christ. In returning to this proper trajectory, they 'take hold of life that is real': they see things as they really are. They begin to realize that their wealth was always only ever a form of participation in God's good trajectory for them. They receive back their present, and from it springs a kind of generosity that has been formatted by grace.

The linchpin of hope. But what could make this future hope seem so real to the New Testament Christians? After all, people dream up all sorts of 'hopes' all the time, but unless we're capable of extreme self-hypnosis or self-deception, these 'hopes' have little real traction in our lives. How is Christian future-talk different?

The resurrection of Jesus Christ (ch. 16) gave early Christians their hope. This event that had the same currency and reality for them as the Apollo lunar landings had for my own generation. They know the folly of pinning present courses of action on imaginary ideas: 'if in Christ we have hope in this life only, we are of all people most to be pitied' (1 Cor. 15:19; cf. 15:32). It's beyond the scope of this book to examine the New Testament's certitude about Jesus' resurrection. Like the Apollo landings, the event of Jesus' resurrection was so momentous that some simply couldn't accept it. Like the Apollo landings, the event of Jesus' resurrection requires us to trust witnesses who went through it. Both events confront us with our view of how knowledge works. We either proceed in partnership with others, or sceptically reject claims that don't accommodate to our powers of individual evaluation. Also, both cases show the way evidence alone cannot suffice to persuade without an entire gestalt shift (p. 72). (In Jesus' case, the gestalt shift needed includes changes to what I allow myself to love.)

Those who undergo this shift, after reading the early Christians' accounts of the risen Christ, now share with them in hope. Jesus' resurrection functions as a kind of 'first fruit' for what's to come (1 Cor. 15: 20, 23), a metaphor referring to the earliest ripe apple or orange in an orchard. It's our linchpin for the future.

A new kind of restfulness. But does this trajectory entail arduous labour? We've seen that it entails behaviours contrary to those around us. The stakes are so high as to create 'fear and trembling'. We've seen that it includes love, alertness, self-discipline and generosity, none of which come particularly easily to most of us. Is the trajectory just too hard?

A most delightful New Testament moment remembers the old Jewish habit of complete restfulness on their seventh 'Sabbath' day', and pictures the new future in such terms. 'So then, a Sabbath rest still remains for the people of God; for those who enter God's rest also cease from their labours as God did from his. Let us therefore make every effort to enter that rest' (Heb. 4:9–11, NRSV).

Rest comes to meet us. Our present experience includes effort; there's no pretence that it doesn't. But the passage doesn't only dangle rest as 'carrot' tomorrow for arduous toil today. Rather, it signals that *God's entire economy is restful.* Our end, our goal, our final trajectory is restful, which is *also* played out as we inhabit that trajectory today. Christians often glimpse that rest in moments of joy, in periods of deep contentment, in spaces filled with adoring worship, and in very literal moments of physical rest. We rely gladly upon the truth that the future isn't merely a project of *our* own making. *Our* performances and projects don't construct reality.

Christians have always been an 'apocalyptic' lot. But technically, the term 'apocalypse' comes from the Greek word for 'revelation' – the final unveiling of things as they really are. As we begin to see, so we begin to participate. In Christian thought, the ends don't *justify* the means. The ends *determine* the means.

Further reading

* Dickson, John, and Greg Clarke, *666 and All That: The Truth about the Future* (Sydney South, NSW: Aquila, 2007). Online: <http://www.publicchristianity.org>.
** Wilcock, Michael, *The Message of Revelation* (Leicester: IVP, 1989).

25. JESUS-SHAPED COMMUNITY

In Part 4 we're examining how ethics emerges from five 'things that matter', which recur throughout the Bible's story arc and remain relevant. This chapter examines the last of these: Jesus Christ, who brings the other four into focus and whose redemptive work and new inclusion creates community.

My intention in this chapter is to show how everything about Jesus covered in chapters 12–18 comprises a fifth 'thing that matters', which I label as 'Jesus-shaped community'. It offers a way into the first four.

I've already said a lot in Part 3 about Jesus Christ's centrality to any Christian conception of ethics. But I observed in ch. 19 that although Christians think that ethics springs from Jesus Christ, we're also interested in other parts of the Bible. We can summarize them under the four 'things that matter' seen so far in Part 4:

1. The character of God (ch. 21).
2. Creation and 'moral order' (ch. 22).
3. Commands that reveal (ch. 23).
4. A new future (ch. 24).

Christians are as prone as anyone else to reductionism (ch. 1). Christian reductionism often tries to make one 'thing that matters' the key to unlock every ethical problem. The trick is to develop the kind of complex discernment (ch. 10 and p. 312) that keeps all these angles in the frame.

However, even that way of putting it is presumptuous, because none of us really has what it takes to do that. As beings in 'flesh' (ch. 9), we cannot always see how our desires and current networks of inclusion (chs. 7–8) affect our judgment. So we don't have the necessary purity of access or clarity of vision about any of these four things, and we're not clever enough to compute easily how all four relate to a given situation. Figure 1 represents the potential for incoherence between these four poles:

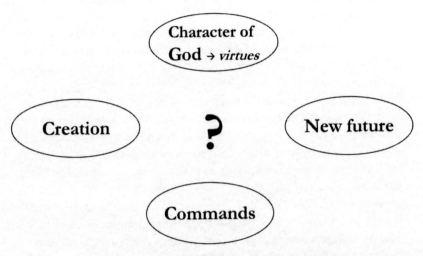

Figure 1: Four poles in Christian thought about ethics. (It's not always easy to see how these poles connect to each other.)

I began our reflection on the centrality of Christ (ch. 12) with a brief look at the 'Christ hymn' of Colossians 1. In this same letter, we also see his centrality to a proper conception of ethics. He's someone 'in whom are hidden all the treasures of wisdom' (Col 2:3, NIV), where 'wisdom' alludes to the great Old Testament category for living well. 'In him' is 'all the fullness of deity' (v. 9), which is why he also encapsulates all wisdom. Woven like a golden thread throughout this reflection is the breathtaking possibility that *we* may be 'in him' and are 'given fullness in Christ' (v. 9; cf. ch. 14), the possibility, in other words, that we may *find our completion* in this one who has all wisdom and fullness of deity. This strange and seductive idea becomes our antidote to bad ethics, false inclusion and manic loves. We may 'continue to live in him' (v. 6) and be 'rooted and built up in him' (v. 7), metaphors that picture our very identity organically connected to Jesus Christ. Only in him do we shed the old understanding of ourselves and the desires of our 'flesh' (v. 11).

In Christian thought, then, Jesus Christ is *our way into* the complex task of finding coherence between the four poles pictured above. Another way of putting all that is to say that Jesus brings those four 'things that matter' into focus in a way we cannot achieve alone. For example:

- Jesus *reveals God's character* when he announces to his followers that 'anyone who has seen me has seen the Father' (John 14:9). A person who humbly serves now refracts the Old Testament excellences of God (Phil. 2:3–11).
- Jesus *restores created order,* as when he rails against the religious strictures of his time that had eclipsed the basic preciousness of a woman who needed healing on the Sabbath (Luke 13:16). He's eventually regarded as the one in whom 'all things hold together' (Col. 1:17, NIV).
- Jesus *interprets and reframes God's commands* when he declares himself to be the greatest fan of the Old Testament law (Matt: 5:17), who yet can discern within all this complex literature that just *two* of its commands – both concerning love – sum up the rest of them (Matt. 22:36–38). Hence when we 'carry one another's burdens', we can be said to 'fulfil the law of Christ' (Gal. 6:2).
- Jesus *receives God's future promises,* believing and trusting that the Father's trajectory for him is good when in the moment of supreme trial he prays 'not my will, but yours be done' (Luke 22:42). And so Jesus is evermore celebrated as the Son whose obedience was perfected in suffering (Heb. 5:8–9), who's given kingly rule (p. 91), and who deserves our constant attention as 'the author and perfecter of our faith, who for the joy set before him endured the cross, scorning its shame, and sat down at the right hand of the throne of God' (Heb. 12:2, NIV).

We can picture Jesus' relationship to the four poles below as in Figure 2. But even this way of looking at it doesn't sum up all the aspects of Jesus' work and of the pinnacle achievements of his life. His death, resurrection and gift of the Spirit enable the formation of a *new community* (chs. 15–18). To add to the points above:

- Jesus *reconciles relationships and creates true community* when he joyfully tells of outcasts returning home (Luke 15:1–31). Via the pinnacle achievements of his life, hate-fuelled people become Spirit-fuelled and are reconciled to one another. 'For he himself is our peace, who

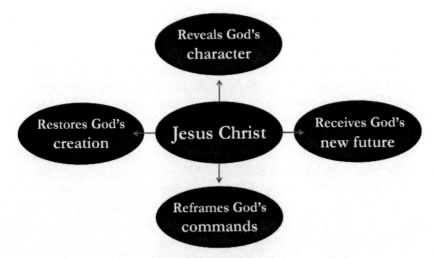

Figure 2: Jesus Christ's relationship to the four poles of Figure 1.

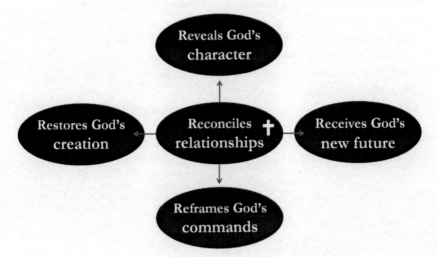

Figure 3: Jesus Christ's relationship to the four poles of Figure 1,
once the pinnacle achievements of his life are taken into account.

has made the two one and has destroyed the barrier, the dividing wall of
hostility' (Eph. 2:14–15, NIV).

We could therefore expand the picture of Jesus' relationship to the other four
poles (Figure 3).

Above, I called Jesus our way into the complex task of finding coherence between the four poles. This human access doesn't consist merely in *knowing about* Jesus, or even in following Jesus (ch. 13). In the New Testament, it takes the form of nothing less than a set of amazing societies called 'churches' (ch. 34): bands of people 'in Christ' (ch. 14) who came together to learn, train and grow the Jesus-shaped version of their identity in small, reconciled groups.

We catch a glimpse of such a group in the Christians of Colossae, who are 'united in love' (Col. 2:2) and for whom obsessional desire, false belonging and false humility are becoming eclipsed by new affections for each other. Jesus has become the focal point of access for how people are to dwell together in community. It turns out that life in one of his churches will thereby shape our conception of how humans in general should live together in society.

Hence Jesus and his reconciling, including work, summarized as 'Jesus-shaped community', should be regarded as the fifth 'thing that matters'. 'Jesus-shaped community' includes *everything* about Jesus covered in chapters 12–18 – the way he

- brings into focus and gives access to the four poles listed above (beginning as we 'follow' him, ch. 13);
- includes us 'in' himself (ch. 14) and shares with us his pinnacle achievements (chs. 15–16) through the Holy Spirit (ch. 17);
- trains us in new ways of being human through his new community (ch. 18);
- all because the planet is ultimately 'Christ powered' (ch. 12).

In the next chapter (ch. 26), I'll present the five 'things that matter' in a 'unified field'.

26. A 'UNIFIED FIELD'

In Part 4 we're examining how ethics emerges from five 'things that matter', which recur throughout the Bible's story arc and remain relevant. This chapter shows how these five combine to give a new 'gestalt' (p. 72) within the complexity of ethics.

In Parts 1–3 we saw how messy it is to think about ethics. Rules, rights, values and results often compete as *the* way to approach ethics, while the contribution of our desires and our need for group inclusion goes unnoticed. I suggested (p. 81) that Christianity offers a richly unifying way to organize and handle the complexity of ethics, offering new gestalt awareness of yourself and your conduct while you move about in whatever surrounds you (ch. 10). To begin finding this new gestalt, we began with Jesus (Part 3) and then looked at five 'things that matter' across the Bible's story arc (Part 4), depicted below in Figure 4.

But the Bible's story arc (ch. 19) includes an unflattering narrative of humanity's pitiful contribution to the ethical history of the planet, represented in Figure 5.

In the 'Fall', we see humanity living 'according to the flesh' (ch. 9). The opening pages of the Bible celebrate desire and sociality. The tragic 'Fall' of Genesis 3:6 pivots on the corruption of both. Christ's intervention rescues people from the result, and by the power of his Spirit (ch. 17) we learn again how to desire well, and how to participate in his true new inclusion through

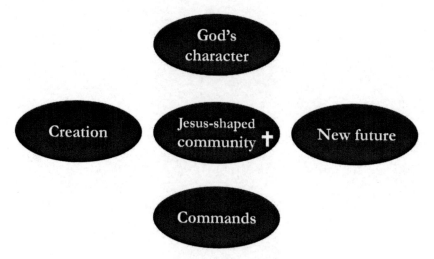

Figure 4: Five poles for Christian thought about ethics.

Figure 5: The human element in the Bible's story arc.

love toward God and others. We can add this human dimension to the five poles, as in Figure 6 (below).

Figure 6 reminds us of the Bible's story arc. The horizontal axis in the middle row alludes to the chronological unfolding of Scripture's story. The stable and good character of God is above this entire axis, emerging in several ways throughout it. (Our knowledge of the character of God emerges only from the unfolding story.) Various commands throw light on how to live at different moments in the story arc. The five dark poles remind us of the five 'things that matter'. These are the 'objective' elements of Christian ethics. Just as I can walk no farther than the North or South Pole, so also here: moral reality doesn't extend beyond these five things that matter. There are no human-invented improvements, replacements or extensions to these poles. They're the boundaries, if you like, of moral reality.

The lighter boxes remind us of the ways humanity moves among these poles, according to 'flesh' or Spirit. They represent our 'subjective' partici-

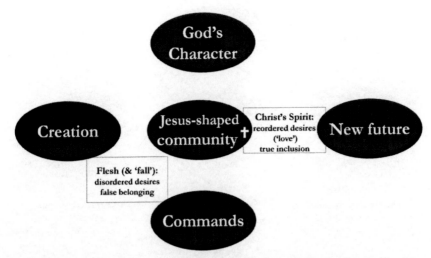

Figure 6: The five poles of Christian thought about ethics, including human participation.

pation in the overall story. The annoying offset of the 'Fall' in the diagram symbolizes a seeming detour in God's plan for the planet.[1] Our participation with Christ's Spirit is located to symbolize our participation in Christ's new community while we expect the new future.

Figure 6, then, shows why I think Christianity acts as a kind of 'unifying field theory' for the complexity of ethics. It offers an interlocking account of the nature of the cosmos we inhabit. (I'll also suggest that secular ethical concepts partly arose from this account, ch. 27.) Like all diagrams, Figure 6 is an overview and approximation. Diagrams are helpful when we need orientation to a bewildering environment; they cannot show everything. But this one is intended to show how life 'in Christ' (ch. 14) offers an orienting field of moral reference to whatever is going on around us.

What results from this way of seeing? What might it look like, in a lived life, to move within this 'unified field'? I've been using the chapters of Part 4 to describe this 'look'. Figure 7 summarizes those summaries:

---

1. Some theologians debate the extent to which God foresaw or planned the Fall. But those discussions have no place in the discussion of ethics, because Scripture portrays God as rescuing us from the effects of this human folly, while he recreates according to his good intentions. Whatever his 'inner counsel' on this Fall, humanity is called to participate in his reversal of it in Christ.

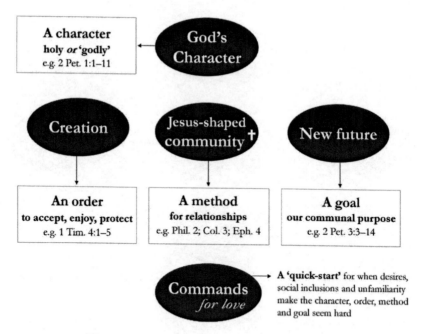

Figure 7: Some lived results of the poles of Figure 4.

Creation (ch. 22) gives an *order* or moral ecology for us to accept, enjoy and protect. So, for example, 1 Timothy 4:1–5 defends the good of food and marriage against ascetics who tell people not to enjoy them.

The new future (ch. 24) reveals the *goal* of human existence – our communal purpose, where people are with and for each other, enjoying God and one another in God.[2] So, for example, in 2 Peter 3:3–14, a prospect of the world's end results in people living in peace together (v. 14) as they 'wait for new heavens and a new earth, where righteousness will dwell' (v. 13).

From the character of God (ch. 21) arises a *character*, the sum of settled habits and patterns of action and feeling that are 'godlike' (or 'godly' or 'holy', to use the New Testament's more helpful descriptors). So, for example, in 2 Peter 1:1–11 a lived set of 'virtues' (vv. 5–8) directly parallels and mirrors the activity of God (vv. 3–4), so that people 'become partakers of the divine nature' (v. 4, ESV).

---

2. I've borrowed this phrase from Augustine, *The City of God against the Pagans*, tr. R. W. Dyson (Cambridge: Cambridge University Press, 1998), pp. 938, 940, 947 (§§19.13, 19.17).

From the cross and resurrection of Jesus (chs. 15–16) come a particular *method* by which to conduct relationships (ch. 25). The new community he forms (chs. 18, 34) becomes the 'training ground' for this method.

Commands (ch. 23) throw light on this order, character, way and goal. While the new gestalt in Christ is unfamiliar, commands offer us a *quick start* and promote a new kind of love.

In other words, Figure 6 offers us a summary of how to begin seeing ethical problems differently, as shown in Figure 7. I've found it helps me to keep remembering and learning my new identity in Christ. It describes the new gestalt by which I see, although, like all learners, I'm like one of those footballers on Jesus' 'team' (p. 114) who cannot play as the Master can.

In a different context, the social anthropologist Professor Tim Ingold describes the way we move about our environment. It's

> an immensely variegated terrain of comings and goings, which is continually taking shape around the traveller even as the latter's movements contribute to its formation. To hold a course in such an environment is to be attentive at all times to what is going on around you, and to respond in ways that answer to your purpose. . . . To find one's way is to advance along a line of growth, in a world which is never quite the same from one moment to the next, and whose future configuration can never be fully known. Ways of life are not therefore determined in advance, as routes to be followed, but have continually to be worked out anew.[3]

The 'unifying field' and its poles are a Christian description of the way we advance. In Part 5 we consider some approaches to the daily details of life for someone in this gestalt. Part 6 considers some outcomes that arise from this way of seeing our lives.

---

3. Tim Ingold, *The Perception of the Environment: Essays on Livelihood, Dwelling and Skill* (London: Routledge, 2000), pp. 223, 242. I'm indebted to Brian Brock for this reference, and the insight arising from it.

27. ETHICS SECULAR AND CHRISTIAN

In Part 4 we're examining how ethics emerges from five 'things that matter', which recur throughout the Bible's story arc and remain relevant. This chapter outlines why there are some points of contact between Christian and secular accounts of right and wrong.

We've seen (ch. 26) how Christians are oriented to the way ethics works. But how does this orientation connect to the way others think ethics works? Later we'll touch on some practicalities for Christians relating to others (chs. 35, 46–47). This chapter seeks to discern why Christians agree and disagree with 'secular' others about right and wrong. (I'm commenting only on what I know about Anglo-American cultures.)

'Secular' is a term that can be used a few ways. Here I'm referring to those modern Western approaches to ethics that explicitly exclude any reference to theology. Proponents of these approaches often hold the naive view that right and wrong is more or less self-evident. On this kind of view, people of all cultures everywhere can understand ethics. The late arrivals on this scene are religions, which simply pick up and amplify bits of what everyone already knows.

If this view has a bit of truth, it would be because we all inhabit the same created moral order (ch. 22). Of course we can expect to find some agreements about right and wrong. But the view is also naive, because it fails to take into account Jesus' striking new intervention into human affairs (ch. 11), and fails to recognize how powerfully Christianity has shaped Western assumptions over two millennia. (Some secularists overtly seek to minimize this Christian impact, and to maximize the contribution of, say, Greco-Roman thought upon us. We cannot examine here whose account of Western history is right, but the readings below may help.)

In Part 1 we saw that modern people usually have some awareness of ethics in terms of rules, rights, values or results. Either the complex task of making these coherent confronts us; or we become reductionist, where we press into service one way of looking at ethics to unlock every problem. Figure 8 depicts this modern state of affairs.

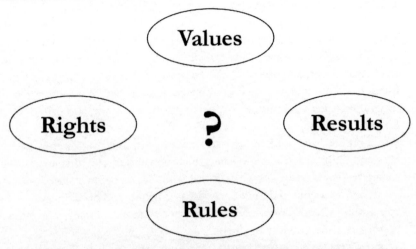

Figure 8: Popular modern approaches to ethics that are hard to make coherent.

The placing of the four poles in Figure 8 reminds us of the outer four poles of Figure 6 (p. 175), because I believe that what Figure 6 depicts is the ancestor to the methods shown in Figure 8.

- The concept of values derives from the virtues of God's own character (ch. 21), expressed through Christian communities (ch. 18) that nurtured virtue (ch. 30).
- The concept of rights has come down from the Christian concept of a good created order (ch. 22), expressed historically in Christian communities where everyone mattered.
- The use of rules sometimes has its roots in older Christian uses of commands (ch. 23), expressed in Christian communities that took biblical commands seriously.
- Our attention to results is similar to the way future-oriented Christian communities organized their acts to 'match' their new future (ch. 24).

Many ethical concepts you and I take for granted today arose, in more ways than we're aware of, from the Christian account of how ethics works. In the interests of brevity I've oversimplified; there were other currents in Western thought. But my general claim accounts for why Christians and others often agree about right and wrong:

- When others promote values such as excellence, self-discipline, responsibility, fairness, inclusion and tolerance, Christians can agree (because God's just, merciful and steadfast character became expressed in communities that learnt virtues of inclusion, respect, care and fairness).
- When others defend someone's right to live, to protection from torture, or to the freedom to marry and reproduce, Christians can agree (because God created humanity so well). When others defend someone's right to freedom of thought, expression or peaceful assembly, Christians agree (because participation in the gospel is a gift of the Spirit, and cannot be forced on anyone).
- When others want policies, laws and rules to stop bullying, exploitation, rape and theft; or to promote safety, inclusion and care, Christians can agree (because we know that commands are sometimes needed to cut across wayward desires and false inclusions; and because our communities need some rules to find order while each member 'catches up on' his or her identity in Christ, p. 98).
- When others urge concern for future results ranging from community provision of food and water through to preservation of the planet and maintenance of social order, Christians can agree (because these future results don't contradict the trajectory of God's new future, and because their own communities prosper with future hope).

Of course, I've oversimplified, because I know that Christian communities haven't always excelled in these matters (cf. ch. 34). I know also that the processes that have formed Western culture were complex. But would the West have been the same without the appearance of Jesus, and without his effects rippling out of many thousands of churches over the years? I doubt it.

The philosopher Alasdair MacIntyre thinks that secular ethics cannot really explain why it knows what it knows about right and wrong. He offers an analogy to describe why. He pictures a technologically advanced society that suddenly disintegrates into social chaos. If, decades later, people picked through the rubble and tried to make sense of each technical artefact, they'd argue endlessly over their incoherent and competing accounts, because they had no picture of the whole. MacIntyre thinks that something like this has happened in Western secular ethics. He later concludes that the Christian story of ethics is the lost whole.[1]

But there are dissimilarities between Figure 8 and Figure 6. 'Mainstream' Western culture has no direct analogue to Jesus-shaped community (ch. 25). The radical Enlightenment explicitly rejected the thought that a community, particularly a Christian one, might be our best school of moral formation (chs. 8, 25). The view eventually emerged that we should all choose our own values.

(I realize there remain some intensely communitarian communities professing an ethno-religious self-identity. They strongly hold their own community to be the best school of moral formation. The gospel challenges Western individualism by asserting that we need Jesus-shaped community. It also challenges ethno-religious communities to honour individuals who follow Christ, and who therefore differ from the community norms they were born into.)

This denial of the formative role of community upon us has driven the effects of group influence (ch. 8) into our unawareness (Part 2). Also, by magnifying individual autonomy, the disordering of love (ch. 7) also drifts into unawareness. Modern secular ethics therefore rarely considers or challenges life according to 'flesh' (ch. 9). So there's no real secular analogue to the 'Fall' box of Figure 6.[2] Likewise, without much sense of the immensity of this human difficulty, there need be no real secular analogue to the 'Christ's Spirit' box of Figure 6. The conceit of most secular talk about ethics is that we should simply learn to make choices that are more rational. As a result, people usually discuss ethics as if clearer thinking will yield better lives. (Atheists often support their assertion that religion is unnecessary for ethics by proclaiming their own goodness. They seem quite unreflective about whether their desires and group inclusions influence them. They regularly attack the covert desires and group effects of the religious, but rarely interrogate whether atheists experience something similar. Self-questioning isn't an obvious strength of this movement.)

---

1. Alasdair MacIntyre, *After Virtue* (Notre Dame: University of Notre Dame Press, 1984); and *Three Rival Versions of Moral Enquiry* (London: Duckworth, 1990).

2. Ad hoc depictions of our evolutionary messiness are the nearest equivalent. For example, the concept of our 'lizard brain' is becoming popular. On this view, surges of passion come from parts of the brain that evolved first, but these responses are now maladaptive.

Further reading

** MacIntyre, Alasdair, *Three Rival Versions of Moral Enquiry* (London: Duckworth, 1990).

*** O'Donovan, Oliver M. T., *The Desire of the Nations: Rediscovering the Roots of Political Theology* (Cambridge: Cambridge University Press, 1996).

*** Taylor, Charles, *A Secular Age* (Cambridge, Mass.: Belknap Press of Harvard University, 2007).

*** Taylor, Charles, *Sources of the Self: The Making of the Modern Identity* (Cambridge: Cambridge University Press, 1989).

PART 5 LIVING OUR LIVES

In Part 4 we examined how ethics emerges from five 'things that matter', which recur throughout the Bible's story arc and remain relevant. They're elements in a unifying field (ch. 26) from which emerges an *order* to enjoy and protect, a *method* for personal relationships, a community *goal* and a *character* to become. But we move through our part of this story via detailed, daily lives. Part 5 examines some approaches to this detail.

These approaches will seem quaint to anyone involved in 'serious' ethical discussions. If you've argued lately about rights, laws, values or some chain of consequences, it may seem strange to consider forgiving and reconciling (ch. 29), virtues and vices (ch. 30), true 'freedom' (ch. 31), imitating Jesus (ch. 32), obeying God (ch. 33), or life in and out of churches (chs. 34–35). But these are some of the *basic building blocks* for a Christian's *moral imagination* (chs. 2, 10). You'll need to know something of each if you are to inhabit your new identity 'in Christ' (ch. 14).

Oddly, though, I'll begin this section by considering 'drunkenness and rage' (ch. 28). I don't plan to commend them! Rather, the Bible's treatment of these vices illustrates how its 'unified field' upsets and changes how we see the little things in life.

28. DRUNKENNESS AND RAGE

Having discovered a 'unified field' by which to discern moral reality in Parts 3–4, Part 5 considers some approaches to the details of our lives. But the way we see some details may first need a massive change – as illustrated when the Bible's 'unified field' unmasks drunkenness and rage for what they really are.

Many are unconvinced that drunkenness and rage are wrong. 'I love to party,' one asserts. 'I'm a bit fiery; that's just who I am,' another explains. These behaviours straightforwardly express the immediate desires (ch. 7) and systems of inclusion (ch. 8) he or she has become accustomed to – the immediate recommendations, that is, of a person's body and brain (their 'flesh', ch. 9). These behaviours may even have settled into habits of action and feeling that contribute to someone's character (ch. 30) and identity (ch. 14). Biblical commands against drunkenness and rage therefore seem offensive, ridiculous or irrelevant.

In contrast, those 'in Christ' (ch. 14) receive commands against drunkenness and rage. They're commands that sound arbitrary and absurd at first. But over time it becomes evident that they unveil aspects of reality previously unseen. These commands act as a kind of gateway to the discovery of a new identity in Christ. I'll try to picture that process unfolding.

Drunkenness. Consumption of alcohol is uncontroversially permitted in the Bible, but drunkenness is consistently condemned and lampooned (e.g.

Prov. 20:1; 23:20–21, 29–35; 31:4–9; Isa. 5:11–12, 22; 28:1–7; Luke 21:34; Rom. 13:13; 1 Cor. 5:11; 6:10; 11:20–22; Gal. 5:21; Eph. 5:18; 1 Tim. 3:3; Titus 1:7; 1 Pet. 4:3). The attack on drunkenness sometimes takes the form of a direct formal command (e.g. Eph. 5:18). But not all biblical commands are direct: sarcastic portrayals (e.g. Isa. 5:22) and the appearances of drunkenness in vice lists (e.g. Rom. 13:13; see ch. 30) effectively function as commands against it. This animosity remains throughout the Bible's story arc (ch. 19).

Many in alcohol-loving Australia and in the pub-laden United Kingdom find this stance completely ludicrous at first. But a little detective work shows that it doesn't come from an *anti-pleasure* stance. That much is clear when the psalmist lists everything worth praising God for, including 'wine that gladdens the heart' (Ps. 104:15, NIV; the argument by some anti-alcohol Christians that this wine is non-alcoholic has no basis in fact). Rather, this biblical rule interrogates our desires (ch. 23), expands our moral imagination (ch. 2) and gives us a necessary 'building block' for loving others (ch. 18).

The stance against drunkenness unveils, and relies on, three facts of human structure (ch. 22). First, intoxication dulls our senses to the point of complete self-absorption. Secondly, others need our engagement with them, not our disengagement from them. Thirdly, others always matter greatly. In contrast, drunkenness expresses self-fulfilment at the expense of others, and so destroys community.

If that much is obvious to us, then we don't need this command and may be tempted to groan that 'surely the Bible is a bit moralistic' about the matter. But if we like to get drunk, then none of this reasoning has become obvious to us yet. Since we think there's no problem with drunkenness, the existence of this rule seems to us either ridiculous, or disastrously unfair and brutal. The command shocks us into a re-evaluation.

For, according to Christian thought, like addicts we're all in the grip of desires we feel are beyond our control (ch. 7). Rules therefore cut across and shock us. We hate them at first, but they invite us to begin the long journey of discovering the Jesus-shaped version of ourselves in Christ. His death severs the connection between my performance and my acceptability to God (ch. 15). God can love and accept me, even with this addiction. His Spirit then works to transform us in ways we never thought possible (ch. 17); and, eventually, we begin to find our desires rearranging themselves as our new identity emerges. To anyone in the grip of any addiction or obsession, this process seems unbelievable at first. But sufficient of us can testify to this surprising experience of change. We therefore surround the addict with our love, care and encouragement to press on so that they may continue to inhabit and participate in Christ's good work within them.

Christians are relearning the preciousness of others (ch. 18), and so over time the 'rule' can be seen as an intelligible expression and revelation of a wider moral order. As we apprehend the goodness of this stance against drunkenness, we internalize it as deeply right, and learn a little more of what to love and how to love. Over time, the alcohol addict learns new patterns of love. Her hope for reconciled, caring relationships in restored communities (chs. 25, 29, 39), finally to be experienced in her new future (ch. 24), actually becomes vastly more interesting to her than the short-term pleasures of alcohol.

These realizations are straightforwardly extensible to other drug users. Marijuana, methamphetamines and narcotics each produce a different style of disengagement, but all amplify the impulses of the 'flesh' and eventually result in the addict's social disengagement. Tragically, addicts often use drugs in order to dull the extraordinary pain perpetrated upon them by the evils of others. Christianity doesn't simply belittle their pain or condemn their pleasure. In the short term, it seeks to protect others against the results of the addict's social disengagement. In the long term, it hopes for addicts to discover their true inclusion, new future and true identity in Christ, and finally to heal their pain.

Rage. My own story unfolded around a habit of uncontrolled rage, where I'd ardently defend this practice as being 'just who I am'. In the early years of my marriage, my wife would quietly insist that this practice was wrong, and that I should not subject her to these bouts of rage. 'Deal with it,' I'd arrogantly declare to her, with a powerful identity claim as justification: 'You knew what you were getting. This is who I am.' (Thankfully, no physical contact was ever involved; but I was verbally and psychologically abusive.)

I was then confronted with biblical condemnations of 'outbursts of anger' (2 Cor. 12:20; Gal. 5:20; Eph. 4:31). The constant and petulant 'fits of rage' attacked by biblical authors relate to our obsession with our precious selves when we live according to the 'flesh'. We fixate on minor goods and overreact, usually only on our own behalf. I hated and rejected these biblical condemnations.

In this example, the Bible's story arc becomes quite important. It might be easy to look at some examples of God's extreme hostility in the Old Testament, and conclude that I can be as angry as I want whenever I want. But the Bible's story arc doesn't mediate the character of God (ch. 21) to me in this way. I cannot simply take this facet of God and make it my own. God's wrath is disclosed to be pure and orderly in a way that mine isn't. The 'story arc' leaves wrath to God, and discloses God's mercy through Christ as *the primary pattern of my existence* (Rom. 12:14–19; Col. 3:13; see ch. 15). It also closely circumscribes whatever may be good about my anger (Eph. 4:26; Jas 1:19–20), for anger *may* sometimes be justified (see below); but that was not what *I* needed to hear about in the *first* instance. I needed the Bible's story arc to disclose that my new future (ch. 24) is a place free of wrath, and that I now participate in a community (ch. 25) whose polity is never governed by rage, but by peace (e.g. Ezek. 37:26; Mark 9:50; John 14:27; 16:33; Eph. 4:3).[1]

Once I took this story arc seriously, I could take no shelter under isolated biblical texts that might have seemed to justify my rage. Eventually, I accepted that these commands and this 'rule' had interrogated my desires and found me out. The subsequent two-year period, when it seemed impossible to change, was one of my life's most miserable. It was a veritable war of identity, for I'd slip back into the angry claim that 'this is who I am'. My 'alien' identity in Christ would then confront me once again. At my worst, I could take shelter only in belonging to his 'team' (p. 98) despite my abject failure. I'd received his 'alien righteousness' (to borrow Luther's language), which severed the connection between my performance and my acceptability to God (ch. 15). But it was alien to my usual way of being.

Yet I woke one day to realize that, strangely, I really had become different – some six months had passed without one of these 'fits'. Somehow, Christ's Spirit had been at work to reorder what I loved (ch. 17). Since then I've learnt many other and more helpful strategies to deal with what used to enrage me, and I now prefer my new identity in Christ.

In this new gestalt (p. 72), anger can become a powerful and proper resistance against the loss of something good. That remains the good, created and closely circumscribed element of my anger (Eph. 4:26; Jas 1:19–20). Anger may be *the best and most proper response* when another's goods are taken and threatened – the kind of response seen when God is aroused in response to injustice (ch. 21), or in response to mockery of his glory and goodness. Similarly, some anger is a proper defence against the denigration of God's 'image' in us, and against deep or constant insults to it. This is a dangerous thought, for too often we overreact, or forget our callousness to others. Yet anger for ourselves may be appropriate when someone maliciously denies us a God-given good (e.g. when we're slandered, belittled or excluded; or bashed, robbed or raped).

This way of seeing anger doesn't contradict what I said above. We don't

---

1. Jesus also surprises us with news that he did *not* come to bring peace (e.g. Matt. 10:34–39; Luke 12:51–53). Here Jesus claims our total allegiance to himself. I'll touch on this disturbing division of humanity below (ch. 46).

get to enact *wrathful condemnation*. But what matters to God begins to matter to us. When threats elicit energetic action to protect what's good, *then* our anger echoes God's character.

The occasional moments of anger in Jesus' life (e.g. Matt. 23:23–39; John 2:14–17; 11:38), and the moments when he refrains from anger (e.g. Matt. 12:24–25; Luke 6:27–28; 23:34), become our human point of access from which to learn this properly circumscribed anger. In this way, the imitation of Jesus (ch. 32) contributes to our renewed moral imagination of anger.

But I owe all of these conclusions to an initial rule that shocked me. Without it, I wouldn't have discovered an entire new angle on being human. I've also begun to discover, in a way I'd been quite blind to, that rage really doesn't advance the cause of love very effectively at all. As Jesus' brother put it, 'the anger of man does not produce the righteousness of God' (Jas 1:20, ESV). That insight may be obvious enough to you, but it was not always to me: I needed this command. Interestingly, though, the way I *now* need it is changing. Now that its point is clearer to me, it's become less like a cattle prod directing me away from specific actions, and more like a lens through which I now see people and relationships. This command is no longer a burden (1 John 5:3); in fact, it's become a bit like honey (Ps. 19:10). It now burdens me that I forgetfully lurch back to the angry responses of my 'flesh'.

29. FORGIVING AND RECONCILING

Having discovered a 'unified field' by which to discern moral reality in Parts 3–4, Part 5 considers some approaches to the details of our lives. This chapter considers the practice of dealing with others called 'forgiveness and reconciliation'.

Churches begin to train people in the skills of forgiveness and reconciliation (p. 108). Since 'compassion and forgiveness belong to the Lord our God, though we've rebelled against Him' (Dan. 9:9), it follows that the practice of forgiveness and reconciliation shapes and forms communities in Christ (e.g. Matt. 6:12–15; Mark 11:25; Luke 6:37; Col. 3:13).

The practice of forgiveness is both simple and complex. Biblical exhortations to forgive interrogate and challenge our desire for revenge (cf. Rom. 12:17–21). But a complex of factors lies beneath that simple challenge.

From where does our longing for vengeance spring? When someone hurts us, we experience in a flash something of the great preciousness with which God has made us. We experience a truth about the created order itself (ch. 22): that we're a part of God's good creation, and aren't nothing. Anger can be a powerful and proper resistance against the loss of something good (see p. 188), and our outraged reaction and demand for justice springs finally from our being made in God's very 'image'. Our longing for infinite vengeance is an overreaction; we forget our injustices against others; but in our angry cries for justice, we glimpse the same impulse that makes God hold each human to account for his or her evil.

The psalmists' cries of lament are the biblical archetype for this proper longing (e.g. Pss 74, 79, 94). These cries seem stark to us, even too harsh. But they're no less than today's cries by the victim of a betrayal, a theft or an assault, or the murder of a loved on. When talk of forgiveness slips too quickly past this cry, we negate the essential good of what has been lost and the proper responses of the person enduring the loss. Crass, instantaneous calls to 'forgive and forget' are false. We violate victims a second time if we suggest that forgiveness entails acting as if nothing really happened. There's a proper time for anguished imprecation and lament.

Yet in Christian thought that cry for justice is *best* answered by the judgment of God, not by our own action to hurt our oppressor (Rom. 12:19). Christ's death (ch. 15) becomes the central venue where God expresses just judgment (cf. Rom. 3:25–26). I know Christians for whom it's made deep sense to cry out in anguish to God, calling for a justice either to be expressed upon Christ at his cross, or upon the person who did the harm as he or she faces God alone.

At the same time, Christ's cross also becomes the powerhouse of forgiveness. The call to practise forgiveness adds a new finding to the cry for justice: that to participate in the sufferings of Christ (p. 105) may include taking the hurt we long to put on another.

There emerges a further complexity to the practice of forgiveness. When people believe they've done us no wrong, our practice of forgiveness can seem irrelevant or meaningless. Where 'repentance' is absent, forgiveness doesn't quite seem to apply to the person. (Analogously, God isn't said to forgive those who show no sign of repentance.) Never are we more reliant upon the justice of God (perhaps via his appointed 'ruler', Rom. 13:4). When someone rejects our forgiveness, it can seem cheapened; we don't know what to do with it, and we don't know where to take it. Forgiveness needs repentance and reconciliation for it to seem complete.

Yet many find *that* analysis incomplete. Even while Christ's killers are utterly enmeshed in their self-justifying action of killing him, Christ's magisterial prayer pleads with the Father to forgive them anyway (Luke 23:34). This beautiful *willingness* to forgive, despite the unrepentant wretchedness of the wrongdoer, is an important, significant and often difficult moral task.[1] Gordon Wilson's daughter, Marie, was slain in the 1987 Enniskillen bombing. His response was sincere and compelling: 'I bear no ill will to anybody,' he said. 'I certainly don't feel bitterness. Maybe you're surprised that I don't, but

---

1. I'm indebted to Rick Creighton for this insight, and for the example following.

I don't. I prayed for them last night, sincerely, and I hope I have the grace to continue to do so.' Such an extraordinary and in a sense *unnatural* response is learnt at the foot of Christ's cross.

So although I maintain a technical distinction between 'standing ready to forgive' an unrepentant person, and 'forgiving' and reconciling with a repentant person, I wouldn't put too fine a point on it. When anyone can say, 'I've forgiven them; I've moved on,' they've enacted the same mercy as Christ embodies, and left the final accounting to God.

But there remains a good reason to keep the technical distinction. Just as forgiveness isn't the pretence that nothing ever happened, neither is it finally an individual journey, a therapeutic end to bitterness. The goal of forgiveness and reconciliation is *restored relationship*. Like the two ingredients in epoxy-resin glue, forgiveness needs a corresponding repentance to bond a broken relationship. Indeed these two 'ingredients' are the only known 'fuel' by which a broken relationship can be propelled into a new future. Repentance, forgiveness and reconciliation are the practices that keep alive the Christian dream of a restored, desirable community (chs. 18, 25, 34). Without these practices, there can be no such community. All that remains is a collection of people who navigate around each other, suspiciously keeping each other at a distance.

Some may conclude that the quest for reconciled relationships doesn't apply to relationships beyond the Christian community. That view could be argued on semantic grounds, since the biblical texts addressing forgiveness apply it to intrachurch or intra-Israel relationships. Construing these texts as narrow commands or duties enables the reader to believe that there's no obligation to forgive anyone beyond the Christian community (as if Christian moral imagination is solely a list of 'obligations'). Or, we may infer that since 'unity' is a gift of the Spirit (Eph. 4:3; cf. ch. 17), there isn't much point trying to reconcile with those who don't identify 'in Christ' (ch. 14).

But these conclusions strike me as blinkered, and I see no reason to agree with them. The relationships being addressed were intrachurch or intra-Israel – yet all humanity participates together in a created moral order that *includes* our inbuilt need for sociality (ch. 8), recreated in Christ (ch. 25). Intrachurch relationships (ch. 34) train those in Christ in the practice of forgiveness. It then ripples out to bless those who know nothing about it. We'll see how our dealings with others include cooperation and grace (ch. 35). Forgiveness and reconciliation can form a part of those dealings (and in a proper understanding of the Spirit, he can be present in these dealings, not only among those who identify in Christ).

I may finally discover how, in blindness and self-deception, I've also wronged my neighbour. Cocooned in the gestalt created by our loves (chs.

7–10), we regularly participate in scenarios where we're indignant at how someone treated us, with no insight into the provocation we gave another. In the complexity of forgiveness, reconciliation necessitates exploring the faults on *both* sides. At first I simply thought I was demanding and expecting repentance, but it turned out I needed to repent.

A man came to me recently. I'd slandered him casually and callously, and word of it had returned to him. But he did no retaliatory slander in response. His next action was a strong and gratifying, if rare, obedience to Jesus' words in this area (Matt. 18:15). He came to me directly and 'showed me my fault, just between the two of us'. My evil action was indefensible; I said so, and he willingly granted his forgiveness. The short email correspondence that followed ended with his joyful and gracious declaration: 'This matter is officially over!'

Further reading

** Cameron, Andrew J. B., 'The Hearing of "Sorry"', *Social Issues Briefing* 71, 14 Dec. 2007. Online: <http://www.sie.org.au>.

* Richards, Kel, *Forgiving Hitler: The Kathy Diosy Story* (Sydney: Matthias Media, 2002).

* Smedes, Lewis B., *The Art of Forgiving: When You Need to Forgive and Don't Know How* (New York: Ballantine, 1996).

*** O'Donovan, Oliver M. T., *The Ways of Judgment: The Bampton Lectures, 2003* (Grand Rapids: Eerdmans, 2005), chs. 6–7.

*** Volf, Miroslav, *Exclusion and Embrace: A Theological Exploration of Identity, Otherness, and Reconciliation* (Nashville: Abingdon, 1996).

** Volf, Miroslav, *Free of Charge: Giving and Forgiving in a Culture Stripped of Grace* (Grand Rapids: Zondervan, 2005).

30. VIRTUES AND VICES

Having discovered a 'unified field' by which to discern moral reality in Parts 3–4, Part 5 considers some approaches to the details of our lives. This chapter examines virtue, which does a lot of 'heavy lifting' in thinking about and practising what's good. We also consider the opposite of virtues – the vices.

'Virtue' isn't really a very helpful word nowadays. In popular parlance, we might speak of the ultra-saintly or the sexually abstinent as 'virtuous'. But deep down, everyone knows this is a word for weirdos. Normal people do well to stay right away from it.

But virtue has been a very important concept in ancient and modern ethics. We need it in order to think about *settled patterns and habits of action and feeling*. For since ancient times:

- 'Virtues' described a person's *settled patterns and habits of good action and proper emotions* (their 'affections').
- 'Vices' described a person's *settled patterns and habits of bad action and improper emotions* (their 'passions').

I've already touched on how virtues and vices get at the 'vibe' of a person (ch. 5) or group (ch. 18). They're about a person's style (or a group's culture). They don't predict specific actions, but they do predict the *type* of action a person is likely to take. Virtue and vice words sum up someone's history as observed over time by those closest to them.

Since virtues and vices tell of what each person does habitually, they start to tell of *who each person is*. The sum total of his or her virtues and vices becomes their *character*. The biblical authors have no direct equivalent for this modern word. But across the Bible's story arc (ch. 19), they refer hundreds of times to *the heart*. It's their metaphor for what drives our inner self.

> As the water reflects the face,
> so the heart reflects the person.
> (Prov. 27:19)

The heart combines our affections and passions, our values and fixations, our commitments and inclusions, and it propels our acts. Hearts can be bad, good, true, deceptive, pure or evil. They're always messy. Virtues and vices come from hearts (e.g. Gen. 6:5; Deut. 8:14; 1 Kgs 9:4; Ps. 64:6; Jer. 17:9; Mark 7:21–23; Luke 6:45; 12:34; Heb. 3:12; Jas 3:14; 1 Pet. 1:22; 2 Pet. 2:14). So if you're to begin to know yourself (your 'heart'), you'll need to know how virtues (and vices) work.

Each virtue is highly compressed and morally dense. Each is a rich and complex aggregate requiring further reflection and analysis. To practise a virtue requires close attention to the components of the moral field (ch. 10) before us. Consider 'kindness'. In a way, it's a simple enough idea. We know kind acts when we receive them. There may be some to whom we try to be kind (e.g. children). Yet if we try to analyse kindness more deeply, we realize that a lot is going on beneath the surface. We need each of the following if we're to act kindly:

1. We need a general working knowledge of people as *creatures with proper desires* (we'll always need food, shelter, health), including the differences made by age (babies need milk and cuddles, not steak and witty repartee).
2. We require a general working knowledge of people's *created sociality* (we'll always need inclusion, affection and the interest of others), including those created cues that enable connection with others (a smile accompanies kindness; a scowl turns it into something else).
3. We need particular knowledge of each person's *individual foibles*. (I don't experience tickets to the opera, or the gift of camping equipment, as 'kind'.)
4. We need some knowledge of cultural differences arising from various

group inclusions. (A Russian or an Englishman may prefer me to make tea in a samovar or a pot, rather than with a teabag.)

5. Ideally, we cannot be kind without a degree of *affection* for the other person. (People seem to know if we're just 'going through the motions', rather than helping because we like them.)

6. Whether we realize it or not, our kindness also pivots on a vision of *what people are 'for'*. (If I think people exist *in order to* be with and for one another, then I may judge it kinder to sit with a sad person. If I think people exist *for* individual self-fulfilment, then I may judge it kinder to offer them some happy activity.)

This one 'simple' virtue contains several different considerations about right and wrong. The mixture of general and specific knowledge seen here reflects the complexity of each moral field we encounter (ch. 10). The last point, about what people are for, demonstrates that different views of reality generate disagreements over what makes a virtue good.

In addition, kindness is the sum total of dozens of different kind acts, each of which may actually be quite different in type (e.g. giving a suitable gift, rescuing someone from drowning, aiding someone in an excluding or embarrassing social situation, offering to listen, administering first aid, providing good working conditions, etc.).

So this one small word, 'kindness', is actually incredibly dense. According to the Oxford English Dictionary, the kind person is 'naturally well-disposed; having a gentle, sympathetic, or benevolent nature; ready to assist, or show consideration for, others'.[1] The use of other overlapping virtue words in this definition highlights the moral density of this kind of language. In the language of the New Testament, 'kindness' overlaps with the very general virtue of 'goodness', and with the more specific virtue of 'mercy' – that unexpected goodness offered by someone I've wronged.

We've seen virtue-language throughout the Bible's account of ethics (e.g. chs. 14–18, 21, 28). Virtue and vice language does a lot of moral 'heavy lifting' in the Bible. The densest occurrences of such language occur in about twenty lists (see appendix to this chapter). Borrowing from the NIV translation (and turning its adjectives into nouns), these lists include

---

1. *Oxford English Dictionary Second Edition on CD-ROM* (v. 4.0) (Oxford: Oxford University Press, 2009).

endurance, faith, gentleness, godliness, goodness, holiness, hospitality, humility, impartiality, joy, kindness, love, mercy, obedience, patience, peace, purity, righteousness, self-control, sincerity, submission, truth . . .

The vice lists are longer and more action specific. That is, they're more likely to attack particular bad actions than the virtue lists are to promote particular good actions (so the vice lists also function as commands against various actions, chs. 23, 28.) Here are some of the more commonly appearing vices (NIV):

adultery, anger, debauchery, deceit, drunkenness, discord, envy, greed, idolatry, impurity, lust, lying, malice, murder, pride, rage, sexual immorality, slander, swindling, violence, wickedness, witchcraft . . .

The virtues are shorthand for life springing from Jesus Christ (Part 3), and the vices are shorthand for what we can otherwise expect to happen regularly (cf. ch. 9). Each list describes some overarching moral categories; some habitual patterns of relationship to God and to other humans; some inner emotions, desires and impulses; and some propensities toward particular types of action. The density of these lists is also daunting (perhaps because we've become unused to this way of thinking about right and wrong).

I'll briefly summarize and respond to four kinds of objection to this kind of language.

The psychologist's objection. A psychologist might claim that we cannot sum people up in these ways. The various words overlap too much to be useful. Each word incorporates too many different actions, behaviours, attitudes, emotions, and so on. I'd respond that the historical reappearance of this language suggests that it retains use and meaning as a kind of 'top level' moral language, and that psychologists may need to adjust *their* theoretical assumptions in order to investigate what gives it such traction in human affairs. Their second objection might be that in different settings, no one displays the same virtues and vices: different environments affect us differently. Of course, that's true, but the New Testament's virtue and vice language still enables us to be more reflective about what we often do in various settings, to discern and enact better responses there.

The 'values' objection. The discussion so far has included the controversial assumption that there's such a thing as 'proper' and 'improper' emotions – the 'affections' of the virtues and the 'passions' of the vices. (Today we generally consider passion a good quality; but until recently, a passion was a runaway, destructive desire or emotion.)

Since the beginning of the twentieth century, we've come to think of the emotions as an entire, morally neutral, category. But for most of Western history, that was not the case: 'affections' were seen as the feelings that propel us toward something good, and 'passions' as those that propel us to something bad.[2] It followed that we could evaluate emotions by deciding whether what they sought (or defended) was good or bad.

But we're no longer willing to label an emotion as good or bad. Indeed, many modern people have become *emotional essentialists*, where 'what I feel is who I am, and that's all there is to it'.[3] Hence we've become content to refer to someone's settled patterns and habits of action and feeling as their values (ch. 5). This term avoids judging whether some pattern is good or bad. Take *ambition*. If ambition is a 'value' for Nathan, we avoid a lot of controversy in comparison to calling it a 'virtue' (or a 'vice') of his. One person's 'virtue' is another person's 'vice'; so let's just call them 'values' to avoid thinking too hard and fighting about it. To speak of people's values emphasizes their choice in deciding on an ethic for themselves, and avoids having to discuss whether their action or emotions are right or wrong.[4]

The theologian's objection. Virtue thinking has a serious image problem among theologians. They notice how good we are at self-deception. We're very poor at evaluating our own settled patterns and habits, both of our actions and our feelings. So we delude ourselves that the lie we just told couldn't have been

---

2. For a detailed account of this distinction, see Thomas Dixon, *From Passions to Emotions: The Creation of a Secular Psychological Category* (Cambridge: Cambridge University Press 2003), pp. 45–61.

3. Here I'm borrowing and extending Diane Tice's concept of 'mood purism', the view that 'emotions are "natural" and should be experienced just as they present themselves'. Cited in Daniel Goleman, *Emotional Intelligence* (London: Bloomsbury, 1996), p. 58.

4. Hence it becomes quite strange when a group, such as a school or corporation, tries to name '*our* values'. Of course, there is nothing wrong with the managers of a group saying what they think is good or bad. But the word 'values' is about what *individuals* choose, and has evolved to *prevent* discussion about whether they're right or wrong so to choose. So when managers tell us 'our' values, they declare some values better than others. Practically no one in the group is convinced. A manager's declaration cannot overturn values *I* have chosen! The manager has tortured the language of 'value', and would be better off to be honest. Managers should simply state what they expect people to do, how they would like them to be, and offer reasons why.

dishonest because 'I'm an honest person'; or that the snub I just offered was not important because 'I'm a hospitable person'; or that we're not morally culpable for the slander or murder we just committed, because 'I'm a good person'.

Protestants have reacted against virtue language, because people congratulate themselves with it too easily. In short order, we start to imagine that the death of Jesus Christ (ch. 15) must have been for others, because we're better than that. These are serious objections. However, they're also overreactions, if only because the New Testament *has so much* of this important moral shorthand. I think it has two uses.

First, virtues function as *statements of aim*. We expand our moral imagination if we're aiming to become an honest, humble, hospitable, contented (and so on) person. I mentioned Ben (p. 18), whose boss, Zeke, asked him to amend some figures in order to win a contract. In the heat of the moment, all Ben had to work with was 'No, Zeke. I can't: I'm an honest person.' This reaction meant Ben didn't start thinking about whether the ends justified the means. He was then able to check if the amendments would break faith with the client, and eventually to come up with a better solution than lying.

Secondly, virtues are used to *describe others*. People in the New Testament frequently praise one another's virtues. They don't think that they thereby risk creating arrogance in the other, because these praises are offered in the context of a community that knows the necessity of Christ's death (ch. 15), and that expects the Holy Spirit to work among them (ch. 17). We would do well to resurrect this way of encouraging one another. ('I've been watching you for many years now, and I'm so thankful for what a kind and gracious person you've become. I saw it when you smiled at those children and took an interest in their toys; when you offered tea to that old person; when you listened carefully to that haggard young mother.')

We do well to retain a healthy awareness that we're not innately true, pure, humble or kind. We retain the usual human propensity to serve our immediate desires (chs. 7–9). But we may be cautiously optimistic that in Christ, we can begin to glimpse something of the virtues of *his* character in our own messy life. That's what happens to 'players' on his 'team' (p. 114).

The shortcomings of 'virtue ethics'. Anyone who plans to think more about virtue needs to be aware of the explosion of *virtue ethics*, a recent re-emergence of an older style of thinking about right and wrong. It contends that we need to place almost sole emphasis on questioning and evaluating who a person is, rather than evaluating his or her specific acts. It also contends that we should look to respected thinkers of the past (such as Aristotle) for guidance about how to do that.

I believe this body of thought has been immensely helpful for expanding moral imagination. However, I also believe that it makes two errors. First, by focusing upon virtue itself these thinkers don't help us to make particular judgments about particular acts in particular situations. To do that, we need to have some knowledge of the moral field before us. In this book I've suggested (ch. 26) that this knowledge comes via the Christian account of creation, Jesus-shaped community, the new future and the character of God, with biblical commands revealing aspects of these. Virtues are the *practices* over time that spring from taking seriously these aspects of the moral field.

The second error follows: not just any virtue will do. Aristotle's moral field was significantly different from that of the early Christian thinkers. The virtues that emerge in the pages of the New Testament spring, ultimately, from Jesus Christ. Virtue ethicists need to wrestle with New Testament virtue-language much more seriously and specifically on its own terms

Further reading

*** Dixon, Thomas, *From Passions to Emotions: The Creation of a Secular Psychological Category* (Cambridge: Cambridge University Press, 2003).

** Himmelfarb, Gertrude, *The De-Moralization of Society: From Victorian Virtues to Modern Values* (New York: Knopf, 1995).

** Wright, Tom, *Virtue Reborn* (London: SPCK, 2010).

Appendix to this chapter: virtue and vice lists

There are approximately twenty each of virtue lists and vice lists in the New Testament. (The exact number depends on how they're counted.) There's more to its language of virtue and vice than just these lists, but they're the core of it.

Virtues: Romans 13:13; 2 Corinthians 6:6–7; Galatians 5:22–23; Ephesians 4:32; 5:9; 6:14–17; Philippians 4:8; Colossians 3:12; 1 Timothy 3:2–12; 6:11; 2 Timothy 2:22, 24; 3:10; Titus 1:8–9; 2:2–5, 7, 9; 3:1–2; James 3:17; 1 Peter 3:8; 2 Peter 1:5–7.

Vices: Mark 7:21–22; Romans 1:29–31; 1 Corinthians 5:10; 6:9–10; 13:4–7; 2 Corinthians 12:20; Galatians 5:19–21; Ephesians 4:31; 5:3–5; Colossians 3:5, 8–9; 1 Timothy 1:9–10; 3:2; 6:4–5; 2 Timothy 3:2–5; Titus 1:7; 2:3, 9–10; 3:3; 1 Peter 4:3; Revelation 21:8; 22:15.

Of course, we should remember that the occasion and purpose of each list is different. Some examples will illustrate this point.

1. The list in Philippians 4:8 has always been of particular interest to scholars, with interpretations ranging from a Pauline affirmation of local secular virtue to the contemplation of abstract goods. A third reading is more plausible: that Pauls exhorts the warring parties in a dispute (Phil. 4:2) to find 'whatever' of these excellences resides in the other. That will help create the relational 'peace' of verses 7 and 9. Virtue is used here to describe another.

2. The qualities of Christian community leaders found in the Pastoral Epistles are tailored to a particular role description. But in the logic of New Testament community, leaders model virtuous behaviour like someone teaching a 'craft-skill' does.[5] Leaders demonstrate the Christian life (although the community can further improvise). Interestingly, the few behaviour-specific virtues (such as 'hospitality') appear in this connection. The example of these elders forms part of an answer asked by any bewildered members of the community, such as 'How can I be kind?'

3. Other virtue lists seem specific to the difficulties of local addressees, as sometimes revealed in the vice lists addressed to them. Thus, for example, Galatians 5:22 is (in part) a reply to the factions evident in verses 19–21, which in turn reflects the occasion of the letter. Thus, while such lists contribute toward a wider profile of New Testament ethics, they're not exhaustive. They illustratively address particular scenarios.

4. Some lists clearly function as general statements of aim rather than of present status (Eph. 6:14–17; Col. 3:12; 2 Pet. 1:5–7; and possibly Titus 3:3 and Jas 3:17).

5. The 'ladder' of 2 Peter 1:5–7 deserves special attention, because it isn't a ladder at all. It can look as though Christians have an arduous self-improvement programme. But it turns out that *each* term in it (except 'love' – see below) corresponds to God's character and work as outlined in verses 1–4. The 'faith' to be supplemented is already given (v. 1); 'goodness' parallels God's own 'goodness' (v. 3); 'knowledge' increases that which has already been given (v. 3); 'self-control' responds to the escape God effected from 'the corruption that is in the world because of evil desires' (v. 4); 'endurance' is a response to promises (v. 4); 'godliness' reflects our sharing in 'the divine nature' (v. 4), and 'brotherly affection' follows from the participants being a

---

5. This metaphor is popular among leading virtue ethicists; e.g. Alasdair MacIntyre, *Three Rival Versions of Moral Enquiry* (London: Duckworth, 1990), pp. 82–83; Stanley Hauerwas, 'Discipleship as a Craft, Church as a Disciplined Community', *Christian Century*, 2 Oct. 1991, pp. 881–884.

group, not an individual. The ladder is in fact a mirror, a pattern of fitting response to divine reality.

6. We should pause to notice the way 'love' works in these lists (Gal. 5:22; 2 Cor. 6:6; Col. 3:14; 1 Tim. 6:11; 2 Pet. 1:7). In the 2 Peter list, love summarizes the other virtues. Robert C. Roberts notes that love is neither a distinct emotion nor a distinct virtue but is rather 'a kind of summary term for virtually the whole range of proper attitudes and action dispositions with respect to God and neighbour'[6] (some of which are explicitly outlined in 1 Cor. 13:4–7). Love is 'the unitary orientation that lies behind all the uniquely varied responses to the generic variety of the created order'.[7]

---

6. Robert C. Roberts, 'Emotions Among the Virtues of the Christian Life', *Journal of Religious Ethics* 20 (1992), p. 43.

7. Oliver M. T. O'Donovan, *Resurrection and Moral Order: An Outline for Evangelical Ethics*, 2nd ed. (Leicester: Apollos, 1994), pp. 223–224.

31. FREEDOM

Having discovered a 'unified field' by which to discern moral reality in Parts 3–4, Part 5 considers some approaches to the details of our lives. This chapter examines 'freedom'. New Testament authors are passionate about freedom; but the order in which they approach it (spiritual, social then physical) is the opposite of what we're used to (physical, social and then spiritual).

Do you want to feel freer? Much leaves people feeling controlled. You may feel *physically* constrained. A compromised body frustrates you, and you wish you could move or see or hear like those around you. Or you're in the grip of a habit, addiction or obsession that overrules your thoughts and directs your actions. Or you're terminally ill, and feel like you are under a death sentence.

Perhaps the constraints on you are *social*. The group surrounding you at school, work or home has patterns and influences you don't like (ch. 8). Or you feel trapped under a load of routine and responsibility you wish would go away. A bully rules your workplace, region or country, dictating every aspect of life, and tolerating no rivals. Areas where you feel you could make a difference aren't open to you, due to your age, gender or skin colour.

Less tangibly, but no less corrosively, the constraints might be *spiritual*. A religious ideology dominates your every choice and action, as if your eternal destiny hangs upon everything you do. You constantly feel guilty (and books on ethics only make it worse!). You're terminally ill, and the prospect of what might come next haunts you.

The biblical authors are passionate about freedom, but it turns out that the first freedom they speak of is spiritual. Straightaway this will be a disappointment to some. We move in an age that values physical and social freedom far more than spiritual freedom. We're like those who took a crippled man to see Jesus, but were nonplussed when Jesus at first offered only spiritual freedom (Mark 2:1–5). But if we work with the logic of the biblical authors, we may be surprised. For they thought that by securing spiritual freedom, we thereby secure some social freedoms – and even make inroads into our physical constraints.

Spiritual freedom. Jesus introduced himself as a liberator. His first hearers were offended (John 8:31–36), because they didn't believe they needed to be released from what Jesus thought controlled them. But he insisted that he knew what sets people free. Once the pinnacle achievements of Jesus' life unfolded (chs. 15–16), the clarion call becomes 'for freedom Christ has set us free; stand firm therefore, and do not submit again to a yoke of slavery' (Gal. 5:1, NIV).

Provocatively, Paul thinks that the control of the Old Testament law (ch. 24) over these people is 'slavery' and that anyone who relies on it is basically sunk (Gal. 3:10).[1] In contrast, we're spiritually free when we accept God's promise to love and accept us despite our regular weakness and failure (Gal. 3:18, 29). The New Testament vision is of Jesus releasing us into 'sonship' with God (Gal. 3:26; 4:7; Eph. 1:5). What we hear as sexism is actually the opposite. Jesus subverts the traditional privilege of sons when women *and* men receive the privileges traditionally due to sons. Here's the best of family relationship – the kind of love and acceptance we can trust and depend upon, even at our worst. The way Christ gives 'glorious freedom of the children of God' (Rom. 8:31), mesmerized the early Christians.

In the history of Christian thought, freedom from Old Testament law has extended to the lessening of rules in general, particularly religiously motivated

---

1. There's a lively debate about what Paul was challenging. Some (like me) think he was challenging their allegiance to every aspect of the Old Testament law, and offering what I'm calling a spiritual freedom. Others think he challenged their view that this law defined their group inclusion, and offered instead a kind of social freedom. It is a complicated discussion beyond the scope of this book. But either way, the take-home point is that the Old Testament law no longer binds or directs people, and, even if some elements of it remain relevant to moral discussion (ch. 20), it is not the code by which Christians live.

ones (e.g. Col. 2:16–23). Overreliance on rules is often called *legalism*. By the Spirit (ch. 17), we become those who can *discern* what really matters (p. 312) rather than being automatons programmed by lists of rules (ch. 3). Freedom in the Spirit includes a growing capacity to respond properly to our surroundings, rather than responding out of the immediate gestalt (p. 72) of our 'flesh' (ch. 9).

Social freedom. Since Christ cuts the link between performance and acceptability to God (p. 67), *every human attempt to condemn us before God is doomed*; and when people experience 'the glorious freedom of the children of God', *every human attempt to claim us is doomed*. Our social freedoms come from this central reality.

That every human attempt to condemn us before God is doomed becomes expressed in discussions about morally indifferent things (or *adiaphora*, to use theology's technical term). Several New Testament discussions secure people's freedom to enjoy good created things, particularly food and married sex (e.g. Acts 10, 15; Rom. 6, 14; 1 Cor. 8 – 10; Gal. 4 – 5; 1 Tim. 4:1–5; 1 Pet. 2:16). We may step lightly through all sorts of false moral claims against us on the proviso that this freedom isn't for flaunting. Love for others sometimes entails the avoidance of whatever they might misinterpret, and of whatever distresses them.

The case of the slave shows how human attempts to claim us are doomed. When Paul exhorts slaves to work enthusiastically for their masters (Col. 3:22–25), he isn't legitimating and enforcing some ancient view of human hierarchy. For he reasons that the slave has *effectively been released* to a new Master, Jesus Christ. This slave is now freed to treat his human master as a spiritual equal, and uses his or her labour for the master's good – but 'as something done for the Lord and not for men' (v. 23). It follows that masters 'in Christ' (ch. 14) can only give justice and fairness to slaves (Col. 4:1).

This reframing of the master–slave relationship isn't mere sophistry. Neither Paul nor slaves could change ancient social structures of slavery (partly because their society was utterly reliant on this workforce). But this reframing did put a ticking time bomb into the heart of slavery as an institution, as it inexorably became clear that adoption by God, and spiritual freedom, eclipsed all ownership claims people might try to make on each other.[2] The true inclusion experienced by 'children of God' trumped all other inclusion claims.

---

2. See the discussion in Oliver M. T. O'Donovan, *The Ways of Judgment* (Grand Rapids: Eerdmans, 2005), pp. 247–248; and in Brian J. Dodd, *The Problem with Paul* (Downers Grove: IVP, 1995), ch. 5.

Luther famously describes the paradox seen in this social freedom: 'A Christian is a perfectly free lord of all, subject to none. A Christian is a perfectly dutiful servant of all, subject to all.'[3] In other words, those in Christ step lightly past all sorts of claims that others make on them – yet at the same time continually invest themselves in the good of others. This interesting New Testament paradox (e.g. 1 Cor. 9:19; Rom. 13:8) forms a significant plank in Christian political thought. 'Submit to every human institution because of the Lord,' says the apostle Peter (1 Pet. 2:13). 'As God's slaves, live as free people, but don't use your freedom as a way to conceal evil' (1 Pet. 2:16). To 'submit' and to 'live free' seems contradictory. But Christians are able to accept human authorities as (very) rough copies of Christ's rule, and so can cooperate as subjects. But when the same authority stops resembling Christ, it has no claim on us, as when two of Jesus apostles declare 'we must obey God rather than any human authority' (Acts 5:29, NRSV). It turns out that this paradox has significantly shaped Western democratic traditions.

Physical freedom. I said that Pauls' reframing of the case of the slave isn't mere sophistry, but that comment may seem defensive. Someone will object, 'hang on. The slave *is still a slave. Nothing has changed* for him or her.' The case of the slave highlights the very great emphasis we place on freedom's most basic level – the freedom to move through and to act unencumbered in space. Just as we resent it when sickness, disability and death limit this very great good, so also do we resent social obligations or roles preventing any expression of our bodily selves. What are we to make of this longing for freedom? Can spiritual freedom touch it?

When we despise our illness, mourn our disabilities, lament oppression and fear our deaths, we long to be truly human. The Bible's interesting and extensive treatment of trials and suffering (cf. p. 105) shapes us to experience our physical unfreedom with optimism and hope, while not always expecting immediate physical restoration. For, due to the resurrection of Christ, these failures of freedom are ultimately temporary: the God who raised Jesus Christ undertakes to remake us. In one of the Bible's most mysterious passages (Rom. 8:18–25), someone – God himself, it seems – subjects the creation to 'futility' so that it 'groans'. At this stage we're not free from this environment. Yet there's hope, because the one who subjects it will release it, reveal his children and redeem their bodies and social relationships. Christians know

---

3. Martin Luther, 'The Freedom of a Christian', in *Luther's Works*, vol. 31, ed. H. Grimm (Philadelphia: Fortress, 1957), p. 344. Online: <http://www.fordham.edu/halsall/mod/luther-freedomchristian.html>.

physical unfreedom as hard as any, but the new future (ch. 24) causes us to receive it differently.

The problem of physical constraint is reshaped in a solution that addresses and reshapes our desires. When some physical constraint saddens us, the biblical authors bring our desires from unawareness to awareness. They acknowledge and affirm our appropriate sadness as we participate in a 'groaning' creation. Yet they don't let us imagine that we always become free simply by meeting some immediate desire. Otherwise, the hope for physical freedom can morph into a false quest. Peter speaks of this quest when describing those who promise freedom, but who are themselves 'slaves of corruption; for people are slaves to whatever masters them' (2 Pet. 2:19, NRSV). The pleasures of physical freedom and the freedom for physical pleasure are lost and barren on their own, and only find their proper home within the social freedom to love others, and within spiritual freedom before God.

Yet within that home, physical freedom *does* emerge. It emerged when Christian communities created places of care that sought healing (Jas 5:13–15), fed the hungry (Acts 6:1–3) and rejoiced when even slaves, of either gender, deliberated aloud over the word of God (Acts 2:18). This Christian community (chs. 18, 25, 34) revels in spiritual freedom, and then becomes a space for social freedoms that enable much physical freedom.

The sixteenth-century theologian John Calvin cleverly challenges another kind of physical bondage that we all experience, but which can masquerade as a quest to be free.[4] We each have a compulsion not to miss good experiences. 'There is almost no one whose resources permit him to be extravagant,' Calvin says, 'who doesn't delight in lavish and ostentatious banquets, bodily apparel, and domestic architecture; who doesn't wish to outstrip his neighbours in all sorts of elegance; who doesn't wonderfully flatter himself in his opulence.' People defend these choices as *adiaphora*, a technical term for something morally neutral or indifferent. 'I admit it,' responds Calvin, 'provided they are used indifferently. But when they are coveted too greedily, when they are proudly boasted of, when they are lavishly squandered, things that were of themselves otherwise lawful are certainly defiled by these vices.'

We may enjoy God's good gifts. 'We have never been forbidden to laugh, or to be filled, or to join new possessions to old or ancestral ones, or to delight in musical harmony, or to drink wine.' But our desires fixate obsessively on these things (ch. 7), and 'under coarse and rude attire there often dwells a heart of

---

4. John Calvin, *Institutes of the Christian Religion*, vol. 1, tr. Ford Lewis Battles (Philadelphia: Westminster, 1960), p. 841 (§3.19.9).

purple, while sometimes under silk and purple is hid a simple humility.' People know true freedom, says Calvin, when they've learned 'in whatever state they are, to be content' (Phil. 4:11–12).

Calvin models a kind of discernment about our response to the material order. We'll be frustrated if we try to encapsulate his comment into a code, formula or rulebook about what to possess. The Jesus-shaped version of us joyfully participates in an order full of goodness, and is free to do so, yet is also free to stop, to not need every experience or have every good. Our Jesus-shaped self knows how to be content with a song once heard or a meal we'll never have again. The Jesus-shaped version of you or me can look at a neighbour's husband or wife, at their social standing, their beauty or at their prosperous family – and simply be happy for the neighbour. We practise a new Christian identity when we pray, talk and buy with *this* kind of freedom.

The oddball Christian philosopher Søren Kierkegaard imagines the *knight of faith* along similar lines.[5] This person is completely at home in the everyday world. He isn't easy to spot in a crowd, since he isn't obviously religious. He jovially greets children in the street on his way home, and he looks forward to seeing his wife and enjoying the roast dinner she's prepared. But these joys don't define him, because he's done business with salvation in 'fear and trembling' (Phil. 2:12). He's engaged with 'the infinite' God in faith and now has an awestruck confidence in God. Kierkegaard suggests that the young virgin who bore Jesus, Mary, was just such a knight of faith. She attracts us because, despite the constraints of her situation, her trust in God set her completely free from the twisted compulsions that so easily could have defined her.

In this connection, I offer a word to those who work hard in evangelical churches, as either members or leaders. They're not legalists, and have a healthy sense that they may enjoy morally indifferent goods. They also have a strong sense of being the 'perfectly dutiful servant of all, subject to all'. But oddly, we sometimes drift into a new form of anxious entrapment. The obligation of 'service to all' totally dominates us, so that our leisure-time uses of *adiaphora* must erupt with urgent intensity in order that we may feel free. Paradoxically, these preachers of freedom can feel quite trapped.

But freedom in Christ means that every human attempt to condemn us or to claim us is doomed. Not even the claims of those in a church, or in a church hierarchy, can eclipse the claim of Christ: we also remain the 'perfectly free lord of all, subject to none'. We may say 'no'; we may rest (p. 167); we're

---

5. Søren Kierkegaard, *Fear and Trembling*, tr. Alastair Hannay (Harmondsworth: Penguin, 1985), pp. 67–70.

free to discover that we're only 'co-workers' with God (1 Cor. 3:9); we find that our leadership and influence only touch people for a season. We, too, may discover what it looks and feels like to become a knight of faith like Mary, or like the Colossian slave.

Further reading

** Ellingsen, Mark, *Sin Bravely: A Joyful Alternative to the Purpose-Driven Life* (New York: Continuum, 2009).

32. IMITATING JESUS

Having discovered a 'unified field' by which to discern moral reality in Parts 3–4, Part 5 considers some approaches to the details of our lives. This chapter examines whether imitating Christ is helpful for deciding what to do and how to be.

'A disciple is not above his teacher, but everyone who is fully trained will be like his teacher,' declares Jesus (Luke 6:40). I've already touched on 'following' Jesus (ch. 13). I concluded that we don't truly follow Jesus merely by attending to his words and deeds as recorded in first-century Palestine. This chapter considers an approach to ethics connected to following Jesus – that we should explicitly pattern our lives by a direct imitation of him wherever possible.

Some think *imitating Christ* is a sufficient approach for finding how to live well.[1] The approach is popularized in those wristbands that ask 'What would Jesus do?' in each moment of the day. The real problem with the wristband isn't so much the question, but that within a day or two we stop noticing it on

---

1. Theologians tend to refer to the risen and ascended Lord as 'Christ', reserving 'Jesus' for his earthly ministry. If we accept this usage, those who speak of 'the imitation of Christ' almost always mean 'the imitation of Jesus' in his first-century Palestinian ministry.

our body. As a result, the wristband doesn't create the kind of attention to the moral field (ch. 10) that we hope to achieve.

This approach is often associated with the extremely influential handbook of Christian piety called *The Imitation of Christ*, written by the fifteenth-century monastic Thomas à Kempis. But ironically, this work has scant specific data about copying Jesus and doesn't outline a method for answering 'What would Jesus do?', except perhaps in relation to suffering (cf. p. 105). The book is an interesting compendium of scriptural insights and of Thomas's advice for how to be a Christian, and represents a significant departure from a rule-based approach to life. Thomas promotes several virtues for use in various situations, and treats mystical and religious themes in a way that provokes Protestant disagreement. As a result, the book's misleading title has rendered the whole idea of imitating Christ guilty by association among evangelical Protestants. But this suspicion of the idea is unwarranted, since *The Imitation of Christ* isn't actually a helpful place from which to begin any close consideration of what's really meant by imitating Christ. The book is, however, an interesting and sometimes helpful Christian exploration of how ethics works. It deserves more engagement than it receives.

Is 'What would Jesus do?' a helpful question? It has some impeccable biblical credentials:

1. Jesus follows the example of his Father (John 4:34; 6:38), and is himself seen as the human 'image' of God (John 14:9; 2 Cor. 4:4; Phil. 2:6–7; Col. 1:15; Heb. 1:3).
2. He himself promoted the imitation of God's character (ch. 21). In his farewell discourses, Jesus follows the Father's works of love, and the disciples then copy Jesus by loving him and each other (John 13:13–16, 34–35; 15:9–10; 20:21). This chain of imitation weaves a unity between Father, Son and disciples, all empowered by the Spirit (John 14:17; see ch. 17).
3. Nuances in the book of Acts suggest that the followers perpetuated Jesus' example. For example the apostles' strategy in Acts 6:1–4 is reminiscent of Jesus' own (Luke 10:38–42; Mark 1:35–38); and the death of Stephen (Acts 7) contains many allusions to Jesus' way of suffering (cf. p. 105).
4. Paul motivates others by use of the example of Christ (2 Cor. 8:9; 10:1; Rom. 15:1–3; Phil. 2:5), for he takes the imitation of Jesus to be an extension of the imitation of God (cf. Eph. 5:1). He even calls others to imitate his own imitation of Jesus (1 Cor. 4:16–17; 11:1), which seems arrogantly audacious to us. Yet this chain of imitation only

restates the logic of 'oneness' Jesus outlined in his farewell discourses (John 14 – 17).

5. Peter, John and the author to the Hebrews all straightforwardly commend the imitation of various aspects of Jesus (1 Pet. 2:21; 1 John 2:6; 3:16; 4:17; Heb. 3:1; 12:2–3).

6. Biblical authors conceive of our new future (ch. 24) as the final expression of a Jesus-shaped version of ourselves (Rom. 8:29; 1 Cor. 15:49; 2 Cor. 3:18; Col. 3:10; 1 John 3:2–3).

But how should such imitation proceed? No one in the New Testament imagines that we merely parrot Jesus' every action. The imitation is a taking up of his *character and virtues* such as his readiness to serve; his patience; his endurance of suffering; his gentleness, compassion, humility, obedience and love; his intolerance of injustice, religiosity, and opposition to God; his concern for the poor and vulnerable; and his consistent return to teaching and evangelism. But as we've seen (ch. 30), the language of character and virtue is a high-level moral language, which requires close attention to the ingredients of the moral field before us.

Therefore, the 'What would Jesus do?' approach is insufficient if it proceeds 'simply by allowing the imagination to sketch rather a hazy and romantic picture of Jesus moving about in the situation within which we find ourselves, and almost magically handling the problem in question,' as Melvin Tinker puts it.[2] The approach also requires imaginatively transporting Jesus from his first-century Palestinian context to our twenty-first-century context. That's a difficult exercise, and we can be prone in such moments to invent a Jesus who suits our own desires and social systems of inclusion (chs. 7–8).

Hence the seemingly simple advice to 'do what Jesus would have done' sometimes only complicates the process of moral discernment. At worst, we simply may not have all the relevant data to know how to imitate Christ, either because we don't have the full details of the current situation, or because we're as yet unfamiliar with all the details of Christ's character available to us in the Bible, or because we're limited by not having been given an exhaustive biography of Jesus, or because Christ never dealt with a similar situation. The imitation of Christ is an important line of Christian ethical reflection among many others. But Jesus' human example occurred as an episode in the Bible's (and his) overall story arc (ch. 19). Our task is

---

2. Melvin Tinker, 'The Priority of Jesus: A Look at the Place of Jesus' Teaching and Example in Christian Ethics', *Themelios* 13.1 (1987), p. 9.

to *discern* the moral field in front of *us* (p. 312), by reference to that *overall* story (ch. 26).

And yet, biblical exhortations to imitate Christ are present for a reason. Among the complexities (ch. 10) of moral deliberation, to wonder what Jesus might have done can expand our moral imagination. His example gives more options than our desires and schools of moral formation offer us (chs. 7–8). Christian readers of the Gospels have often noticed Jesus' enjoyment of God's good creation, his enjoyment and depth of human relationships, his lack of greed, his steely determination, his spontaneous love of children, and much more. We would be fools to think that these impressions are irrelevant moral data. Indeed, perhaps rather than wondering what Jesus would do, the real trick is to wonder *who Jesus would be.*

My beloved pastor, Barry, has an ingenious method for starting down this new road of moral imagination. Rather than reading the Gospels and asking, 'What would Jesus do in Barry's life?', Barry reads them and asks 'What would Barry do in Jesus' life?' That is, he puts his own anxieties, hang-ups and foibles onto Jesus' situations and experiences. What would Barry do, when confronted by a lame man, a difficult religious leader, or a Roman ruler? I doubled over in laughter at Barry describing himself ludicrously running about these scenes pleasing people, or losing patience, or having a meltdown. 'I'm so *glad* I don't have to follow *that* "Christ"!' he chortles. In this way, he stops assuming his own identity, and begins to see Jesus' way of being.

Further reading

** Griffiths, Michael, *The Example of Jesus* (London: Hodder & Stoughton, 1985).

** Jensen, Michael, 'Imitating Paul, Imitating Christ: How Does Imitation Work as a Moral Concept?', *Churchman* 124.1 (2010), pp. 17–36.

** Tinker, Melvin, 'The Priority of Jesus: A Look at the Place of Jesus' Teaching and Example in Christian Ethics', *Themelios* 13.1 (1987), pp. 9–19.

33. OBEDIENCE TO GOD

Having discovered a 'unified field' by which to discern moral reality in Parts 3–4, Part 5 considers some approaches to the details of our lives. This chapter examines obedience to God, particularly for those who find it difficult.

Many people's first encounter with Christian thought about ethics is around the practice of 'obedience' to God. Although some come to terms with such obedience and love it, others hatefully reject it. Yet others try it uncertainly, not quite sure how or what to obey, or why. For how can obedience cohere at all with a life lived according to the Spirit (ch. 17), or with freedom (ch. 31)? In this chapter, I'll attempt to interpret obedience using themes covered so far.

Some may relate to my own early experiences of obedience. My father was stern, intimidating, a little erratic and big enough to enforce obedience to him. The moments he did so aroused a lot of anger in me, and from that angry perspective what I was 'obeying' seemed to be only his own self-interest. I now believe that he loved me through these conflicts, although it took a long time to believe that. However, it's also clear that his recourses to enforced obedience were sometimes a desperate short cut. As he anxiously surveyed the moral field before him (ch. 10), a raised voice and sometimes a heavy hand were the only options he had for piloting his family through the complexities of life. For some reason, these conflicts usually erupted every

Saturday, when his plans and purposes for an old house and an unruly yard were very far from my own. So for me, obedience was for a long time the sound of those who, at best, couldn't explain why they wanted what they wanted; or at worst, simply used force to enslave me to their interests.

Not everyone will relate to my kind of upbringing. Some of us come from the opposite direction, experiencing few expectations to obey and finding the Christian notion of obedience simply bizarre. (Why start 'submitting' to God when you have never been expected to submit to anyone?) Although we come at it from different directions, I suspect obedience also sounds to you like a failure to give proper reasons, and an attempt to advance interests at your expense.

These two suspicions about obedience – that it substitutes for thoughtful reasons, and that it enforces someone else's interests – turn out to be a potent summary of the thought of Immanuel Kant (ch. 3) and Friedrich Nietzsche (ch. 11). Nietzsche isn't very surprised that people try to enforce obedience on each other. That's just what people do. If you're in a position not to obey, just don't. If you're too powerless to resist, too bad. Kant, on the other hand, deeply resents the 'laziness and cowardice' he thinks obedience represents. 'If I have a book which understands for me, a pastor who has a conscience for me, a physician who decides my diet, and so forth, I need not trouble myself. I need not think.'[1] In opposition to such stupidity, the radical Enlightenment called for a total rejection of religious authority. (Kant actually went on to defend the duties of clerics and public officials, but argued that reasoned public discussion was required in order to justify the truth and morality they uphold.)

Such thoughts are our inheritance. What then are we to make of the appearance of 'obedience' in Scripture and in Christian thought about right and wrong? I've already said something about the way biblical rules are embedded in a wider reality (ch. 26), while also interrogating our emotions (chs. 3, 23). I've broadly outlined this wider reality and the way commands function to unveil it. We've also seen how Jesus embodied several 'virtues' that add up to a 'character' we may also embody (chs. 13–17, 21, 28, 32).

Many of these themes are woven together in Jesus' extraordinary farewell discourse (John 13 – 17), where he makes ample use of the language of

---

1. Immanuel Kant, 'What Is Enlightenment?', tr. Lewis White Beck, in *On History*, ed. Lewis White Beck (Indianapolis: Bobbs-Merrill, 1963), p. 3. Online: <http://www.fordham.edu/halsall/mod/kant-whatis.html> (accessed 15 July 2010).

command and obedience: 'If you love me, you will keep my commandments' (14:15, NRSV). But we also begin to see an extraordinary interplay between obedience and the nature of loving relationship: 'If you keep my commandments, you will abide in my love, just as I have kept my Father's commandments and abide in his love' (15:10, NRSV). As people learn this Godlike love (ch. 21), the community becomes united. 'Those who love me will keep my word, and my Father will love them, and we will come to them and make our home with them' (14:23, NRSV).

This interplay is typical of biblical command and obedience language, which I suggest is a special case of obedience. It doesn't suffer from the flaws we see in other human experiences. It doesn't fall foul of Kant's suspicions, for we see repeatedly that biblical commands operate intelligibly within the matrix of nature, community and future. A good created order needs our defence and protection (ch. 22). Some kinds of vices damage human sociality in this order. Other kinds of virtues defend and protect it. A Jesus-shaped community learns which does what (ch. 25). We can resist or promote humanity's purpose (ch. 24), and Christian obedience is a response to the news that this is how things are.

Nor does biblical command and obedience language fall foul of Nietzsche's suspicions, for we begin to see that neither Father nor Son command obedience from mere self-interest. As in all relationships, trust that this is so can emerge only from a history of trustworthy disposition and activity. Gradually, Christians realize that these persons *do* know how to act for the best interests of others. This history has begun to emerge in this book (in Part 3 and ch. 21). I eventually became convinced that God's call to obey had none of the difficulties associated with my early experiences of obedience. Responding, then, to those reactions to obedience I began with:

- To those who've come to terms with obedience and love it: congratulations, as long as you also realize that this obedience includes the call 'that your love may abound more and more in knowledge and depth of insight, so that you may be able to discern what is best' (Phil. 1:9–10, NIV). Love governs our response to each moral field (ch. 10), and includes a responsibility to watch, think and discern (p. 312). In this respect, Kant was right to attack lazy and thoughtless forms of obedience.
- To those who try obedience with uncertainty, not always knowing how or why: try thinking of each rule as a 'tool of reasoning which is capable of embracing even the unpredictable particular case and rendering it intelligible'. As we apply it to a particular case, 'we come

to understand not merely the case but [each tool], too, better than we did before'.[2]

- To those who hatefully reject obedience to God: consider the possibility that your moral imagination is stunted by this rejection. Could it be that your existing desires and systems of inclusion (chs. 7–8) are never properly interrogated? If so, you may know less than you think about how to be truly human. That said, don't assume Christian obedience also entails obedience to every *human* claim. Jesus agrees with Nietzsche: some authority claims are illicit, only serving to advance the self-interest of the one who commands (e.g. Matt. 23:3–6). Kant was correct to argue that we need to reason publically together about what justifies a rule, precisely in order to curb illicit authority claims.

I owe it to a good man finally to admit that his efforts to raise me well *were* loving. He *did* need to use commands and require my obedience. I now see how much I resisted him, due to some very short-sighted desires. I generally only succeeded in increasing this good man's participation in Christ's sufferings (p. 105).

---

2. Oliver M. T. O'Donovan's account of Paul Ramsey on rules. Oliver M. T. O'Donovan, 'Obituary: Paul Ramsey (1913–88)', *Studies in Christian Ethics* 1.1 (1988), p. 85.

34. LIFE IN CHURCHES

Having discovered a 'unified field' by which to discern moral reality in Parts 3–4, Part 5 considers some approaches to the details of our lives. Churches have regular and terrible flaws, yet are our 'school' for learning the communal nature of identity in Christ and of true human being.

I often find churches maddening. I've had a fair bit to do with them over my time, in roles ranging from member, to volunteer worker, to mid-level leader and pastor, to trainer of pastors. I've been involved in eleven local churches of five different denominations (wider associations of local churches) in Australia and the UK.

I don't always find them maddening. My current local church exhibits friendliness, grace and a continual knack for helping me to discover my identity in Christ. I actually jump out of bed each Sunday morning to get there. I love it. Likewise, the small group of Christians who cared for my family in the UK remain a highlight in our lives, and proved how good a church could be.

But experiences like that come and go, and being a member of a church can be quite hard. Each case would need its own analysis but the main problem is that a church is like a hospital for sick sinners. Hospitals are always intense places, but my wife Mary-Anne once worked in a hospital that illustrates the point particularly well. This place cared for people who had experienced a specific kind of head injury. They had each received a severe blow to the front of their skull, which houses the brain's frontal lobes. This area of the brain governs our social behaviour. It gives us insight into how we're coming across in social situations, and enables us to rein back our actions when a strong emotion surges up. The damaged frontal lobes in these people impaired their performance of those tasks.

Hence their 'community' made for a lot of black comedy. They would each do outrageous things to one another, yet with no insight into how outrageous. Each would then express utter indignation at the insults they had endured. Jim would storm up to Mary-Anne complaining that Bob had punched him. She would try to point out that Bob had punched him because Jim had insulted Bob, or stolen from Bob, or exposed himself to Bob. But Jim couldn't see the significance in any of that. He only remembered Bob's punch.

This sad place has become for me a kind of dark parable about what goes on in the hospital for sick sinners. We each bring to it our weird fixations and social aspirations (chs. 7–8). We remain poor at noticing how we come across to others, or what other people need and how to give it. It's taken me decades even to begin seeing the pathologies I bring to this hospital, many of which affect others.

That is why the New Testament's communities in Christ took on a 'vibe' (ch. 18) that included mercy, humility, grace, empathy, equity, inclusion, honour and submission, care, sexual self-restraint, hospitality, sharing and mutual service. Nearly fifty 'one another' sayings continually create a new gestalt (p. 72) in which to construe true humanity: that we *inhabit reciprocal relationships*, and are not just lone atoms wandering detached through a crowd. Against the backdrop of constant human failure, these relationships rely upon the 'fuel' of repentance, forgiveness and reconciliation (ch. 29) to propel them into a new, non-vengeful future.

Each church is an extraordinary project of Jesus-shaped community (ch. 25), a network of relationships in which to learn endurance in difficulty while still pursuing peace and love. In other words, they become an *alternative* school of moral formation (ch. 8), where people are apprenticed to different settled habits and patterns of action and feeling (ch. 30), as expressed through various speech acts, money acts and other acts (ch. 18).

Since Jesus Christ gives truest access to true humanity, this 'vibe' pivots on learning from, praying to and praising God in Jesus Christ and through the Spirit (ch. 17). That's why many churches, then as now, take 'truthful' doctrine very seriously: if the Bible's account is correct, we simply revert to all the usual ways of being human without the continued close examination of Christ's identity in a church's agenda. When the membership or leadership of a church becomes uninterested in Jesus Christ, the result is a toxic environment and wordy bombast (1 Tim. 6:3–5; 2 Tim. 2:12–15; 2 Pet. 2:18–20). New Testament communities saw the rise of exploitative rhetoricians who had no real knowledge of Jesus Christ. That can also occur today, although I suspect these New Testament discussions equally apply when members and leaders have a deep interest in 'truthful' doctrine but without any interest in *inhabiting* their new identity in Jesus Christ. Either way, churches become toxic when they lose their moorings in Christ.

But for all their desperate human faults, churches are meant to operate as Christ's earthbound school of moral formation. To put that a little more technically, *the unique 'polity' of the church, with its structures and practices, is a Christian's first and last 'school' for properly understanding social order.*[1] God is said to have 'put everything under [Jesus'] feet' and to have appointed him 'head over everything', for, surprisingly, the church 'is His body, the fullness of the One who fills all things in every way' (Eph. 1:22–23). In other words, these strange groups of oddballs function as a living, breathing advertisement of Jesus Christ. Amazingly, 'every ruler and authority, power and dominion, and every title given' (v. 21) becomes subservient to the church's Lord. Rulers and authorities don't tell us how to live together. Those in churches find how to live together from him.

Measured from the usual human perspective, that idea seems preposterous. How could it possibly be true? Three kinds of problems intervene against the audacious claim that a church is a Christian's first and last 'school' for properly understanding social order.

First, people learn so much about society and about personal relationships from family, school and media, whereas churches often seem only to be small marginalized groupings in a wider complex society. Principles of orderly social life seem to be available to all people, and our introduction to them occurs through our upbringing in a family and a society. Christian churches don't seem very radically opposed to all this. Indeed, they often only seem to function because of the social norms everyone brings to church, not instead of those norms.

Secondly, churches differ so much in how they're ordered and governed that they don't seem to offer any general pattern for social structure. Indeed,

---

1. I've borrowed this insight from the famous declaration by US Christian theological ethicist Stanley Hauerwas: 'Put starkly, the first social ethical task of the church is to be the church . . . the church doesn't have a social ethic; the church is a social ethic' (Stanley Hauerwas, *The Peaceable Kingdom* [Notre Dame: University of Notre Dame Press, 1983], p. 99).

they often borrow various governance structures and cultural practices from the surrounding society, so they don't seem to bring any innovative patterns for social structure.

Finally, churches are often so far from social excellence. Even at their best, these hospitals for sick sinners are regularly quite poor in some aspect of their social functioning. At their worst, they become toxic. The recent all-time nadir has been when completely underspecified notions of 'forgiveness', 'compassion' or 'fellowship' perverted various churches to become havens for sexual predators and abusers, particularly of children. With tears, we recognize the validity of Peter's ancient polemic: 'They are blots and blemishes, delighting in their deceptions as they feast with you, having eyes full of adultery and always looking for sin, seducing unstable people, and with hearts trained in greed' (2 Pet. 2:13–14). With anger, we remember Jesus' chilling words that 'whoever causes the downfall of one of these little ones who believe in Me – it would be better for him if a heavy millstone were hung around his neck and he were drowned in the depths of the sea!' (Matt. 18:6).

We should not forget that these offenders exist on the same continuum of human failure as ourselves. Nonetheless, in responding to them, generations of church members and leaders took their cue from false and distorted notions of church group identity. They acted to cover up, save face and protect the image of the group, in a false system of inclusion (ch. 8) no different from any other. Their identity had not 'caught up' (p. 98) with the One who loved the vulnerable with total sexual self-discipline. Those who have suffered under the depredations of these habitual users of others have the hardest task of all in believing a church could ever be good.

In the face of these grinding human failures, there's only one possible defence of church: that in making their claims about churches, the New Testament authors are actually talking about Jesus Christ. They don't deny that people bring a variety of other influences to church. Nor do they think a church ever arrives at simple excellence. Friendliness, generosity, care and holiness never quite become natural properties of churches. They knew and wrestled with how sordid churches can be. But they point to what theologian P. T. Forsyth described as the gospel's 'creative, self-organizing, and self-recuperative power'.[2] Jesus Christ regularly intervenes through his Spirit, generating new forms of life, unmaking and remaking churches, creating social structures fit for his 'body'.

---

2. P. T. Forsyth, *Lectures on the Church and the Sacraments* (London: Longmans Green, 1917), p. 42.

Hence these authors want us to see how each church is intended to become Christ's venue for gathering and healing people. I may find churches maddening, but by hanging around them long enough, I find unassuming giants of people – *knights of faith* (p. 208) who mediate to me the Spirit's fruit of 'love, joy, peace, patience, kindness, goodness, faithfulness, gentleness and self-control' (Gal. 5:22–23, NIV).

The sociology of the modern West is very complex, since the stories of wider Western society and Christian churches have been intertwined for so long. People argue about how much one has affected the other, and about whether the best in our society comes from Greek, Enlightenment or Christian ideas. I don't believe we'll ever settle these arguments, because we all interpret historical data from within the gestalt awareness (p. 72) we bring to them.

As churches regularly go toxic and revert to regular ways of being human, it does sometimes take other people's rules, rights, values and results to snap us out. Secular others remind us, paradoxically, of our heritage (ch. 27). What, for example, were nineteenth- and twentieth-century Australian churches thinking, when they complied with various state agencies to remove indigenous children from their families for placement in other settings?[3] It took the rights-based indignation of a wider society to remind churches that they had forgotten to defend and protect the orderly created structure of the indigenous family. These practices of removal were typically justified by appeal to cases where families were unable to offer proper care, although these appeals evidence a failure of moral imagination to change the conditions under which such families were forced to operate. In reality, the practice was sustained by rigid patterns of white-group belonging that were unrelated to identity in Christ.

Conversely, the Christian concept of community has deeply affected Western thought about the best way to be human, as embedded in many of the rules, rights, values and desired results that surround us (ch. 27). Every other group is a school of moral formation, but Christians test the goods and evils of each against their school of moral formation in Christ (ch. 14). Even the humblest Jesus-shaped community can become an engine room for learning how to approach communities and groups in general. Several strategies then spring up for engaging with others who don't identify with Christ (ch. 35).

---

3. For a longer discussion of Australia's national apology to these people, follow the link to 'The Hearing of Sorry' (on <http://www.sie.org.au>) under 'Further reading' in ch. 29.

Further reading

** Peterson, Eugene H., *Practice Resurrection: A Conversation on Growing up in Christ* (Grand Rapids: Eerdmans, 2010).

35. LIFE OUTSIDE CHURCHES

Having discovered a 'unified field' by which to discern moral reality in Parts 3–4, Part 5 considers some approaches to the details of our lives. This chapter considers our relationships to others who don't identify with Christ. We consider four strategies for relating to them.

Augustine's favourite way of describing human society was that despite all our diversity, there are 'only two orders, as we may call them, of human society: and, following our Scriptures, we may rightly speak of these two as cities'. That is, it's as if two groups are tangled together. There are those with an eye on the new future (ch. 24), the members of 'the heavenly city'. There are those with an eye on their 'flesh' (ch. 9), the members of 'the earthly city'. 'Each desires its own kind of peace, and, when they have found what they sought, each lives its own kind of peace.'[1]

---

1. Augustine, *The City of God against the Pagans*, tr. R. W. Dyson (Cambridge: University Press, 1998), p. 581. Augustine has a number of Scriptures in mind, many of which picture the citizens of these two 'cities' living alongside each other in a sort of a tangle: Ps. 119:19–20, 54; Matt. 5:13–16 (perhaps); Rom. 12:2; 2 Cor. 6:14–18 (but noting the 'entanglement' seen in 1 Cor. 5:10); 2 Cor. 10:2–3; Eph. 2:19; Phil. 3:20; 1 Pet. 1:1, 17; 2:9–11; and Heb. 11:13.

Citizens of the heavenly city traverse among those of the earthly city who don't identify with Christ. But how? Various groups become schools of moral formation that imperceptibly alter what we and others think and do (ch. 8). We cannot antisocially deny our sociality; we have to move in these groups, and they do affect us.

But we find our truest inclusion 'in' Jesus Christ (ch. 14), and we learn new patterns of relationship in his school of moral formation (ch. 34). Once this process has begun, the Christian community – the 'heavenly city' – 'live[s] an alternative way of life in the present social setting, transforming it, as it [can], from within'.[2] These words are a neat summary of what happens as people gradually find their true human identity in Christ, and live a truth not yet known by the people around us.

The biblical authors present a spectrum of responses to the wider social environment. This set can act as a useful toolkit for imagining and discerning what might be the best and most useful response to various neighbours in various situations. We'll each tend to have a favourite on this spectrum, but the expansion of our moral imaginations will consist in becoming more skilled at the other responses.

Cooperation is the default posture. 'If it is possible, as far as it depends on you, live at peace with everyone' (Rom. 12:18, NIV). Christians are uncontroversially able to cooperate with many people and their various plans and purposes. The prophet Jeremiah's exhortation to Jewish exiles to seek Babylon's welfare (Jer. 29:7) is an Old Testament analogue.

We see this cooperation when slaves wholeheartedly assist masters, knowing Christ as their new, true Master (Eph. 6:5–9; Col. 3:22–23; 1 Tim. 6:1–2). In this new knowledge, the master is actually an equal of sorts (ch. 31). Similarly, Peter exhorts cooperation with various humanly constituted expressions of authority (literally, 'every human creation', 1 Pet. 2:13).

This relaxation about cooperation relies, it seems, on humanity's participation together in a created order (ch. 22). We often agree to cooperate with another's sharing of created goods, or with their view of proper sociality, or with the conditions they set for it. This posture also frees Christians from expectations to overturn systems, as in the case of the socially powerless first-century slave (ch. 31). The effect upon social settings of these apparently powerless people will be intangible and long term – an unpredictable 'ripple effect' (p. 124).

---

2. Miroslav Volf, 'Soft Difference: Theological Reflections on the Relation Between Church and Culture in 1 Peter', *Ex Auditu* 10 (1994), p. 20.

However, this default response easily becomes the only response conservative Christians practise. Well-resourced modern Christians do need to experiment more with the other responses I'll outline.

Subversion isn't always a negative social force. The classic Old Testament subversive is Daniel, who willingly cooperates with the Babylonian regime, yet conducts his practices of diet, prayer and integrity so cleverly as to shock the despot Nebuchadnezzar to his core.

Jesus' metaphor of light shining in darkness (Matt. 5:14–16) describes lives so attractive that others cannot help themselves: 'they may see your good works and give glory to your Father in heaven' (v. 16). As an example, he promotes and attends lavish dinner parties for outcasts rather than merely for friends, family and rich contacts (Luke 14:12–14; cf. 5:29–32; 7:34).

Jesus spoke in a context where the Father to be praised was generally known. The apostles Peter and Paul extend his concept to settings where God was unknown. Peter pictures Christians responding to contempt with hopeful gentleness (1 Pet. 3:14–16), and Paul pictures Christians responding to wariness in others with the salty speech of grace (Col. 4:5–6). Speech that's 'always full of grace' (Col. 4:6, NIV) reminds us of the allied practice of forgiveness and reconciliation (ch. 29). Christians gracefully subvert vengeful and meritorious cultures through practices of forgiveness, and by their thirst for reconciliation.

The philosopher Wittgenstein, known for his quirky insights, makes a comment that helps me visualize what's going on in these practices:

> We must begin with the mistake and transform it into what is true. That is, we must uncover the source of the error; otherwise hearing what is true won't help us. It cannot penetrate . . . To convince someone of what is true, it is not enough to state it; we must find the *road* from error to truth. I must plunge again and again in the water of doubt.[3]

So neighbour A listens to talkback radio's narratives of strength, and promotes an ideology of vengefulness. Neighbour B listens to narratives of random human origins, and has an ideology of futility and despair. Neighbour C listens to economic narratives of growth amid scarcity, and lives out an ideology of endless acquisition. Neighbour D feeds on magazine narratives of individual beauty and merit, and arduously pursues an ideology of self-improvement.

---

3. Ludwig Wittgenstein, *Remarks on Frazer's Golden Bough*, tr. A. C. Miles, ed. Rush Rhees (Retford: Brynmill, 1979), p. 11e.

But gentleness, hope, generosity and grace uncover an error at the root of his and her conception of true humanity, plunging each neighbour into doubt about his and her ideology. We may also *speak* this gentleness, hope, generosity and grace into situations at work, in schools, hospitals, political parties and businesses. Christians are joyfully subversive in these off-balancing, atypical responses. Neighbours will probably censor us in these moments, since we *will* be undermining some dominant school of moral formation. But someone will quietly listen and may, like Nicodemus, creep up at night to find out more (John 3:1–2).

There's no guarantee that these neighbours will always respond with interest or praise to God, and we don't subvert only to achieve that result. Others may just as likely respond in sharp defence of their ideology, as when my friend proposed 'grace' and 'forgiveness' as candidates for his children's school's list of values. 'They fell on me like wolves,' he recounted. But even so, when Christians are gentle, others can start to doubt their muscular systems of vengeance. When Christians are joyfully hopeful, others may doubt their despair. When Christians are lavishly generous, endless practices of acquisition are destabilized. When Christians are graceful, it becomes possible to loosen the bonds of self-improvement.

Exposure is the 'whistle-blowing' posture of open challenge and rebuke to others. Although some modern Christians specialize in it, this posture appears infrequently in the New Testament letters. Its deeper roots are in the prophetic literature of the Old Testament (such as the 'watchman' metaphor of Ezek. 3:16–19 and 33:1–9), and in the polemical aspects of Jesus' own ministry (e.g. Matt. 23:12–35; Luke 6:42–52).

But those attacks have a particular place in the Bible's story arc (ch. 19), so exposure was not Paul's primary posture for relating to others (1 Cor. 5:9–10, 12). Even so, Jesus' light metaphor is extended in the exposure of 'fruitless works of darkness' (Eph. 5:11), and such moments of exposure seem to have been the flashpoint for the outright disagreements and return expressions of contempt seen in the starkly polarized communities of 1 Peter 4:3–4 (a text that also hints at the next posture, separation).

But what would trigger such exposure of others? It relies upon a capacity to discern (p. 312) a practice as 'fruitless' and 'dark'. The moral meaning of the metaphor 'fruitless' is technically hard to pin down. What distinguishes a 'fruitless' from a 'fruitful' practice, and what makes a practice 'dark'? In Titus 3:14, continued involvement with those who have serious needs is not 'unfruitful'; and 'dark' practices seem, roughly, to be those that no one wants seen. However, we need more than a semantic analysis to find the substantive moral content of these metaphors. We need a 'unifying field' (ch. 26) in order to gauge what constitutes the kinds of evil that deserve exposure, and to focus our mind on evaluating the actions, culture or policy of some group in which we're situated:

- We might confront refusals to acknowledge the good *order of creation*, whether in practices of (e.g.) rapacious strip mining, unsustainable logging, excessive biomedicine, or the complete refusal of sexual propriety. (In Australia, Melinda Tankard Reist has launched a sustained assault on bizarre social trends to 'pornify' women and young girls.[4])
- We might confront narratives of society that don't understand how people are to be with and for each other, as learnt in *Christian community* and by attention to the *new future*. We might oppose practices of deliberate exclusion, or contrived competition, or the glorifications of isolation or tribalism or xenophobia. (At every federal election in Australia it becomes necessary to oppose the political exploitation of latent racism against asylum seekers.)
- We might confront refusals of the just and merciful *character of God*, whether in practices of extremely vengeful justice, or in practices of lax injustice. (In my home state of New South Wales, prisons have become holding pens for difficult people who struggle with mild intellectual disability and multiple substance abuses. Many within the system do their best to help these people. But the people of my state prefer simplistic 'law and order' policies to properly devised care for these difficult and troubled people.)

Of course, the Christian logic of exposure will always prompt the mantra that 'we have no right to impose our values on others'. I'll return to this objection later (ch. 47).

Separation appears as almost a 'monastic' option in 2 Corinthians 6:17 – 7:1. It alludes to Old Testament covenant-restoration after idolatry, but Paul doesn't specify what moral referent is analogous to fleeing idolatry. He does warn against too-close associations with those of an opposing world view (vv. 14–16), and then refers more generally to 'washing ourselves clean from every impurity of the flesh and spirit' (7:1). The Corinthians' temptation to follow teachers that were more glamorous may also lie in the background.

Therefore, we cannot encode the moral referent in this section into a set

---

4. Melinda Tankard Reist (ed.), *Getting Real: Challenging the Sexualisation of Girls* (North Melbourne, Vic: Spinifex, 2009). Online: <http://www.melindatankardreist.com>.

of rules. That is, we cannot simply dream up some list of bogeys from which to separate (e.g. dancing, smoking or drinking). Rather, the possibility of separation helps us to avoid passively endorsing or participating in social evil solely because our moral imagination has not extended to *exiting* the group that sponsors it. The time comes simply to refuse playing by the rules of some other group's school of moral formation. When the apostles declare 'we must obey God rather than any human authority' (Acts 5:29, NRSV; cf. 4:19–20), they serve notice that they're taking a different path. Others must then determine whether to oppose them, join them or leave them alone.

Sometimes, a literal geographical separation may be the best response. A Dark Ages monastery, a modern Christian school, a hospice or a home for pregnant women who wish to keep their children may become the best expression of Christian polity. Such communities can operate as islands of life shaped by the gospel. (However, we must note the danger of idiosyncrasy and abuse when separation cuts others *and their leaders* off from accountability to a wider church, so that these communities degenerate into mere sects: terrible prisons of body and spirit.)

Less dramatically, separation may take the form of leaving a job, moving house or refusing further contact with some acquaintance. But in the light of Paul's passing remark that Christians don't voluntarily 'leave the world' (1 Cor. 5:10b), this posture cannot possibly be the default. At most, separation is an emergency condition.

In summary, then, New Testament authors can imagine a variety of postures towards others. Settling on which posture to deploy is a context-dependent act of discernment (p. 312). We each tend to have a favourite, with various edifices of justification based on this favourite. Therefore, we may each need to experiment with our less-favoured options, in order to have a better 'tool set' for use when the time requires it.

PART 6 LIFE-PACKAGES

So far, this book has spoken only in general terms about ethics. That can be frustrating if you're looking for specific guidance in some area of your own life. Life comes in different packages for different people, and those differences seem to require something less general.

So we arrive at a more practical part of the book. Actually, I reckon it's all been practical, but that's just my view. I know you'll want to picture living it out in your particular package of life. There are more practical matters in the later 'hot spots' sections, but, for all their drama, I don't think focusing on hot spots is a particularly useful way to join up your life. You'll spend much of your life among aspects of your life-package we'll now consider.

Until recently, Christians have used the language of *vocation* to describe your life-package. The word has now degenerated to refer to people's job in a high-sounding kind of way, particularly if that job is religious, well paid or obviously helpful. (A low-paid cleaner, who's extremely helpful, doesn't get to refer to her 'vocation'. But she should!)

This term arose from a part of the Bible. When people are 'called' to identify with Christ (1 Cor. 7:20), they're advised not to change their life situation suddenly. The intention is not to lock people into their situation forever, but to free them from the worry that finding a new identity in Christ (ch. 14) means leaving a spouse, or finding one, or changing jobs or whatever. The journey to that new identity can continue in the same life-package as where it began. (So Christianity is delightfully free from the kind of control and manipulation that occurs when people join sects.)

These life situations have aspects we can discuss in general terms. We can 'compare notes' on how to be single or married; how to care for children, friends or the creation; and how to go to work each day. Of course, differences remain between us, but we can travel together anyway, even across our differences. (Christians use the almost worn-out word 'fellowship' for this kind of sharing across difference.)

We do long for someone to know and decode *our particular* life-package. We'll consider singleness; but what about the unique contours of *my* singleness? We'll consider marriage; but what about the intricacies of *my* marriage, *my* children, friends, work, and so on? I'm sorry I can't help more – but someone *does* know every tiny aspect of your world (Luke 12:6–7; John 10:14, 27; 1 Cor. 8:3; 13:12; Gal. 4:9; 2 Tim. 2:19). So whatever we don't get to, remember Peter's kind suggestion to 'cast all your anxiety on him, because he cares for you' (1 Pet. 5:7, NRSV).

36. SINGLENESS

In Part 6 we're applying the account of how ethics works in Parts 1–5 to aspects of our 'vocation', or life-package. There are stretches of our lives where we may have many good relationships, but not a sexual relationship, and are 'single'. But society holds singleness in contempt.

The two creation accounts present the invention of marriage as God's pinnacle creative act. He makes humanity in his 'image' (Gen. 1:26), and then makes a procreating pair. Likewise, a man *alone* introduces the first note of imperfection (Gen. 2:18–25). He meets the appearance of a woman with exultation. After those creation accounts, the Old Testament doesn't commend singleness. Widows are honourable yet tragic figures, and the Old Testament doesn't otherwise refer to a single adult. We could easily conclude that to be a complete adult human, we need to be married.

Many single people will be seriously annoyed to have read that paragraph. They have had a gutful of the Christian praise of marriage. Many of them want in, but have found no way in. They're sick of us telling them it's the best place to be.

But there's good news for them. The overall story arc of the Bible (ch. 19) contains a twist. It doesn't conclude that we need to marry to become a complete adult human. Neither marriage nor singleness will give us our true selves. We can do singleness or marriage well or badly, but we find our true humanity as we identify with Jesus Christ (ch. 14). It turns out that *both* marriage and singleness are good, although in different respects.

Western societies praise sexualized coupledom so much that celibate singleness has become weirdly suspect in some quarters. In this school of moral formation (ch. 8), it seems impossible to believe that singleness could ever be good. Jesus opens up new terrain. He certainly affirms marriage as an element of creation (Matt. 19:4–6; Mark 10:5–9) by his presence at the wedding in Cana (John 2:1–11); in his use of bridegroom imagery (Matt. 9:15; 25:1–10; Mark 2:19–20; Luke 5:34–35); and in his promotion of deep marital faithfulness (Matt. 5:27–32; 19:8–9). But his new initiative is also to commend chaste singleness. (I could also say *celibate* singleness here, but 'celibate' sometimes implies a lifelong vow against marriage. No one in the New Testament advocates such a vow, so *chaste* singleness describes a life without sexual relationships for people who are always free to marry.)

Jesus surprises everyone by describing heaven as a place where 'they neither marry nor are given in marriage, but are like angels' (Matt. 22:30; cf. Mark 12:25; Luke 20:34–36). Is he simply saying that new *weddings* cease, but *marriages* perhaps remain? That reading would make less sense of 'like the angels'. More importantly, it would rob his response to the previous riddle of any force. (Jesus' riddlers sought to disprove that God raises the dead. God's so doing, they claimed, would create an abominable situation where remarried people had many partners. Jesus simply reverses their presumption: there *will* be a resurrection, but surprisingly, human marriages won't be reinstated.)

His other references to singleness are more oblique. His return will interrupt regular activities, such as weddings (Matt. 24:36–44). In an odd metaphor, some have 'made themselves eunuchs' (Matt 19:12, ESV). It must describe chaste singleness because the topic has already already come up (v. 10), and Jesus may be including himself in this class of people. (We never see evidence of a wife in his life. Theories that Jesus married Mary Magdalene have no basis in history. They reflect our society's praise of sexualized coupledom and contempt for chaste singleness. Many want a romantic Jesus.)

Jesus' new teaching arises from the new future (ch. 24). It turns out that human marriages are not reinstated in the new future, because they point to the ultimate 'marriage' – a final union between Christ and his people (Eph. 5:29–32; Rev. 19:6–8; 21:2, 9–11; cf. 22:17). But we need a little more theological detective work to determine how chaste *singleness* points to the new future. Here's my best guess.

In the new future, John looks and sees 'a vast multitude from every nation, tribe, people, and language, which no one could number, standing before the throne and before the Lamb' (Rev. 7:9). The significance of normal social identity markers (nation, tribe, people and language) has melted away. The markers remain visible – but people now gather on a *new* basis *other* than ties of culture, genes or kinship. These structure social life now, but not then. As theologian Oliver O'Donovan puts it, 'Humanity in the presence of God will know a community in which the fidelity of love which marriage makes possible will be extended beyond the limits of marriage.'[1]

Single people offer a glimpse of this kind of society. They're harbingers of an aspect of heavenly community, because they're not constrained by family boundaries of genetics and kinship. They show how care and intimacy can go beyond family boundaries. They nudge members of families out of the introverted obsession with family life that becomes its dark side. They remind families that God calls everyone into the 'great multitude', and they call couples and families to attend to the wider community, and to point to heaven. The single person's focus upon 'the affairs of the Lord' (1 Cor. 7:32, 34a) reminds married people of what's cosmically at stake. Jesus Christ saves and serves a world; the single person mirrors his concern, and leads the married person to do the same (within the proper limitations and responsibilities that come with marriage, 1 Cor. 7:33–34).

'Hang about,' someone will object, 'that justification for chaste singleness is a bit fanciful. Those ancient texts just came from people who hated their bodies, disliked sex and were suspicious about marriage.' This is exactly the kind of slur you would expect from a society that only praises sexualized coupledom. But we find that the Hellenistic world was as interested in sex as are we, and was not a uniformly body-hating or sex-hating society.[2] In fact, onlookers were suspicious of single Christians, because the Christian's new future meant there was less interest in continuing his or her family line. Christians also had no interest in helping to populate the empire, and that seemed weird. (You can almost hear their talkback radio jocks griping in Latin over how 'un-British' or 'un-Australian' were these Christians.)

The pinnacle achievements of Jesus' life unveiled a new way to be human (Part 3). It's strikingly different to its competitors. It includes the honour of chaste singleness. Therefore, single people should expect and even plan for the obsession with couples and families that surrounds them. Rather than sinking into anger or despondency at these obsessions, single people can work to subvert these obsessions joyfully (ch. 35), since they know the new future.

---

1. Oliver M. T. O'Donovan, *Resurrection and Moral Order: An Outline for Evangelical Ethics*, 2nd ed. (Leicester: Apollos, 1994), p. 70.
2. Cf. Peter Brown, *The Body and Society* (New York: Columbia University Press, 1988).

But Jesus' way doesn't include any notion that singles should be *lonely*. We're all social beings (ch. 8), and it isn't good for a single person to be alone (Gen. 2:18). In Christian thought, our loneliness isn't finally met in marriage, but in our enjoyment of Christ the 'groom' and through his community (chs. 18, 25, 34). When single people believe this community can meet loneliness, they begin to conduct a symphony of satisfying friendships. Marriage is no longer their sole solution.

Of course, the single person may marry, though! In one well-known treatise (1 Cor. 7:8–40), Paul practically does somersaults to convince his readers that *there's such a thing as two right answers.* No vow should ever prevent marriage, nor should any compulsion force someone to it. The single person is free to marry, and free not to marry. (However, as Christopher Ash helpfully notes, marriage isn't a *choice* but a form of *consent.* Two people *graciously offer* to marry the other. No one *chooses* anyone.[3] We control our choices, but we have no control over who offers to marry us, to whom we may then consent, or not. The point is painfully obvious to anyone who wishes someone would make the offer. The language of choice does many single people no favours, for they haven't always chosen their situation.)

These interesting ideas can enable single people to be joyfully, contentedly single. But they face two roadblocks: sex and churches.

Sex is *so* good, yet we're being asked to accept that single life can be good without any sexual activity with others. That sounds ludicrous if I view my sexual thoughts and feelings as 'needs' (ch. 43). Chaste singleness simply seems cruel. But our sexual feelings are not a 'need' for 'fuelling'; they're to help cement a relationship (chs. 37–38). So to have sex bonds the single person to one or a few without the safety of marriage, and distorts their network of relationships.

Single people who have no sexual relations remind everyone that intimate relationships don't have to be sexual to be complete. They confront and subvert the notion that every good has to be possessed (cf. ch. 7) and that everything good has to be sexualized (ch. 43). They also proclaim that sex is *so* good, it deserves a better home than they can provide. In this way, they honour marriage (Heb. 13:4) as that home, and call on married people to make their sexual relationship the best it can be.

If I've described the single person's vocation regarding sex correctly, then what's masturbation? Some argue that masturbation is wrong because it

---

3. Christopher Ash, *Marriage: Sex in the Service of God* (Leicester: IVP, 2003), pp. 215–232.

dissociates sex from procreation. At least this view resists the modern conceit that our sexuality has nothing to do with a created ecology. But throughout the Bible's story arc, nothing of its command structure addresses masturbation. Sexual acts with others always generate the high-stakes discussions. Although arguments from silence are risky, I conclude that the biblical authors did not worry about masturbation assaulting the created order. Indeed, it seems to me that a single person masturbates because sex, and their embodiment of it, is excellent. So, residing in masturbation is both danger and possibility. The danger is the same as we always face when something excellent mesmerizes us (ch. 7). The possibility is that we discover the good purposes of sexuality. Anti-masturbation stances inevitably degenerate into a view that sexuality is bad. The practice straightforwardly expresses sexual thoughts and feelings that were created good.

But to say that something seems straightforward may only regard ourselves according to the 'flesh' (ch. 9), where my imagination shrinks to the immediate recommendations of my body. When my attitudes and relationships are becoming sexualized, masturbation can amplify that view. I then project my sexual longings on anyone I'm sexually attracted to, imagining that the same desire as consumes me also consumes them. I can never then know who they *really* are, and I fail to notice anyone I'm not sexually attracted to. So I forget my true vocation as a single person – to lead symphonies of intimate, caring relationships that model the nature of true community.

At the risk, then, of irritating those looking for a rule on this matter, I won't specify whether and under what conditions someone should or should not masturbate. People are going to masturbate from time to time, since our embodiment includes a sexual aspect; I'd never say never. But how we masturbate, like how we do anything, contributes to settled patterns and habits of action and feeling that eventually describe *who we are*, our character (ch. 30). I've hinted at a kind of character that masturbation can amplify. But equally, the making of rules about when or when not to masturbate may only generate a person whose character is to obsess over when and when not to masturbate. Rather, we simply aim to be those who don't view others primarily as sexual, and who don't continually convert our attractions to others into sexual fantasies. We also aim to become people who live for many other things, so that our sexual thoughts and feelings don't get to dominate our consciousness.

There's a second roadblock faced by singles: churches. I've insisted that churches are Jesus-shaped communities where all of us, single and married alike, learn a new and true sociality (ch. 34). Churches are meant to be the first venue (although not the only venue) where single people model the nature of true community. But I'm painfully aware that many churches exclusively praise marriage, and treat singleness as a problem to be solved. Christians can patronize single people, or declare them inadequate. ('What he/she needs is a nice wife/husband.') They tell single people to be 'less choosy' in their choice of partner. (Some are unrealistic in their expectations, but many simply honour marriage by taking care among limited options. In any case, marriage isn't finally a *choice* but an act of *consent* to someone who offers.) They tell single people that participation in Christian ministries will increase their chances of finding a spouse, as if Christians are to become consequentialists (ch. 6). Single people have to endure 'family' services', 'family picnics', 'family values', marriage guidance, sermons on marriage and sermons on children in an endless rhetoric and practice that pays no attention to their vocation. These are people who often support marriage and family strongly; they may even think of church as their 'family'; but this endless torrent becomes too much.

In my view, church members and leaders need to rediscover all the ways that a single person teaches us that true community is bigger than our families. Churches also need to reframe the problem: the single person's problem isn't *singleness*, but *loneliness* (just as, at its worst, a marriage becomes two people alone). I don't mean that churches should set up clever programmes to 'fix' single people's loneliness – that usually only rubs it in. I do mean that church overseers need to set the conditions under which relationships of service and friendship can form as accessibly for single people as for anyone.

It will take some decades of patient teaching and new practice, though, to change the cultural landscape of our churches. Christian singles need to perceive themselves as happy warriors for such change – not for their own legitimation, but so that the people of God might better reflect God's dream for a community where both singleness and marriage testify to the nature of affectionate community.

There will be a brilliant outcome of such change. Our societies abhor singleness and hate chastity – yet the numbers of very lonely people are rapidly escalating. Our churches can become oases of welcome for them, in a way that will be a wonder to all who look on.

Further reading

* Adeney, Tim, 'Making Singleness Better', *Briefing*, May 2009. Online: <http://matthiasmedia.com.au/briefing/library/5571> (accessed 12 Sept. 2010).
** Colón, Christine A., and B. Field, *Singled Out: Why Celibacy Must Be Reinvented in Today's Church* (Grand Rapids: Brazos, 2009).

** Danylak, Barry, *A Biblical Theology of Singleness* (Cambridge: Grove, 2007). Online: <http://www.grovebooks.co.uk>.

*** Danylak, Barry, *Redeeming Singleness: How the Storyline of Scripture Affirms the Single Life* (Wheaton: Crossway, 2010).

** Hsu, Al Y., *The Single Issue* (Leicester: IVP, 1997).

* Winner, Lauren F., *Real Sex: The Naked Truth about Chastity* (Grand Rapids: Brazos, 2005).

37. MARRIAGE

In Part 6 we're applying the account of how ethics works in Parts 1–5 to aspects of our 'vocation', or life-package. Society upholds and mocks the second of these: the joining of a man and a woman into the lifelong, sexual and procreative form of life we call 'marriage'.

In Christian thought, God steers us toward a new future (ch. 24) that opens the way for chaste singleness and makes it intelligible (ch. 36). But this future never overturns, annihilates or displaces the structures of the present. One of these structures is marriage. The Bible's overall story arc interprets our marriages – what they're for, and why they go sour. Here I'll do an overview of marriage by using the terms of the 'unified field' introduced earlier (ch. 26).

Marriage is presented as stitched into the *order of creation* (ch. 22), and as God's ultimate creative act (Gen. 1:26–28; 2:18–25). These texts carry overtones of a rich and joyful human connection, of erotic fascination and fecund procreativity, of daily labour gladly conducted in close company, and of simple friendship. But marriage also becomes the venue of aimless complicity, alienation and blame (Gen. 3:6–12), and then later of grinding domination (e.g. Gen. 4:23–24).

Here's an extraordinary depiction of marriage at its best and worst. The monogamy of first marriage is also extraordinary. (Polygamy only emerges as human affairs deteriorate.) This text may have been written when polygamy was common and acceptable. Yet it starkly challenges the practice.

Marriage, then, becomes ambiguous, like a cut crystal with light and dark faces. So as the Bible unfolds, the *character of God* (ch. 21) focuses the way toward good marriage. A favoured trope for his steadfast love pictures God as the faithful husband of Israel (e.g. Ezek. 16; Hosea). The structure of redeemed marriage springs from God's capacity for faithful relationship, first seen in covenant with Israel and then through Christ's marriage to the church. Human marriage is a reflection of this character (Eph. 5:32).

The *Jesus-shaped community* (ch. 25) begins to rediscover marriage as it was meant to be. Jesus gives marriage back to humanity in its proper form of faithful monogamy (e.g. Matt. 5:27–32; 19:3–10). The pinnacle achievements of his life pioneer a method for flawed people to continue in good relationships: repentance, forgiveness and reconciliation (ch. 29). Each married couple becomes a micro-community encapsulating the faithfulness of God, enacted over myriad instances of repentance, forgiveness, reconciliation and the other virtues of Christian community (ch. 18). Some think the virtue of *hospitality* is the template by which married people welcome little strangers – children (ch. 38). (The biblical authors don't directly make this connection.)

This community receives and celebrates gender difference in marriage as a great good. A man uses his strength to become a loving, serving 'head'; a woman willingly receives this service in the supportive loyalty of 'submission'. Later I'll touch on these concepts that we find so supremely problematic (ch. 42). But the safeguards of equality also thread the discussions of difference. Both genders are known and called by God without distinction, with men and women needing and serving one another reciprocally (e.g. 1 Cor. 7:3–5; 11:11–12; Eph. 5:33).

But marriages do end. Some Christians think divorce doesn't end marriage, odd though that may sound. This view is based on Jesus' words (Matt. 5:31–32; 19:3–12; Mark 10:2–11; Luke 16:18), and holds that God considers a person to remain married to their first spouse until one or the other dies. On this view divorce or remarriage is a kind of human pretence. Others say that for Jesus, a divorce is real if and only if adultery has entered the fray (with Paul adding desertion). I respect the way the holders of these views are searching for the Jesus-shaped version of marriage. But I suggest they forget to read Jesus' words in the light of the abuses of the men of his time, and in the light of the Gospels' place in the Bible's story arc.

Jesus certainly opposed the use of divorce law (Deut. 24:1–4) as a quick way into a new marriage – a kind of 'legal adultery' game that was practised then as now (cf. Matt. 14:3–4; Mark 6:17–18; Luke 3:19). But divorce is the bitter fruit when 'hearts' (p. 195) have gone wrong, and one or both married people practise no repentance, forgiveness or reconciliation (ch. 29). A marriage

dies without these; divorce certifies the death; and Jesus recognizes as much
(Mark 10:5). Remarriages were accepted in the history of Israel (Deut. 24:2),
possibly by Jesus himself (in John 4:18), and possibly by an apostle. (In 1 Cor.
7, 'unmarried' includes the divorced, v. 11. In v. 11, Christians don't initiate
divorce, and do aim for reconciliation. Yet all 'unmarried' may marry in v. 8;
and to be 'not bound' in v. 15 is to be free to marry.) I think these remarriages
were considered as real as first marriages. However, these comments touch on
several knotty controversies among Christians. Only a more lengthy analysis
can tease them apart (see 'Further reading').

Almost all agree that death ends marriage (cf. Rom. 7:2). But oddly, it turns
out that in the *new future* (ch. 24) human marriages are not reinstated (ch. 36),
for our marriages are primarily an advertisement of the intimacy between
Christ and his people. This intimacy shapes the way human marriages are
conducted (Eph. 5:22–33).

Commands (ch. 23) about marriage across the Bible reinforce and promote
faithfulness, care and affection (e.g. Exod. 20:14, 17; Deut. 24:5; Prov. 5:18–20;
Matt. 19:6; 1 Cor. 7:3–5, 10–11; Eph. 5:22, 25; Col. 3:18–19; 1 Pet. 3:1, 7). The
specifics of each are particular to its place in the story arc. Yet they all educate
us in some way about the nature and practice of marriage.

As Christians integrated this way of seeing marriage, they concluded that
marriage has *three purposes*. The first purpose, *procreation*, is integral to the creation accounts (Gen. 1:28; 2:24). The man leaves mother and father (almost a
kind of 'divorce') to make 'one flesh' with another – a metaphor for founding
a new family, not just for having sex. The arrival of children is celebrated and
honoured (e.g. Deut. 4:9–10; 6:7; Ps. 78:1–8). In this procreative purpose of
marriage, the biblical authors connect our sexuality (ch. 43) with the natural
order we inhabit (ch. 22). (Later I'll return to the pain and grief of those
whose marriage doesn't result in children, ch. 38.)

A second purpose becomes *lifelong faithful companionship*. One exultant statement says it all: 'This one, at last, is bone of my bone, and flesh of my flesh'
(Gen. 2:23). It echoes similar statements (e.g. Gen. 29:14) emphasizing the
way kin help one another, sharing strength ('bone') during the good times, and
faithfully helping during weakness ('flesh').[1] This companionship is observed
and affirmed across the whole Bible: in long honeymoons (Deut. 24:5); in old
people's marriages (Gen. 23:2; 35:7); in young people's sexual passion (Song
of Songs); in simple joys (Prov. 5:18; 12:4; 18:22; 19:14; 31:10–31); as a relief

---

1. Walter Brueggemann, 'Of the Same Flesh and Bone (Gen. 2:23a)', *Catholic Biblical
Quarterly* 32.4 (1970), pp. 532–542.

from emptiness (Eccl. 9:9); and in the assumption that it proceeds until death (Rom. 7:2–3; 1 Cor. 7:39).

Thirdly, marriage is to be the *safe-haven for erotic love* (1 Cor. 7:2, 5, 9). An old Anglican way of putting it goes too far when this safe haven becomes a sexual outlet for 'such persons as have not the gift of continency'. This notion derives from the view that some need sex more than others, and that Paul has them in mind when he writes 'it is better to marry than to burn with desire' (1 Cor. 7:9). In fact, he simply says 'than to burn', a metaphor that could mean a few different things. (Our modern translators add, 'with desire'.) But even if he were referring to powerful sexual longings, he wouldn't mean to negate the expectation for all to avoid sexual voracity (1 Thess. 4:1–7). So men in particular are called to gentleness toward wives (Col. 3:19; Eph. 5:33; 1 Pet. 3:7), even while both are reminded that their marriage needs sex in order to thrive (1 Cor. 7:3–7).

I suspect that marriage becomes a school of moral formation where men especially are trained that they don't have sexual 'needs' that always deserve to be quenched (ch. 43). We men learn that *our sexuality is the servant of a relationship*, and that our sexual thoughts and feelings exist *to create joy in a particular other* – our wife. This revolutionary concept – that a marriage, not an individual, has sexual 'needs' – is what makes the chastity of singles thinkable and liveable (ch. 36). It also creates the realistic expectation that a man will control his sexuality when his wife is absent or unwell, and it helps some women to remember that sex is more important for the emotional togetherness of her marriage than her libido might suggest. (This comment assumes that men generally want sex more than women do. Of course, a man may also have to go beyond his 'needs' for the sake of his wife.) Rather than a *personal* need for sex, there's a *marital* need for sex. A marriage is distinct from other relationships precisely because it's sexual and sexualized. Marriages need sex as a divinely given adhesive to enable lifelong steadfast love.

It follows that we're not free to reinvent our marriages into something sexless. The micro-community called marriage always drives the relationship toward a closer connection, primarily through repentance, forgiveness and reconciliation, and with sex ably assisting. I recognize that this is a hard word for couples who avoid sex. Whatever a marriage in pain needs will vary, and will be an exercise of freedom (ch. 31). Couples may need to experiment with a long holiday, decent childcare, medical help, sexual therapy or counselling. They may invent other ways forward. But Christians hope for married people to rediscover each other emotionally and sexually by the power of the Spirit (ch. 17).

Sex, then, is 'for' marriage, while marriage is 'for' many things. By saying sex is 'for' marriage, I mean much more than that marriage should cage a personal 'need' for sex. (There isn't a lot of moral imagination in that view.) Rather, the claim is about the purpose of sex itself: that it exists in order to assist the entity called 'marriage', and that other uses of sex have failed to notice this purpose. By adding that marriage is 'for' many things, I've importantly avoided the assertion that sex is primarily for procreation, or companionship, or pleasure.

These three purposes are a summary of the biblical story arc of marriage, and there are some good summaries of the summary. According to the Australian theologian Michael Hill, marriage and sex within marriage is an external expression befitting our inner nature as persons created for self-giving steadfast love.[2] Similarly, the British pastor and theologian Christopher Ash notices the way a cluster of factors come together in a complex to create and constitute a marriage:

> Marriage is the voluntary sexual and public social union of one man and one woman from different families. This union is patterned upon the union of God with his people his bride, the Christ with his church. Intrinsic to this union is God's calling to lifelong exclusive sexual faithfulness.[3]

Ash's superlative study reveals that sexual relations alone don't automatically create a marriage; that free consent by each person is essential to marriage; that people don't simply declare they love one another, but that they agree to the purposes of marriage; and that these declarations need to be publicly voiced, preferably with families in support.

Far from being a private contract, marriage is the public expression of a particular 'polity'. It is the living embodiment of human community as ordered by faithfulness, service and steadfast love. Cohabiting couples may experience some benefits of marriage, but may also cheat themselves out of its inner logic of gracious, steadfast love. They also deprive themselves of other advantages conferred by the public nature of marriage.

The public statement of consent to marriage by one to another strengthens it, since we easily deny secret promises. Marriage then protects relationships from the painful ambiguities of casual sexual relationships. It can also protect the weak from some forms of coercion, since a family and a community

---

2. Michael Hill, *The How and Why of Love* (Kingsford, NSW: Matthias Media, 2002), pp. 139–154.

3. Christopher Ash, *Marriage: Sex in the Service of God* (Leicester: IVP, 2003), p. 63.

endorse a marriage in the best interests of each man and woman (one hopes). In the worst case, the weak have some hope of support and protection when a marriage dies, since the breakdown is also public. In the best case, marriage creates families and clans that give rise to genealogies, connectedness and a historical element of personal identity (which is de-emphasized in the new future, ch. 36).

Under the tutelage of Jesus-shaped community, married relationships become a school for the moral formation of loving, loyal relationships. That helps to form wider communities. Hence an older style of social ethical language described marriage as 'the basic unit of society', for, at their best, marriages function as stable mini-communities of care and of love.

Further reading

*** Ash, Christopher, *Marriage: Sex in the Service of God* (Leicester: IVP, 2003).

** Ash, Christopher, *Married for God: Making your Marriage the Best it Can Be* (Nottingham: IVP, 2007).

*** Hauerwas, Stanley, 'Sex in Public: How Adventurous Christians Are Doing It', in J. Berkman and M. Cartwright (eds.), *The Hauerwas Reader* (Durham, N. C.: Duke University Press, 2001), pp. 481–504.

** Hill, Michael, *The How and Why of Love* (Kingsford, NSW: Matthias Media, 2002), pp. 139–175.

** Instone-Brewer, David, *Divorce and Remarriage in the 1st and 21st Century* (Cambridge: Grove, 2001). Online: <http://www.grovebooks.co.uk>.

** Instone-Brewer, David, *Divorce and Remarriage in the Church: Biblical Solutions for Pastoral Realities* (Carlisle: Paternoster, 2003).

** Köstenberger, Andreas J., and David W. Jones, *God, Marriage, and Family: Rebuilding the Biblical Foundation*, 2nd ed. (Wheaton, Ill.: Crossway, 2010).

** Powers, B. Ward, *Marriage and Divorce: The New Testament Teaching* (Concord, NSW: Family Life Movement, 1987).

38. HAVING CHILDREN

In Part 6 we're applying the account of how ethics works in Parts 1–5 to aspects of our 'vocation', or life-package. This chapter considers the bearing of children as part of the married vocation.

I was twenty-nine when we had Amy, our first child. She's now a beautiful young woman. I recently bragged of how impressed she should be that we had her. 'But it was *me*!' she exclaimed. 'How could you have lived without *me*!?' I couldn't have had that thought twenty years ago, because I was acting like a child myself. If I'd thought, 'Let's invite a stranger into our marriage for the next two decades,' we would never have met her. I didn't really want children, but our neighbours' gorgeous baby girl won me over. She seemed to be the best kind of hi-tech pet and, like all good consumers, I wanted one.

There's so much wrong with this story. I'm only glad my wife had better sense. (I also recognize how painfully self-absorbed my story must seem to those who long for children but cannot have them. I'll consider their situation below.) But I typified the way many adults think about children. It's as if children must 'argue' harder to be allowed among us, for we're in the grip of a new kind of 'stranger danger'. 'They say of children', says philosopher Michael Novak, 'that they are piranhas, brats, snots.' Novak pinpoints a school of moral formation (ch. 8) that we find in workplaces, at dinner parties and in magazines. 'Children are not a welcome responsibility, for to have children is, plainly, to cease being a child oneself.' 'One tries instead to live as the angels were once believed to live – soaring, free, unencumbered.'[1]

Just as that other baby girl won me over, the 'cuteness' of children is their best shot at winning us over. It's a great good that should not be underestimated. Writing before contraception, the theologian Augustine tells of sexual relationships like one in which he was involved. It was just 'a bargain struck for lust, in which the birth of children is begrudged' – 'though, if they come,' as a son did in his own case, 'we cannot help but love them'.[2] God has made children to be magnificently subversive: they overwhelm the most elaborate defences of the most selfish adults.

But cuteness only helps us to flip from hostility to desire (ch. 7), and a child is at risk of becoming our personal accessory. The German philosopher Friedrich Nietzsche reckoned that 'involuntarily, parents turn children into something similar to themselves – they call that "education"'. We see in 'every new human being an unproblematic opportunity for another possession'.[3] In my part of the world, we call this project 'über-parenting'. Sadly, though, some children will never be very cute, and some will not come close to their parent's wants.

So we don't want the inconvenience of children, and we want to remain free for other things (including Christian 'ministry'). Then we want their cuteness; we want to make an impression on the world through them; we may even want to express our love. But this cluster of thoughts is far from the exuberant welcome to children seen in the Bible. I'll use the five poles of the 'unified field' (ch. 26) of the Bible's story arc (ch. 19) to find a better way to have children.

The main instruction among the *commands* of the Bible (ch. 23) is very famous: 'Be fruitful and increase in number; fill the earth' (Gen. 1:28). These first words to humanity are an explicit word of blessing. They now trigger our 'stranger danger' of children. We cannot hear them without fearing overpopulation. I concede the need to recognize and address population pressures, but not at the expense of blaming and excluding children. God's instruction reveals children to be a wonderful good of the *created order* (ch. 22).

1. Michael Novak, 'The Family Out of Favor', *Harper's*, April 1976, pp. 42, 39, 40. Online: <http://www.harpers.org/archive/1976/04/0022442> (accessed 15 July 2010).

2. Augustine, *Confessions*, tr. R. S. Pine-Coffin (Harmondsworth: Penguin, 1961), p. 72 (§4.2).

3. Friedrich Nietzsche, *Beyond Good and Evil: Prelude to a Philosophy of the Future*, tr. Walter Kaufmann (New York: Vintage, 1989), pp. 107–108 (§194).

Old Testament authors then showcase children as gifts we desire, love and accept. Pregnancy is uncomplicated by any musings about where life begins.[4] Pregnant women think that they simply carry children (cf. Ps. 139:13–16; Isa. 43:1; Jer. 1:5), and in a beautiful metaphor, children are the 'fruit' of their womb (Ps. 127:3, ESV). An 'unwanted child' is as oxymoronic to them as 'unwanted money' to us. When some midwives prevent infanticide, their fitting reward is to receive children of their own (Exod. 1:21). Infertility is lamented (e.g. Isa. 54:1–5), and childbirth elicits praise (Eve, Gen. 4:1; Sarah, Gen. 21:6–7; Rebekah, Gen. 24:60; Rachel, Gen. 30:23; Hannah, 1 Sam. 2:1–10; Elizabeth, Luke 1:25; Mary, Luke 1:46–55). Jesus later trades on this backdrop of praise to predict a bizarre time, when people say 'blessed are the barren' (Luke 23:29). But the desire for anything precious has a dark side (ch. 7), as here. We see women deeply envying the pregnancy of another (e.g. Gen. 16:4; 30:1). There are those who sacrifice children, presumably as a misguided attempt to give their most precious thing to their gods; the practice is condemned (Lev. 18:21; 20:1–5; 2 Kgs 23:10; Jer. 32:35).

The joyful narratives of Jesus' own birth (Matt. 1 – 2; Luke 1 – 2) are the strongest statement God could have offered for the excellence of children. Jesus' perfect humanity included the vulnerability of a tiny child. He went on to exemplify the *character of God* (ch. 21) in relation to children, welcoming them with love even when others tried to exclude them (Matt. 18:1–5; 19:13–15; Mark 10:13–16). He isn't starry-eyed about children: he knows their perversity (Matt. 11:16–17). But he notices how children saw him properly, and pokes obtuse religious leaders accordingly (Matt. 11:25; 21:16). An ancient glimpse of the *new future* (ch. 24) shows the littlest people enjoying the care of God's king. Creation's 'curse' (p. 264) is gone, and 'a little child' leads wolves, leopards, lions and snakes (Isa. 11:1–9). I find it poignant and evocative to find children presented so centrally in this ancient picture of Christ's ultimate rule.

Jesus laid the groundwork for the *Jesus-shaped community* (ch. 25) to learn hospitality. The biblical authors don't directly make the connection; but this virtue (ch. 30) shapes married people to welcome little strangers. As Rodney Clapp puts it:

---

4. The only possible exception I can think of is Exod. 21:22, which may indicate a fetus as having less moral claim than does a born human. Argument over this text is complicated by some uncertainties over its ancient legal meaning, its textual transmission, and the best way to translate it now. It doesn't dislodge the Old Testament's overall celebration of pregnancy and childbirth.

Welcoming the strangers who are our children, we learn a little about being out of control, about the possibility of surprise (and so of hope), about how strange we ourselves are. Moment by mundane moment – dealing with rebellion, hosting birthday parties, struggling to understand exactly what a toddler has dreamed and been so frightened by in the night – we pick up skills in patience, empathy, generosity, forgiveness. And all these are transferable skills, skills we can and must use to welcome other strangers besides our children. We become better equipped to open ourselves to strangers, especially to those strangers who are not our children but our brothers and sisters in Christ.[5]

In an age of contraception, married people need to rediscover the hospitality of marriage. The promises spouses make to one other form the beginnings of an inclusive, hospitable mini-community – a family. A couple's natural yearning to welcome a little stranger is true to the hospitable and social nature of their marriage. (Adoption is also an expression of this hospitality, but is an emergency measure only.[6] Where possible, we support biological parents to care for their child as much as they can.)

It follows from this high praise of children that a purpose of marriage (ch. 37) is procreation. But there are those who grieve over the absence of children. They endure a yearning so fierce that its voracity is like all-consuming fire, or like the thirst of dry ground (Prov. 30:15–16). Their unmet yearning may be their participation in the sufferings of Christ (p. 105), and we 'weep with those who weep' (Rom. 12:15).

But if a purpose of marriage is procreation, could the absence of children imply that the marriage is somehow defective? Even the question is offensive, but some have to endure it. For Oxford theologian Bernd Wannenwetsch, such a conclusion is 'simply wrong'. He points out that the second biblical creation narrative says much about woman and man, but nothing about children or procreation. Therefore, of marriage 'we could perhaps say that it belongs to its substance to be open to children, while this openness need not and cannot in all cases be realized'.[7]

This couple enjoys the core blessings of marriage and some of the possibilities of singleness (ch. 36). It will always be a melancholy kind of freedom.

---

5. Rodney Clapp, *Families at the Crossroads* (Downers Grove: IVP, 1993), p. 148.

6. Gilbert Meilaender, *Bioethics: A Primer for Christians* (Grand Rapids: Eerdmans, 1996), pp. 18–19.

7. Bernd Wannenwetsch, '"Proles": Children, Family and Living out of Control', unpublished lecture. Used by permission. I also quote this source below.

Their proper yearning remains, yet their situation allows interesting new possibilities for the service of others. They may find ways to love and serve the children of others. They may help families to look beyond their usual fixations. They're freer to concern themselves with more 'affairs of the Lord' (cf. 1 Cor. 7:32–34).We ask them, though, not to lie to us. Bearing a pain so great, some involuntarily childless couples tell people that they've chosen not to have children. This lie is understandable as a strategy to avoid pain. But it subverts the practice of Jesus-shaped community (ch. 25), so that those around them cannot 'weep with those who weep' (Rom. 12:15). Their lie of feigned choice worsens the chasm of their isolation.

In the meantime, *artificial reproductive technology* is all our society now offers to meet this longing. I distinguish between the couples accessing this industry and its architects, who avoid some morally troubling aspects of it. There are pornographic triggers for sperm collection, multiple expendable embryos, the selection of 'best' embryos on any number of shifting canons of perfection, the destruction of leftover embryos, and the introduction to a marriage of as many other 'parents' (surrogates or gamete donors) as are technologically expedient. To sustain these practices, clinics treat sexuality and procreation as unrelated to marriage, and pretend no people are involved other than the adults who are paying or being paid. Powerful schools of moral formation (ch. 8) are at work in this industry.

But it doesn't follow that couples should avoid it. There are clinics that listen to couples and respond with moral care, and couples can discern their path through this jungle. Sadly, though, the industry can also blind couples to the most salient point of discernment: *when to stop* accessing artificial reproductive technology. A modern woman often postpones her journey through grief far longer than do the Bible's 'barren' women. In the worst case, a couple becomes fixated on endless cycles of treatment. The sexuality of their marriage becomes mechanized and their hopes dashed for decades.

Just because some married couples have single-like possibilities in their life, it doesn't follow that we may invent childless marriages. Wannenwetsch acknowledges the intrinsic value of the married relationship, but doesn't think of procreation as an afterthought to marriage. He pictures 'an organic connection such as the fruit has to a tree. While one cannot hold that a tree must have fruit in order to be a tree, it would be odd to deny its natural destiny to bear fruit.' I suggest that if procreation is a purpose of marriage, then *God calls married couples to become open to welcoming children.* The statement envisages the possibility of adoption, or of informal care of other families' children. But it also asks married couples to consider ceasing contraception at some point or points in their marriage. Apart from a basic hostility to children, I hear two main arguments against having them.

In the 'argument from disability', a couple feels unqualified to be parents due to age, health or past experiences of abuse. I don't mean to belittle these concerns. Specific weaknesses may need special consideration. Even then, biblical optimism about good generations arising from defective ones (cf. Ps. 78:1–8) may expand our imagination of what's possible.[8]

The second argument is consequentialist (ch. 6): 'We choose not to have children so that we can do more Christian ministry.' The New Testament authors never canvassed this false application of the new future (ch. 24). The apostles could easily have reasoned that the new future displaces the structures of creation, and that celibate marriage would be a neat way to free people for evangelism and ministry. But they made no such moves. If the new future in Christ doesn't overturn the fecundity of marriage, no one should now propose that the invention of contraception overturns it.

This novel argument reverses a couple's public agreement to the purposes of marriage. It ignores generations of welcoming nurture of children as a particular form of service to God (Deut. 6:7; Ps. 78:1–8). It implies other ministries are much more important and noble. It creates the intolerable suggestion that the yearnings of the involuntarily childless are defective or trivial, as if they too should want to 'do ministry' instead. In the end, couples who make this choice probably succeed only in making for themselves a ball and chain of endless productivity, to justify their decision. At its core, this argument really only reproduces the 'pattern' of our world (Rom. 12:2, NIV): contempt for children.

Forgiveness is always on offer for our follies, but I'd plead with a married couple to avoid this one. Of course, I'd never publically hound a couple who made this decision. Paul may say of it, 'who are you to judge someone else's servant?' (Rom. 14:4). However, if a couple publically promoted this reason for choosing childlessness, I'd publically disagree.

Finally, a few words on parenting. The 'über-parent' can never succeed. Parents give to their children from the best they have (Matt. 7:9–11), but the best parents can never erase the imprint of their 'flesh' (ch. 9). Their child will also need to find the Jesus-shaped version of themselves by the power of the Spirit (chs. 14, 17).

Good parenting is a microcosm of the complexity of life (ch. 10), requiring

---

8. For this and the following paragraph, cf. Christopher Ash, *Marriage: Sex in the Service of God* (Leicester: IVP, 2003), pp. 178–179.

the same discernment (p. 312) we bring to life in general. Mary-Anne and I have tried to introduce our children to the created order, to the Jesus-shaped community, to humanity's new future, to God's character and to the way various commands highlight these (Part 4). We discuss the rules, rights, values and results around them (chs. 3–6). In our frailty, we've given our best take on how the world works. What happens next is between them and God.

There are many disputes over raising children, but the practice of parenting is as an arena of freedom (ch. 31). Even so, the friendly sharing of wisdom in a community (chs. 18, 25, 34) would nicely offset the highly strung and brittle defensiveness Western parents bring to the task. Parents can admit their creaturely limitations, and discuss different ways of doing things. For a child's *moral imagination* is at stake. We can help each other to enable our children to expand it.

Further reading

** Cameron, Andrew J. B., and Megan Best, 'Freedom for Gifts of Hope: Revisiting the Ethics of Contraception', *Briefing* 385 (2010), pp. 22–25. Online: <http://www.mathiasmedia.com>, <http://www.thegoodbook.co.uk>.

*** Deddo, Gary W., *Karl Barth's Theology of Relations: Trinitarian, Christological, and Human: Towards an Ethic of the Family* (New York: P. Lang, 1999).

*** Hauerwas, Stanley, 'The Radical Hope in the Annunciation: Why Both Single and Married Christians Welcome Children', in J. Berkman and M. Cartwright (eds.), *The Hauerwas Reader* (Durham, N. C.: Duke University Press, 2001), pp. 505–518.

** Köstenberger, Andreas J., and David W. Jones, *God, Marriage, and Family: Rebuilding the Biblical Foundation*, 2nd ed. (Wheaton, Ill.: Crossway, 2010).

** Novak, Michael, 'The Family Out of Favor', *Harper's*, Apr. 1976, pp. 37–46. Online: <http://harpers.org/archive/1976/04/0022442> (as at July 2010).

*** Martin E. Marty, *The Mystery of the Child* (Grand Rapids: Eerdmans, 2007).

*** Wall, John, 'Animals and Innocents: Theological Reflections on the Meaning and Purpose of Child-Rearing', *Theology Today* 59.4 (2003), pp. 559–582.

39. FRIENDSHIP

In Part 6 we're applying the account of how ethics works in Parts 1–5 to aspects of our 'vocation', or life-package. This chapter is about navigating our friendships.

We have all sorts of friends, from casual acquaintances to relationships where the stakes are high. There are Facebook friends, work friends, old school friends, family friends, best friends. We think a lot about our friendships, but less about the nature of friendship. Like every other group in which we participate, *every friendship is a school of moral formation* (ch. 8).

The idea that friendship is a school of moral formation will seem strange to us, but it was not always so. Ancient philosophers such as Cicero were less casual about friendship. Their expectations upon friendships were higher. They expected friends to stay loyal, and they chose their friends carefully. They thought about their friends in a 'political' way: that if the friendship was to succeed, both needed to 'play' for the same 'team' when it comes to what matters.[1]

The biblical authors are philosophically naive about friendship, in the sense that they don't give it any extended analysis. The relevant Hebrew and Greek

---

1. The relevant works are Plato, *Lysis* (c. 380 BC); Aristotle, *Nichomachean Ethics* 8–9 (c. 350 BC); and Cicero, *De Amicitia* (c. AD 44).

words span the range from casual to close relationships. Yet if we examine friendship using the terms of the 'unified field' introduced earlier (ch. 26), some interesting patterns emerge.

Friendships are a simple outworking of our sociality, and are part of the *created order* (ch. 22). Jesus casually observes that *exchange and reciprocity* are natural to friendships (Luke 6:32–34). For the pattern-observing proverbist, 'a friend loves at all times' (Prov. 17:17; cf. 18:24), which points to the strong *attraction* that's a natural element of friendship. Such an attraction is seen between David and Jonathan (1 Sam. 18:1–5; 19:1–7; 20), and in the profound sense of loss when a friend is gone (cf. Ps. 35:14). Likewise, there was a particular disciple whom 'Jesus loved' (John 13:23; 19:26; 20:2; 21:7, 20).

Our society sexualizes attraction (ch. 43), and so a favourite modern pastime has been to cleverly read sexual overtones into this biblical material. But actually, it has the opposite effect. It pushes us to experiment with the possibility that powerful attractions are not always sexual, and don't need to be sexualized.

But there's a dark side to natural friendship, and many failures of it. The closest friend will persuade us toward moral heinousness (Deut. 13:6). *Attraction* and *exchange* become muddled: then as now, the rich and powerful have more friends (Prov. 19:4, 6). Friendships collapse during severe social stress (Jer. 9:4–5; Mic. 7:5), when everyone fights over scarcity rather than imagining a community that could share whatever is available. The bitterness of David's or Jesus' betrayal by a friend (Pss 41:9; 55:13–14; Matt. 26:50) is matched only by the bitterness of friendlessness (Ps. 88:18; Eccl. 4:10).

As the old adage goes, we can't live with them and we can't live without them. Friendship is a bittersweet combination of attraction, exchange, disappointment and betrayal. But we also begin to see how friendships can transcend these human failures. The Bible's story arc (ch. 19) shows the natural aspects of friendship restored to become stronger.

Friendships can transcend suspicion (Prov. 22:11), and can bear the weight of dispute and disagreement (Prov. 27:6, 9). A friend can identify selflessly with another (Job 16:20–21). These Old Testament foundations are precursors to the redemption of friendship in the *Jesus-shaped community* (ch. 25). Jesus willingly calls his disciples friends (John 15:11–15); but the natural element of exchange is replaced by *gracious giving*, as Jesus willingly lays down his life for his friends (v. 13). At the same time, Jesus never lauds any sense of their indebtedness over them. He implies these people are somehow *equals* (v. 15).

Yet Jesus also dislodges the cosy elitism of ancient friendship. Cicero chose his own circles of inclusion (ch. 8) by choosing his friends. But we're shocked to discover that, according to Jesus, even an *enemy* is as precious as a friend

(Matt. 5:43–48). Jesus acknowledges natural, neighbourly friendship – and then calls us to a kind of love that goes way beyond it, toward strangers and enemies. We're no longer able to treat non-friends with indifference. This radical revaluation of *all* humanity has permeated Western thought (and remains embedded in our concepts of universal human rights, chs. 4, 27).

As a result, communities in Christ (chs. 18, 25) see each other primarily as 'brother' and 'sister', not as 'friend'. Of course, we do find friends in these communities; but our most basic relationship to one another is as sibling, not as friend. This sibling language brings two major advantages. First, it reminds us that every person is as precious as any other. Secondly, these relationships don't always rely on attraction and reciprocity. I might love people to whom I wouldn't normally be attracted; I might care for a sister without expecting much back; but I'm not called to pretend that all these people are my friends.

Jesus de-emphasizes choosy friendship, and directs our attention to non-friends – particularly the socially excluded (Luke 14:12–14). But this stance confuses Christians, because it seems to prevent us loving particular friends. So Christians can drift into some odd places. Some try to turn all relationships into friendships. Others avoid friendships, as when a Christian leader becomes conflicted about nurturing any friendships (because to do so might look like favouritism). In each case the person is trying to live Jesus' rejection of Cicero's elitism, and to avoid the exclusivity Jesus attacks (e.g. Luke 14:12–14; cf. Jas 4:4).

Yet the fact remains that Jesus isn't embarrassed to have a ring of friends, and to express a particular fondness toward one of them. The natural good of friendship isn't a problem to be avoided, but a good to be received, even while at the same time we avoid elitism and favouritism. The Jesus-shaped community learns how to have friends, and how also to be open to other relationships – and perhaps, then, to the unlikeliest of friendships. Although friendship isn't explicitly mentioned as part of the *new future* (ch. 24), I've argued (ch. 36) that single people in Christian communities model this non-partisan openness across many relationships, from which new friendships may blossom.

When God declares Abraham (2 Chr. 20:7; Isa. 41:8; Jas 2:23) and Moses (Exod. 33:11) to be his 'friend', they participate in *God's character* (ch. 21), for there's no relating to God other than by honouring his character. Hence friendship is also revealed to be a kind of *moral community*. 'I am a friend to all who fear You,' enthuses the psalmist, 'to those who keep Your precepts' (Ps. 119:63).

Here's an aspect of friendship with which we're uncomfortable. We're very comfortable with the natural attractions and exchanges of friendship. We also like the possibility that a friend can transcend suspicion, endure dispute and disagreement, and identify selflessly. But to have all that, a friendship needs shared agreements about right and wrong, and we baulk at that. For us, 'morality' represents a kind of lead weight on the carefree joys of friendship. But *each* group, including our groups of friends, is a school of moral formation. Every friendship is based not only on attraction and exchange, but also on rules, rights, values and goals (chs. 3–6) that are agreed, if often unspoken. Friendships break up when someone changes, or challenges, or ignores something in this moral structure. (I remember 'changing the rules' when I expected a friend to listen more to my concerns. The friendship died within days.)

According to the twelfth-century Christian thinker Aelred of Riveaulx,[2] a friendship based on natural attraction 'has a powerful effect for a while; it draws two people fairly close together, it beckons them flatteringly' (2.57). But in the absence of any thought about what matters (Aelred calls it 'reason'), this kind of attraction 'is given to forming attachments that are in many respects illicit – indeed, it cannot tell the difference between the licit and the illicit' (2.57). Such friendships, he thinks, are 'without weight, without moderation, without consideration of whether the friendship will be spiritually beneficial or not' (2.57). He pictures friends who 'catch fire together as one' and will do anything for each other, without any reference to a wider moral compass. This kind of friendship is 'dissolved with the same flightiness with which it was initiated' (1.40) for 'there is nothing certain, nothing constant, nothing secure' in it (1.42).

Aelred is remembering the friendships of his youth. He probably also alludes to the story, from eight centuries earlier, of Augustine's gang stealing pears to fling at pigs (p. 52). Likewise, today's friendships often arise only from attraction, with no thought about what else they're based on or where they're going.

'Often affection precedes friendship,' Aelred admits; but he suggests provocatively that 'it ought never to be followed unless it is led by reason, moderated by a sense of honour, and ruled by justice' (1.57). He probably has in mind the *command structures* of the Bible (ch. 23) when he describes the 'authority of law' regulating what 'nature begins and custom strengthens' (1.61). He's imagining a friendship beginning naturally enough, but needing a kind of *moral scaffold* if it is to prosper.

So he begins to apply his moral imagination to his friendships. A friendship

---

2. The section numbers in the quotations below are from Aelred, *Spiritual Friendship*, tr. Mark F. Willams (London: Associated University Presses, 1994).

needs, he thinks, 'favour that proceeds from benevolence' (3.51). It needs the graceful kindness that Jesus showed to his friends, which is a step up from exchange. It relies on trust: a freedom to reveal 'all one's secrets and purposes without fear or suspicion' (3.51). It also needs affection, and a meeting of minds 'concerning all matters, whether happy or sad, which have a bearing on the friendship' (3.51). Aelred speaks of a friend who helps him make difficult decisions, and who with a just nod can help Aelred to check his anger or tongue (3.103). Aelred's point is that just as a vine grows well in a trellis, an initial attraction can grow within a shared moral framework to become a profound and satisfying friendship.

We easily sneer at Aelred's moral seriousness, yet our often casual and thoughtless 'friendships' are too fragile to last. Therefore, based on all we've seen, I want to offer some suggestions about how to navigate our friendships.

Signalling. It's important to become aware of the intentions we signal when we first meet someone. To be 'friendly' is to respond with civility laced with interest and affection. In my opinion, Australians like me misuse 'friendliness'. We're not offering friendship, for we never make any time for it. Yet we use 'friendliness' to mask this distance. In Britain, I eventually came to respect what initially seemed a kind of general aloofness. These people were being careful not to imply a false promise of friendship. Later, some became great friends of mine.

Beginning. Friendship isn't entirely up to us. We can make an overture of friendship and be disappointed; there's nothing wrong with that. But to pursue a friendship as if we can *make* it happen is too controlling, and often only results in angry sadness. The other doesn't always feel that mysterious attraction, and we cannot control it. Usually, friendships creep up and tap us on the shoulder when we least expect them. (I observed above that not all attraction is sexual. I should add that not all sexual attraction is the spark of friendship – much as we try to pretend so at the time.)

Nurturing. The ancients were too choosy about their friends – but they were on to something. Our technology and mobility generates high numbers of shallow friends. We've an almost allergic reaction to nurturing a few, preferring the endless fake busy-work of 'catching up' with the many.

In suggesting we might nurture a few friendships, I don't mean to ignore Jesus' call to love widely, which includes openness to unlikely friends. I'm trying to draw attention to the moral scaffold Aelred noticed. A shallow friendship has no real future when you differ over what matters most. So before you entrust yourself to someone, you might wait until you know more about what the friendship will be based on. (The call to *love* others doesn't carry with it the expectation instantly to *trust* everyone; cf. John 2:24.)

For this reason, Christians often gravitate toward Christian friends. We should not be nervous, though, about becoming friends with those who don't (yet) identify with Christ (ch. 14). A lot of moral agreement may be on offer. But we need to be realistic – there's a greater likelihood of severe disagreement about what matters, which might later explode the friendship.

Reciprocating. Friendships naturally involve reciprocity and exchange. Christians learn how to go beyond exchange to expressions of *grace* – the kind of giving that doesn't expect a return. They stop keeping a running tally of whether the exchange has been equal, because Christ didn't. But if the giving is *all* one way, then the relationship isn't a *friendship*. It may still be an expression of love. A teacher's main attention is on a student's needs; a nurse's main attention is on a patient's needs; and we sometimes help people who don't give much back. But we wouldn't call it a friendship. (If you're constantly lonely, you need to ask *what you offer* – or whether you just use people. Those with no friendships are often very poor at reciprocity and grace.)

Friends don't have to give the same thing to one another. We give from the strength of our gifts and skills, as needed by the other. I may listen, while my friend is marvellously hospitable. I may care for their children, while they repair my computer or car. I've missed a key aspect of friendship if I grumpily demand what I gave (listening or childcare) while failing to see what my friend gave (hospitality or repairs).

Morally attending. Friendships grow when we navigate moral disagreements well. In one of my oddest friendships, we differ on politics, the environment, and our uses of money. These are moral disagreements, to be sure. But our many points of agreement include the importance of loyalty, truth-telling, harmonious families, and Jesus. These agreements are not lightweight conversation points. They add to attraction and reciprocity to help knit the friendship together.

Repenting and forgiving. Relationships require repentance and forgiveness to propel them into the future (ch. 29). Friendships are no exception. Good friendships are lost when one (or both) is too proud to admit that he or she has gone against what both know matters. The practices of repentance and forgiveness can reconcile friends, and for frail creatures like us that's the only way toward the kind of trust Aelred built with his friend.

Ending. Friendships end due to simple and deeper causes. Some friendships result only from proximity. We can feel burdened to 'stay in contact' with every friend we've ever lived near or worked with. But when we move on, these temporary relationships are simply over. (Of course, you may need to move less.)

A deeper cause relates to the friendship's spoken or unspoken shared moral agreement. You find yourself saying, 'I don't like her any more,' because *someone has changed* when it comes to *what matters most*, and will not budge. Unless you need to repent, it's good to recognize this change. The end of the friendship is probably inevitable.

Or we may notice that the other person *never* reciprocates. They never give time, energy, listening, help or advice. There's nothing wrong with sadly observing that this is no friendship. You may continue to act kindly to them, but you don't have to pretend you are friends.

In both cases, it would be best to explain what you think has changed. You would need to push yourself to such a conversation; although, sadly, others are adept at avoiding them. So friendships often die unsatisfyingly and without words, and we wonder why. The post-mortem should ask who stopped reciprocating. Did someone fail to repent or forgive? Was there a moral roadblock, a disagreement about what matters that was bigger than both of us? Answering these questions may not ease the pain, but we may grow in discernment (p. 312) about how to make other friendships better.

Further reading

** Black, Hugh, *Friendship*, 3rd ed. (London: Hodder & Stoughton, 1904). Online: <http://www.gutenberg.org/etext/20861> (accessed 12 Sept. 2010). Various reprints are available: e.g. BiblioBazaar, 2007; Joshua, 2008.

40. SUSTAINABLE CARE

In Part 6 we're applying the account of how ethics works in Parts 1–5 to aspects of our 'vocation', or life-package. This chapter is about 'care'. It especially refers to care for the created order, but includes our care for other humans.

We're all called to care. That much becomes clear once we discover that human identity 'in Christ' (ch. 14) entails participation in a community (ch. 25). This new school of moral formation shows us how we enact true humanity through care for others (ch. 34) rather than through competition against them, or in isolation from them.

But someone will observe that this concept (and the book so far) is preoccupied with humans and their social relationships. It's had little to say about the *environmental habitat* in which this care occurs. As the anti-Christian utilitarian ethicist Peter Singer puts it:

> Jesus appears never to have addressed the question of our relations with nonhuman animals. This absence of comment – in marked contrast to, for example, the teachings of Buddha – conveys a clear impression that only humans really count.[1]

---

1. Peter Singer, *Rethinking Life and Death* (Oxford: Oxford University Press, 1995), p. 166.

On a quick reading of the Gospels, Singer has a point. But Singer ignores how Jesus' teaching occurs in an overall story arc (ch. 19). So this chapter uses the five poles of this story (ch. 26) to examine our care for the environment as part of a *spectrum of care* that includes care for each other.

We accept, enjoy and protect a *created moral order* (ch. 22) in which care for humans and care for biodiversity are inseparable. City people like me easily forget our interdependence with the natural environment. Yet we grow plants around buildings, keep pets and install water features. We receive food grown by others and then take steps to control the bacteria in it. We channel water toward us and excess water away from us. When the air quality deteriorates, we debate and pass complicated laws and policies to assist the wind to clean it. We constantly subdue, order and reorder the good structures of creation while remaining completely embedded within them.

The machines we use create the illusion that our lives are vastly different from those who live rurally. Our interests also seem vastly different from those, say, who fight for rainforests or whales. But if I may minimize the obvious differences for a moment, the simple point is that we all engage with the creation all the time. Our acts of care for one another usually involve interactions with the environment. Indeed, our care for one another is, in a sense, also an expression of care for the creation. Both kinds of care are an aspect of everyone's vocation.

But *should* we subdue, order and reorder what surrounds us? And *should* we put care for creation into the same conversation as care for one another? That I've put it so will attract the charge that I'm *anthropocentric* – I've presumed to keep human action and human problems in the centre of the frame. By saying that our care for one another drives many of our engagements with the creation, I seem to have reduced the natural order to become a kind of raw material for the advancement of humanity. In a famous 1967 article, Lynn White argued that this kind of Christian anthropocentrism is to blame for environmental degradation. When the God of medieval Christian theology displaced animal and tree spirits, people could use the natural environment fearlessly. We then saw it only as raw material for our use, rather than in terms of any intrinsic value in itself.[2]

I don't completely deny these charges. It would take a historian to evaluate White's argument; but people do fixate on the recommendations of their

---

2. Lynn White, 'Historical Roots of our Ecological Crisis', *Science* 155 (1967), pp. 1203–1207.

'flesh' (ch. 9). It should be no surprise when people consume with infinite greed. Rapacity can easily use Christian slogans.[3]

Yet I defend a kind of qualified anthropocentrism that also upholds and protects the natural order. For only by misanthropy, a hatred of humans, could we properly oppose anthropocentrism. It isn't hard to find people who do so. They speak of humanity as a kind of plague that they hope a massive population crash will cull. Most of us don't really like thinking of ourselves as a kind of bipedal rat – but of course we wouldn't, would we. According to the misanthropic 'deep green' view, the claim for human dignity is just a disguised evil, a verminous will to survive.

Against misanthropy, how may I be glad to be human? Jesus Christ makes me glad to be human. By inhabiting true humanity, God in Christ reiterates that humanity was a good invention. Of course, my deep green opponent groans at this point and says, 'Well, that's exactly what I'd expect of an anthropocentric *religion*, where even *God* is a human.' But since I've more reason to trust Jesus Christ than this opponent, we part company; and I, released from misanthropy and glad to be human, can get on with reimagining a care for creation that also includes care for humanity.

The Old Testament foundations (ch. 20) in this arena are, in a sense, anthropocentric – but not in the sense that they justify environmental rapacity. Rather, the authors simply observe that we cannot be *other* than human. Two very different but highly complementary accounts show how.

In the first of these accounts, God appoints humanity to 'be fruitful, multiply, fill the earth, and subdue it'. They're to 'rule the fish of the sea, the birds of the sky, and every creature that crawls on the earth' (Gen. 1:28), and people are to use plants and, then later, animals for food (Gen. 1:29; 9:3). This language of 'subduing' and 'ruling' is very strong indeed, and is precisely what

---

3. Christians are now more or less obliged to respond to White's charge. The 'Further readings' listed at the end of this chapter offer several responses. For example, Van Dyke et al., and Spencer and White, show that White's charge is not inherent in the logic of the Bible. Bauckham (in Berry, *Stewardship*) argues that an *amalgamation* of Christian theology *with other philosophies* was to blame. Harrison (in Berry, *Stewardship*) thinks the real damage occurred due to a distorted cluster of seventeenth-century theological ideas. Such critiques are important; but White's charge now operates as a 'genealogical' claim – a 'likely story' that casts suspicion on the entire Christian world view, which no amount of argument can dislodge. The only way out from under such a story is to *live* a better one. Spencer and White present an excellent start to such a life.

draws fire from people who think that Judeo-Christianity legitimizes environmental degradation. But the portrayal is simple honesty. We do have the capacity to seek mastery over what we survey, and there's no use pretending otherwise. As God puts it later, 'the fear and dread of you will fall upon all the beasts of the earth' (Gen. 9:2, NIV). This declaration reaffirms the power of human rule – although with some ambivalence, for at this point in the story arc runaway human desires and false inclusions (chs. 7–8) have distorted everything.

And yet a second account of creation complements the first. Humanity is *drawn from* the earth, and humankind's task is to watch over and work a garden (Gen. 2:15) and to name animals (Gen. 2:19–20). To 'subdue' here is to monitor and gently enhance the coherence of the garden.

The marked contrast between these first two chapters honestly highlights a striking human paradox. On the one hand, we're the most sentient, clever, manipulative and powerful beings on the planet (Gen. 9:2). Yet, on the other hand, we're intimately connected to it, made of its very 'dust' (Gen. 2:7). Our Godlike power derives from the one in whose image we're made (Gen. 1:27); yet we share the same weaknesses and vulnerabilities as the species around us. (Scholar Richard Bauckham therefore prefers to speak 'of human authority in creation rather than over creation, because it is vital . . . to recover a lively sense of human creatureliness'.[4])

This biblical material carries no hint of human reinvention or obliteration of the created order. Humanity is part of the landscape, and has limited capacity to alter it. At its best, humanity's enormous power cares for our world while using it, for use and care don't have to be perpetually antagonistic. Israel's wise persons know their place in God's world. They see how the structures of our lives are created, sustained and nurtured by God's just and kind rule.

This knowledge comes partly by reference to natural rhythms:

> Go to the ant, you slacker!
> Observe its ways and become wise.
> Without leader, administrator, or ruler,
> it prepares its provisions in summer;
> it gathers its food during harvest.
> How long will you stay in bed, you slacker?

---

4. In R. J. Berry (ed.), *Environmental Stewardship: Critical Perspectives, Past and Present* (London: T. & T. Clark, 2006), p. 32.

When will you get up from your sleep?
(Prov. 6:6–9)

Intended as an amusing take on human folly, these words have been used to justify an extreme and unbalanced work ethic. But they exemplify the initial affirmations of humanity: that we participate in creation by watching, learning, ordering and reordering. We rely on creation even while we 'master' and use it.

A darker biblical theme also emerges. A kind of a 'curse' scars our cohabitation with the natural order. It's a provisional impairment of the essential good of creation. Putting it bluntly, God 'subjects' his creation to 'futility' (Rom. 8:20). The human defection to 'flesh' (ch. 9) results in God's sentence of painful toil, disordered and invasive 'thorns and thistles', and death (Gen. 3:17–19). It also results in distortions of desire and power between men and women (Gen. 3:16; cf. ch. 42). The natural order is now like the woman in painful birth (Rom. 8:22): beautiful and life-giving, yet threaded with suffering. But this 'curse' isn't like that of a horror film or a Greek tragedy, bleakly hovering above the action and trumping every bright spot with despair. Paradoxically, creation's *best* hope resides in the God who effected this subjugation. 'He who has subjected the creature is God: and thence emerges hope,' observes the theologian Karl Barth – 'hope in the restoration of the unobservable union between the Creator and the creature, through the Cross and Resurrection of Christ.'[5]

We've become used to interpreting the difficulties of the created order in the language of science – the movement of tectonic plates, the evolution of various conflicting instincts, competition among biodiverse elements causing disease and famine, and so on. What Genesis presents as God's doing, we now think we know as mere impersonal outcomes of natural processes. The two ways of viewing it seem incommensurable and become heightened into a kind of warfare between 'science' and 'religion'. But that polarity is overstated. Of course we may observe and catalogue the processes of the natural world. These present no threat to the Christian account of a wider cosmic 'backstory'. We can also listen to the anciently spoken possibility that human desertion from partnership with God has affected the way we appropriate the creation, and the way it's appropriated to us. There's no threat to science in hearing this possibility, or in hearing the hopeful news of rescue.

----

5. Karl Barth, *The Epistle to the Romans*, tr. Edwyn C. Hoskyns (London: Oxford University Press, 1933), p. 309.

Returning to the poles of our 'unified field', the *character of God* (ch. 21) informs human responses to the material order. God has other interests than the human race. He isn't anthropocentric; if anything, he's Christocentric about his Christ-powered planet (ch. 12), for it is to be delivered intact to Christ (1 Cor. 15:24–28). So God's love for humanity never displaces his loving concern for the entire creation. It's all 'very good' (Gen. 1:4, 10, 18, 25, 31). Plants also exist for non-human life (Gen. 1:30), and his covenant of protection applies to non-human life as well as to humanity (Gen. 9:9–10). In moments where the focus is completely off humanity, biblical authors revel in God's creative genius and in his exuberance toward the world. So Psalm 104 retells the story of God's founding the earth (v. 5) through to sustaining its teeming creatures (vv. 27–30). God storms into the confrontation with Job (Job 38 – 40) to drive home how much goes on in the world beyond human knowledge.

It simply pleases God to care, many details of which remain unknown to us. We see an echo of this character in the delight of the scientist, the wilderness activist or the zookeeper. Most of us never see the wonders they see, and when they urgently call for the protection of some species or habitat, they simply convey to us what God knows, begging us not to demolish it out of mere ignorance.

The *command structure* (ch. 23) of Israel's ancient law included provisions to guard the non-human world. The agrarian structure of their society generally made the need for such care obvious. These people had no need to write about their total dependence on the land – it was implicit in everything they did.

But one intriguing moment addresses the heated immediacy of warfare, where people forget everything except immediate human ambitions:

> When you lay siege to a city for a long time, fighting against it in order to capture it, you must not destroy its trees by putting an axe to them, because you can get food from them. You must not cut them down. Are trees of the field human, to come under siege by you? (Deut. 20:19)

Concession is made to cut down some trees (v. 20), but this command highlights the way no human project justifies wholesale environmental destruction. Similarly, various laws protect some animals (e.g. Exod. 20:10; Deut. 22:1–4; 25:4). Humans always 'rule' animals, but this rule is supportive. 'The righteous know the needs of their animals' (Prov. 12:10, NRSV).

What does *Jesus-shaped community* (ch. 25) teach about environmental care? Practically nothing, I must concede. That is the kernel of truth in Singer's point above. But the concession isn't very significant. With the Old Testament foundations secure, there was not much to add. Jesus reiterated the way wise people care for their animals (Matt. 12:11), and noted God's continual care for his world (Matt. 5:45; 6:26; 10:29; cf. Acts 14:17). Beyond that, the town and village settings of the New Testament meant that communities in Christ (ch. 18) would primarily school people in *a method for human relationships* – which are, in their own way, also an aspect of the created order, and which need our constant attention.

This seemingly anthropocentric ethic of the New Testament reminds us that we cannot stop being human. Our sociality is the primary setting of our lives, and a great deal of thought and energy needs to be spent attending to the minutiae of care, inclusion and virtue. Environmental care can flow much more easily from communities that are content and at peace than from communities in uproar over human affairs. In contrast, I find it striking when some environmentally motivated people are impatient when it comes to building quality human relationships. They seem to think that kindness, patience or sexual discipline is trivial in comparison to the enormous needs of the planet. They fail to consider that perhaps we can properly inhabit the planet only when we properly inhabit our human relationships.

The trajectory of the *new future* (ch. 24) includes a renewed and rejuvenated creation (Rev. 21 – 22), although, interestingly, the biblical story arc moves humanity into a city nestled among the rejuvenated creation. This future isn't divorced from the environment. At the centre of this city John sees 'the river of living water, sparkling like crystal, flowing from the throne of God' and down the middle of the main city thoroughfare. 'On both sides of the river was the tree of life bearing kinds of fruit, producing its fruit every month. The leaves of the tree are for healing the nations, and there will no longer be any curse' (Rev. 22:1–3).

Some Christians expect a complete obliteration of the present order, but this view simply evades the biblical story arc. (Some think that 2 Pet. 3:5–13 refers to such obliteration. However its exotic language refers to the 'lid' being ripped off human affairs, to be tested against the fire of God's judgment, p. 163.) We remain embedded in God's renewed world, embodied and material. The new future isn't some disembodied place of spirits. Its transformation brings life, healing and freedom from the curse that currently scars our cohabitation with the natural order.

Given this qualified biblical anthropocentrism, what might we wish to protect in the natural environment?[6] It depends entirely on the specific bit

---

6. The following paragraphs are indebted to Robin Grove-White and Oliver M. T. O'Donovan, 'An Alternative Approach', in *Values, Conflict and the Environment*, ed. Robin Attfield and Katharine Dell (Oxford: Ian Ramsey Centre, 1989), pp. 73–82.

of it under consideration. We might value the size or extent of some area. We might want to keep the diversity of species there, or retain it in a state relatively untouched by humans. The rarity and fragility of a place or species might matter to us, or something might matter because it's *typical*. A species' position in an ecological or geographical unit might be paramount; or the importance of keeping examples of a place or thing for future generations might weigh heavily upon us. Equally, we might worry about the health effects upon humans living near an environmental feature (e.g. a mosquito-ridden swamp). In the case of climate change, as magnified by carbon-dioxide levels, we seriously attempt to attend to the whole.

Sustainable care tries to take into account the unique environmental considerations in a situation, and then ponders how to maintain these for, and despite, human interests. (It also reflects upon how to protect equity between human beings in the process.) This 'pondering' will look different every time. There are no short cuts. This recognition of complexity (ch. 10) is open to abuse, as when someone declares a resource 'sustainable' when there's no way it can replenish itself. But no magic bullet can stop that problem. We can only keep trying to take humanity and the non-human creation seriously.

I don't come from an environmentally aware background. I don't finally know the extent to which global warming, overpopulation or overconsumption is a threat. But I see no reason to rebel against these concepts in some bloody-minded assertion of a human right to consume. I now cooperate with local waste disposal and recycling authorities on the assumption that they may know what I don't. My family no longer owns a car – we use a car-share network instead. We pay for renewable power; we experiment, somewhat episodically, with growing food. (At least the chickens are a success!) But I don't trumpet these endeavours with the competitive piety that often characterizes environmental awareness. Indeed, they sound absurd. They make such a little difference, and I remain dependent upon industrial uses of the land.

But we do these practices to challenge the greed I learnt in the schools of moral formation I inhabited in the 1970s and 1980s. We do them as an experiment in contentment. We do them to expand our moral imagination. I have to say that, at that level, they're changing me. (At first, I couldn't believe I'd remain a man without my big car. As it happens, I still am! I now feel an amazing freedom since losing this monster of consumption and worry from my world.) So I invite *you* to pause and consider:

- How seriously do you take your place in the creation as a dependent co-inhabitant of it?

- Where are you called to watch, order and reorder the created order in your everyday life?
- Are you a unit of consumption and production, or someone who lives sustainably alongside others?
- Are you content, or must you consume?
- Would caring for a plant or an animal expand your moral imagination, while also reminding you of your limits?

The concept of sustainable care is beginning to affect the way I think about care for people. We care sustainably for another when we take care not to become overresponsible for them. The best care blossoms into others caring for themselves, and then for others in their turn. In Paul's interesting contrast, we 'carry one another's burdens' yet 'each person will have to carry his own load' (Gal. 6:2, 5). We also care 'sustainably' for another when we know our own creaturely limitations, rather than being so addicted to 'productivity' that we fail to attend to sleep, nutrition and exercise.

Further reading

*** Berry, R. J. (ed.), *Environmental Stewardship: Critical Perspectives, Past and Present* (London: T. & T. Clark, 2006).

** Berry, R. J. (ed.), *When Enough Is Enough: A Christian Framework for Environmental Sustainability* (Nottingham: IVP, 2007).

*** Brock, Brian, *Christian Ethics in a Technological Age* (Grand Rapids: Eerdmans, 2010).

** Spencer, Nick, and Robert White, *Christianity, Climate Change and Sustainable Living* (London: SPCK, 2007).

** Van Dyke, Fred H., David C. Mahan, Joseph K. Sheldon and Raymond H. Brand, *Redeeming Creation: The Biblical Basis for Environmental Stewardship* (Downers Grove: IVP, 1996).

41. WORK

In Part 6 we're applying the account of how ethics works in Parts 1–5 to aspects of our 'vocation', or life-package. In this chapter, we look at our work, with particular reference to our paid work, although noting that we do other work as well.

If we've left the education system, our daily work has probably become fundamental to what we see as our 'identity' (ch. 14). I 'am', we say, an advertiser, lecturer, actuary, driver or welder. Each workplace promotes and defends some collection of rules, rights, values and results (chs. 3–6). As a school of moral formation (ch. 8), your workplace has likely told you a lot about who you are. But in this chapter, we'll ask how our work aligns to the 'unified field' of chapter 26. We may then become more able to cooperate with a workplace, subvert or expose it, or even to leave it (ch. 35).

One ancient Old Testament treatise (Eccl. 2:4–11) contains a penetrating description of what work isn't. It opposes three common reasons modern people give for why they work. 'What do people gain from all the toil at which they toil under the sun?' begins 'the Teacher' (Eccl. 1:3, NRSV). His treatise describes the way his own work was an invigorating solution to meaninglessness, at first.

His activity was intense:

I increased my achievements. I built houses and planted vineyards for myself.
I made gardens and parks for myself and planted every kind of fruit tree in them.

I constructed reservoirs of water for myself from which to irrigate a grove of flourishing trees. (Eccl. 2:4–6)

'I took pleasure in all my struggles' (2:10b); we would say he became *personally fulfilled*. He makes *a reputation*: 'I became great and surpassed all who were before me in Jerusalem' (v. 9). He sates his *desire to consume*: 'All that my eyes desired, I did not deny them. I did not refuse myself any pleasure' (v. 10a). In sum, he wards off emptiness by working for *fulfilment, reputation and consumption*. Work meets the desires and inclusion systems of his 'flesh' (chs. 7–9). The cocktail of fulfilment, reputation and consumption is intoxicating – for a while.

Yet the final judgment on his life is devastating. 'When I considered all that I had accomplished and what I had laboured to achieve, I found everything to be futile and a pursuit of the wind' (Eccl. 2:11). Work used for fulfilment, reputation and consumption cannot succeed. The collapse of the project is inevitable. The film *About Schmidt* opens five minutes before the end of Warren Schmidt's last day at an Omaha insurance firm. Schmidt (played by Jack Nicholson) has achieved some fulfilment, made a name and amassed some wealth from his work. But within days, Schmidt's ambitious young successor has reduced him to a dim memory, and Schmidt finds the files for his pet project stacked in the foyer for dumping. 'When Schmidt considered all that he had accomplished and laboured to achieve, he found everything to be futile, a pursuit of the wind.'

'The Teacher' concedes the good of work, in its place (Eccl. 5:18–20). It isn't that work never enables fulfilment, reputation and consumption. *But these are secondary outcomes.* We don't understand our work until we understand its *primary* outcomes. We can begin to gauge these using the poles of the 'unified field' (ch. 26).

We inhabit a *created order* (ch. 22) that humanity sustainably cares for and uses (ch. 40). All work has some connection to the structures of the natural order, although with different emphases. A scientist primarily watches and learns. A teacher conveys patterns of order. A cleaner, a pest controller or a doctor stave off disorder and reorder what they see. Some jobs seem quite disconnected from the created order: accountants and fashion designers seem only to operate in the human social world. But the accountant organizes the sharing of resources; the fashion designer brings delight to human senses; and like other workers, they need to know where their endeavours use the created order unsustainably. The first primary outcome of work is the understanding, use and care of the created order, which I'll call 'the work of creation'. Each of us needs to discern what connections our work has to the natural order.

The second primary outcome of work, its social function, is more apparent in modern urban environments. Once we begin to learn true sociality through *Jesus-shaped community* (ch. 25), we also learn to perceive our work as existing, somehow, for others. The following New Testament statements all exhibit the community focus of our work. They also highlight how the *command structure of the Bible* (ch. 23) functions to highlight realities easily missed – in this case, the nature of engagement in a community:

> Make it your ambition to lead a quiet life, to mind your own business and to work with your hands, just as we told you, so that your daily life may win the respect of outsiders and so that you will not be dependent on anybody. (1 Thess. 4:11–12, NIV)

> The thief must no longer steal. Instead, he must do honest work with his own hands, so that he has something to share with anyone in need. (Eph. 4:28)

> Now if anyone does not provide for his own relatives, and especially for his household, he has denied the faith and is worse than an unbeliever. (1 Tim. 5:8)

We read these texts to say that pay received enables families to consume. But that reading, through a post-Industrial Revolution lens, is too limited: *our work directly affects the order and harmony of the wider community*. Hence Paul can describe the Thessalonians' noteworthy 'labour of love' (1 Thess. 1:3), actions done to love others, not merely to consume.

To spell this out a little: once we've watched, learnt from, ordered and reordered creation, we're in a position *to share God's good gifts to promote communities where people care for each other*.[1] The second primary outcome of work is this loving sharing, to care for a community – what I'll call 'the work of community'. Each of us needs to discern how our work enables caring community.

Sharing God's good gifts doesn't necessarily imply giving them away for nothing. Money helps to order the sharing of good things, and we can view markets as venues of organized sharing, including the sharing of intangibles such as knowledge or beauty. Our consumption is a valid participation in this system of sharing. Further, not all work immediately results in people caring

---

1. The notion of work as a system of sharing comes from Oliver O'Donovan, who thinks society is primarily interrelational, and consists in the sharing or 'communication' of goods with one another (Oliver M. T. O'Donovan, *The Ways of Judgment* [Grand Rapids: Eerdmans, 2005], ch. 14). I'm also indebted to his comments on the market, pp. 63–66, 246–250, 255.

for each other. We compartmentalize our work so that some can attend to the work of creation and others to the work of community, with each focus enabling the other. But everyone helps to create the conditions for caring communities. This outcome of work excited the Protestant Reformers, who thought our work simply expressed the love for those next to us that Jesus stood for (e.g. Luke 10:25–37).

My friend Tim tells of stopping at a pretty, shaded rest area during a long drive. It had flowers, a lawn and clean toilets. 'Here was evidence of good work,' says Tim, 'a part of creation ordered and redeemed, kept beautiful and made useful.' The man responsible then arrived. Tim walked over to thank the man for the place and his work. He replied, 'If we make them nice, more people will stop.' He knew the *primary* outcomes of his work, which included *enticing* people to rest, and so bringing down the rate of car accidents. The man probably saves lives, not to mention simply making a lot of kids and parents a little bit happier. He uses and cares for creation to help create a community that cares.[2]

Modern people, Christians included, have become poor at articulating the primary outcomes of their work. When asked 'What's your work for?' most can offer its secondary outcomes of fulfilment, reputation and consumption. Few consider how their work relates to created or social order. I hope we can arrive at a point where each worker can fill in the blanks about his or her work:

1. 'I use and care for creation as I . . .'
2. 'My activity enables caring community by . . .'

Using this analysis, we find substantive criteria for judging our work. That is, we begin to see what makes some work bad. For example:

- Work is bad if it so persistently *disorders creation* as to generate new work for whoever has to clean up the mess.
- Work is bad if it *damages or destroys communities of care* through downstream effects, such as the destruction of people or families or habitats; or the economic disembowelment of other good modes of sharing in a community; or by such enormous time demands that communities other than the workplace become impossible.

---

2. Tim Adeney, 'Clean Toilets Save Lives.' Online: <http://www.timadeney.wordpress.com>.

- Work is bad when it's *nothing but* toilsome and laborious. When workers can find no way that their work assists a community to care, they've found a sad truth about their work.

Workplaces can become places that foster darkness and distortion, and we don't always have to cooperate with bad work. We may subvert it to become good. We may expose its evils. We may walk away from it (ch. 35). The usual language for what I'm describing says that we each need to develop a 'social conscience' (or 'corporate social responsibility') about our work. I don't like these labels, because they sound like boutique-extras to the work of fulfilment, reputation and consumption. The effects of our work upon creation and community are *always* integral to it, and to have a 'social conscience' is merely to notice the cumulative effect of our actions. It's not an optional extra. Whatever our workplace school of moral formation has told us – of rights for shareholders or customers, of compliance rules that must be observed, of values that 'we' stand for, or of results that must be obtained – workers have to learn to discern (p. 312) what's *really* going on there.

Work isn't only about creation and community. The New Testament introduces a third primary outcome for work. It's harder for Christians to discern how this outcome joins to work, but we can try. This third outcome has to do with the *new future* (ch. 24). It's introduced as 'the work of God' when Jesus explicitly moves beyond works of creation and community:

> Do not work for the food that perishes but for the food that lasts for eternal life, which the Son of Man will give you, because God the Father has set His seal of approval on Him. . . . This is the work of God: that you believe in the One He has sent. (John 6:27–30)

The work of God arises from the future judgments of the Lord Christ (ch. 12), which will stand beyond all human activity.

Jesus alludes to this new work in a healing context (John 5:17), in metaphors of harvest workers, who are effectively Christian evangelists (John 4:35–38; Matt 9:37–38; Luke 10:2), and by explicit wordplay: 'My food is to do the will of Him who sent Me and to finish His work' (John 4:34). Others respond to the immediate recommendations of their 'flesh' (ch. 9), striving for food and clothing without any reference to the new future (Matt. 6:31–34). But Jesus' work of God forces us to recognize the limitations of the works of creation and community. Paul enthusiastically expands on this work of God (Rom. 14:20; 1 Cor. 3:8–9, 13; 15:10, 58; 16:9–10, 16; 2 Cor. 6:1, 5; 10:13–16; 11:23; Phil. 1:22; 2:16, 30; 1 Thess. 3:5; 5:12; 1 Tim. 5:17–18; cf. the 'workers' of Rom. 16:3, 6, 9, 12, 21).

In this third primary outcome of work, the project is to bring people into fellowship with God through Christ. A kind of armed standoff has developed between workers who point to the new future, and those who do works of creation and community. In these fights between 'clergy' and 'laity', each tries to trump the other with the greater importance or necessity of their work. I propose we find a better way forward together.

Pastors, priests, bishops, deaconesses, vicars, ministers, youth-workers and the like presumably have the necessary gifts, skills and opportunities to focus on the work of God. But these workers need to recall that in the New Testament, the work of God never eclipses nor displaces works of creation and community. So even though Paul enthusiastically follows Jesus in espousing this new kind of work, his work clearly includes the work of creation to support his endeavours to preach (1 Cor. 4:12; 1 Thess. 2:9; 2 Thess. 3:8). The work of God relies upon the work of creation (1 Cor. 9:1, 4, 7–10); and as we've seen, responding to the gospel generates diligence in works of creation and community (Eph. 4:28; 1 Tim. 5:8; 1 Thess. 5:14; 2 Thess. 3:6–10). The good done in work isn't limited to the work of God (Eph. 6:7–9), and various other tasks are specifically endorsed and promoted (Luke 3:12–14; 1 Tim. 5:14; Titus 2:4–5). Those who focus on the work of God still participate in a created and social order. It requires personal works of creation and community of them. Every meal cooked, desk tidied, lawn mown, person comforted and conflict resolved sets essential conditions under which the work of God can proceed. No pastor can abstract himself or herself from the matrix we inhabit as creaturely social beings.

It follows that pastors do well to help articulate the works of creation and community conducted by those around them. They need to affirm what makes work good, and help analyse what makes it bad. They need to say *much* more about others' work than that 'it enables you to feed yourself and to support the work of God', for *that message would erroneously imply that consumption is a primary outcome of work*. Teachers and theologians need to discuss the primary outcomes of other workers' work, enabling workers to grow into the *real* theological experts of their field. Such thoughtful workers would be a fine expression of what Peter calls the 'priesthood' of all believers (1 Pet. 2:5, 9).

Conversely, the worker who focuses on creation and community needs to recognize (with Jesus and 'the Teacher' of Ecclesiastes) the limitations of this work and the place of the work of God. There's a proper honour for those who focus upon the work of God. All who surround them can uphold and celebrate this activity, partly by assisting them in works of creation and community. The Jesus-shaped community does itself no favours to belittle or sneer at this kind of vocation. 'That would be unprofitable for you,' observes the author to the Hebrews. 'Remember your leaders who have spoken God's word to you,' for they have the particular task of holding us to the new future.

> As you carefully observe the outcome of their lives, imitate their faith . . . Obey your
> leaders and submit to them, for they keep watch over your souls as those who will
> give an account, so that they can do this with joy and not with grief. (Heb. 13:7)

But how does the work of God connect to the daily work of most workers? For two reasons it isn't easy for modern Western workers to see how their own work assists the work of God. First, the Industrial Revolution has segmented the workplace into minutely specialized tasks. We now find it hard to see how our work connects to the created order and to the social order, let alone to the new future. Secondly, modern Westerners are so obsessed to keep 'religion' out of workplaces that it simply becomes easier to stop thinking about how the lordship of Jesus may touch a workplace. I realize these difficulties are very great, and don't want to minimize them. The following paragraphs simply offer a few suggestions for further theological conversation.

People acknowledge the new future when they know their true identity in a workplace. I love this story (possibly apocryphal) of one workplace power play. A corporate recruiter, seeking to entice a man into a better-paying job, suddenly shouts a manipulative and jarring demand: 'What's your purpose in life?' The recruiter had found that this question rattled most people. But this man coolly shot back: 'To get to heaven, and to take as many people as I can with me.' For this 'knight of faith' (p. 208), the workplace school of moral formation had not undermined his deeper identity in Christ (ch. 14).

Jobs may draw upon the new future. Each worker could try to discern how his or her job is 'formatted' (ch. 24) by that future. When a judge judges, when a health professional heals, when a lawyer negotiates peace, they do something of what Christ will complete in the new future. His final work may guide us in how to evaluate a job well done. The judge would learn justice from what Christ defends, the healer from what Christ healed people to become, and the lawyer from the kind of peace Christ will bring. (This kind of thinking should not displace or trump the New Testament's emphasis – that the work of God *verbally* testifies to God's future judgments through Christ.)

We may seek to 'subvert' a workplace with grace (ch. 35). But workplace limitations on the work of God have evolved over many years. They predate our arrival. Managers need to provide a harmonious workplace for people of different beliefs (ch. 46), and that entails boundaries on our expressions of identity in Christ. We may cooperate with some of these (ch. 35): we wouldn't imagine some 'right', for example, to play praise music loudly. But as we discern (p. 312) how to be subversive, we should probably test our plans first, at church and with friends (chs. 34, 39). There are clever and subtle ways to do the work of God while continuing works of creation and community.

I know a teacher who hated his staffroom's crude, corrosive humour. So he began a habit with the morning paper. He would read the opinion page on the way to work, and think through his Christian response. He would then get to the staffroom first, open his paper, and share his view. Others would share theirs. One morning he was on playground duty instead, a task despised by teachers. But a colleague sidled up to join him. With some surprise he asked, 'Umm . . . why are you here?' The colleague shrugged and mumbled, 'That staffroom . . . it's not worth being there when you're not.'

The work of God also takes place in an overall vocation or life-package. Do I support the work of God elsewhere in my life? If not, I may have slipped into the futilities of fulfilment, reputation and consumption, of which Jesus and 'the Teacher' warn us.

We also need to benchmark our work against the biblical vision of *rest* in the new future. It's interesting to consider that while there's no *toil* in this new future, activity such as the singing of praises continues. Could that be a joyous kind of work of God? Even if so, the new future is overwhelmingly a place of rest.

Over the Bible's story arc, God's own rest governs all that follows (Gen. 2:2–3), with humanity on a quest to 'enter' God's rest with him (Heb. 4:1). The quest for rest is seen in Israel's early history and law (the 'Sabbath': Exod. 16:23, 30; 20:11; 23:12; 31:14–17; 34:21; 35:2–3; Lev. 23:3; Deut. 5:14; and other 'rests': Lev. 16:31; 23:24–25, 31–32; 23:39; 25:4–5; 26:34–35). The conquest of Palestine is also, in its own way, a quest for rest (Deut. 3:20; 12:9–10; 25:19; Josh. 1:13–15; 10:23; 14:15; 1 Kgs 8:56). But the rest gained there is lost in the exile (e.g. Lam. 5:5), and only regained by Jesus' ministry and pinnacle achievements (Matt. 11:28–29; Heb. 3:18 – 4:11). Human destiny is to be restless without him, or restful with him (Rev. 14:11, 13).

This scriptural trajectory validates our times of rest, but not merely our leisure. We receive glimpses of true Sabbath rest when we 'worship': that is, when the focus of our activity is upon the praise and enjoyment of God. The works of creation, community and God are finally unintelligible, even futile, without this final Sabbath rest with God. It's traditionally been symbolized in a weekly Sabbath rest, although we miss the point a bit when that practice is dominated by demanding strictness (Mark 2:27; Col. 2:16). But regular worshipful rest glimpses the new future, and reminds us of the ultimate purpose of all work.

While we work, *the character of God* (ch. 21) impinges upon us. We bring to our work settled patterns and habits of action and feeling, the virtues and vices that make the totality of our character (ch. 30). In Christian thought, we learn new patterns of what to love and hate as we imitate Christ (ch. 32) and as his Spirit changes us (ch. 17). *Who we are* begins to change at our core, and it affects what we do.

- Your boss bustles in against a deadline. 'Listen, mate, I need you to change those figures on page 9 before the client gets here, or we'll lose this contract.'
- A knot of women giggle at another woman's weight. They eye you invitingly to join in.
- Two men fantasize lewdly about a woman's body. One casts a comment your way.
- Hatred of customers, with scathing sarcasm, fuels your workmates. They expect you to join their mockery.
- A board meeting inexorably drifts toward a decision that cleverly camouflages an injustice, or makes more money at the expense of some wider community good. Your vote is in doubt. You need to speak. They're eyeballing you.

The power of false inclusion (ch. 8) tears at us intensely in these moments. In the first or last of these cases, wider considerations may change your mind. But in the heat of them, we have only the *who* of our identity in Christ. 'I seek honesty.' 'I don't do slander.' 'I'm going to stay pure.' 'I'm here to care.' 'I want to be just.' In these moments of emergency, *who we are* is our first datum about *what to do*.

The language of virtue is never more mocked as pathetic than in moments like these. The decision not to be involved will cut across us like a hot knife. The person who seeks to grow the character of God in a workplace will most assuredly endure the sufferings of Christ (p. 105). But the virtues of Christ, drawn ultimately from the character of God, hold us through these moments. In such moments, act first to become the Jesus-shaped version of yourself you seek. Over time, people who carry themselves this way grow into the leaders, elders and respected experts in their field.

Now *that* would be fulfilment and a reputation worth having.

Further reading

*** Brock, Brian, *Christian Ethics in a Technological Age* (Grand Rapids: Eerdmans, 2010).

*** Cairney, Trevor (ed.), 'Work in Progress', *Case* 24 (2010). Online: <http://www.case.edu.au>.

** Crouch, Andy, *Culture Making: Recovering Our Creative Calling* (Downers Grove: IVP, 2008).

** Hardy, Lee, *The Fabric of This World: Inquiries into Calling, Career Choice, and the Design of Human Work* (Grand Rapids: Eerdmans, 1990).

** Stapleford, John E., *Bulls, Bears and Golden Calves: Applying Christian Ethics in Economics*, 2nd ed. (Downers Grove: IVP Academic, 2009).

PART 7 SIX HOTSPOTS

The early church had a public-relations problem. Word spread that these communities 'drank the blood of the Son of God' – that is, they drank wine symbolizing the death of Christ (ch. 15). Before long, garbled reports emerged that Christians were baby-eating cannibals. Such an insane evil outraged people, until the record was set straight.

This section takes a short look at some current 'hotspots' in ethics. They're areas of discussion that are most likely to cause a fight. They're flashpoints where, in our time, others are most likely to think Christians are evil or insane.

I definitely don't think these are the *only* areas that matter. I wish I had more pages to consider literally thousands of matters that deserve discernment and action. How to regrow Chilean or sub-Saharan trees when the locals need an energy source; what to do about the stranglehold of a union, a business or a political party over a political process; whether to turn to some safe form of nuclear energy; what to do about ridiculous levels of inequity in our education systems; how to create a regular coordinated international response to earthquakes and tsunamis; how to include and enable many thousands of men, women and children who live marginal existences on the edge of our societies. Many people think about such important and tangled issues, which all create 'hotspots' of some sort. *I don't want this section to suggest otherwise.*

By choosing the hotspots I've chosen, I risk implying that Christians obsess over a small handful of issues. (It could be that these issues obsess our society, and Christians are the resistance.) But I want to show that at these hot points of disagreement, Christians are not necessarily evil or insane. We may even offer something good.

People like to read about hotspots because of the conflict and drama involved. But I don't think they're the best way to approach ethics. The vast majority of what we do consists in how we travel – in the way we orient ourselves to life (Part 4); in our approaches to all its little transactions (Part 5); and in the way we pursue our 'vocation' (Part 6). I've suggested throughout the book that these arenas matter most. They're our primary responses to Jesus Christ (Part 3). But as we'll see, there are competing visions of how to be human and of how to live together. The hotspots disclose these competing accounts.

42. WOMEN

In Part 7 we're looking at some moral 'hotspots' — areas of conflict that often arise between Christians and others. This chapter examines two practices that many find difficult: the 'submission' of married women, and leadership of churches by men.

Even I find it offensive to call 'women' a hotspot. But I saw no point in camouflaging this chapter. As I write, women now occupy the four prime roles of my state and federal governments, and two more women are my parliamentary representatives. Yet some in my own and several other Christian communities continue two practices in connection to women that onlookers find outrageous.

The first is a discourse of 'submission' by women in marriage. The second holds that men should always lead churches. People have heard of these two practices in relation to women, and word has spread that the men of these churches are either bizarrely outdated in their view of women, or simply evil dominators. If you don't agree with these practices, I'm not setting out to persuade you to adopt them. I hope only to show why Christians who do them are not necessarily evil or bizarre, and how the practices may be good. For I'm keen that these practices not be an obstacle to anyone discovering their identity 'in Christ' (ch. 14). I'll use the 'unified field' of chapter 26 to help us.

Proponents of these practices are often content to point to the Bible's *command structure*. They think the Bible has some authority over them; that its commands about gender relations are neither culturally delimited nor self-evidently wrong; and that unlike some other biblical commands, they remain relevant. I won't visit their arguments for these conclusions. My point is that defenders of these practices have grown to trust the followers of Jesus who wrote this material (Paul and Peter), and the God whom they think directed this writing.

But this 'trust defence' will seem thin to anyone who doesn't yet share that trust, which comes from knowing the person of Jesus Christ (Part 3), the character of God (ch. 21), the work of the Holy Spirit (ch. 17) and the credentials of the biblical authors. As one thinker has put it, 'only a perception of truth can lead us to whole-hearted action'.[1] These practices and the commands that lead to them are a case in point. I think it fair, then, for people to ask for more than a 'trust defence'. I've suggested that biblical commands reveal various other aspects of reality (ch. 23). In what way could the commands for these practices possibly throw light on reality? How could they possibly be good?

I find a clue in the writings of Peter, when he directs husbands carefully to consider their wives as 'weaker' (1 Pet. 3:7). Even that statement has become offensive to modern ears. It would be indefensible if Peter were claiming that women were psychologically or mentally inferior to men. But he assumes men and women share the same kind of intelligence, the same kind of responsibility for their actions, and the same status before God, as when he stresses that women are to be honoured as 'co-heirs of the grace of life' (1 Pet. 3:7).[2] Elsewhere, Peter famously celebrated the way young women and servant girls could offer insights into God's word (Acts 2:17–18).

Once other candidates for 'weakness' are eliminated, I think he means simply that men are usually physically bigger and stronger than women. Like all generalizations, we can find exceptions. But most women are smaller than most men. What to do with this difference? It's an aspect of the *created order* (ch. 22) that remains relevant to us. But I'll *not* argue that 'men should rule because the strong should rule'. The physical strength differential between most women and most men will find a radical new interpretation in Christ's community; I'll get to that. But let's sit for a moment with the fact of it.

We live at a time when this difference in strength doesn't govern social relations between men and women, and rightly so. Women expect not to have

---

1. Oliver M. T. O'Donovan, *Resurrection and Moral Order: An Outline for Evangelical Ethics*, 2nd ed. (Leicester: Apollos, 1994), p. 131.

2. Similarly, Paul harboured no sense of any defect intrinsic to women: see above, p. 52 and n. 5.

to think about it. That a man is bigger shouldn't have anything to do with her contribution to a discussion, her opportunity to contribute her gifts and skills, or her freedom to walk safely down the street. We've organized modern Western cultures so that men and women can both helpfully contribute, irrespective of size or strength. The size and strength of a man comes into play only in limited situations where strength is relevant.

I rejoice in all that. However, these social arrangements can also cause us to pretend that male strength is no longer an aspect of the created order. Yet it remains *inalienable* to men. Men cannot be abstracted from the greater power of their bodies. We see this in those infinitesimally subtle moments when a man carries his body, lowers his voice or remains silent so as to leave a woman feeling vaguely intimidated or unexpectedly safer. This power gives men socially influential capacities. When used according to the 'flesh' (ch. 9), men can be callous and brutal, as predicted long ago (Gen. 3:16b). They have to be urged not to be 'harsh' to their wives (Col. 3:19, NIV), specific advice to men, because the option of physical harshness is less available to women.

Western culture has responded with amplified myths of the ultra-strong woman (e.g. *Nikita*, *Elektra*, *Buffy the Vampire Slayer*, *Alias*'s 'Sydney', *Aliens*'s 'Ripley', *Terminator*'s 'Sarah Connor', *Firefly*'s 'River', *Iron Man*'s 'Natalie', *Salt*, etc.). These characters are a welcome relief from the passive and stupid 'femininity' that preceded them. But they often enact fantasies of violent revenge, and embody a wistful longing for women to be able to compete on terms that nullify a male's strength advantage. Most women on most days will never have that option.

In contrast, the *Jesus-shaped community* (ch. 25) approaches this strength differential using Jesus' understanding of power. Jesus saw the powerful of his day doing what their 'flesh' recommended as obvious: 'those who are regarded as rulers of the Gentiles dominate them, and their men of high positions exercise power over them'. With his usual stylish subversion, Jesus unveils a different way: 'it must not be like that among you. On the contrary, whoever wants to become great among you must be your servant' (Mark 10:42–43).

All strength has moral implications – it can be used to dominate or to serve. But it cannot be pretended away. So when men accord to their wives an 'understanding of their weaker nature yet showing them honour as co-heirs of the grace of life' (1 Pet. 3:7), the 'understanding', the 'honour' and the recognition of a 'co-heir' become three interesting and creative modes of care deployed by the possessor of greater strength. Similarly, the consistent command to husbands particularly to 'love' wives (Eph. 5:25, 28; Col. 3:19) depicts possessors of greater strength using it for as many kinds of love as they can invent and enact.

'Submission' simply invites women to celebrate the man's use of his strength – to cooperate with him, and joyously to participate in the man's attempts to care. Women can be freed from the mocking, undermining and controlling responses that may be *their* most straightforward expressions of 'flesh' as possessors of lesser physical strength. The ancient prediction of Genesis 3:16b may allude to these strategies for underhandedly mastering strength. They become uninteresting and unnecessary in the company of a loving, effective man.

We submit when we're ruled (e.g. Rom. 13:1; Heb. 2:8), but there are two reasons to think that a wife's submission isn't like that. First, Paul carefully qualifies the *mutual interdependence* of men and women (1 Cor. 11:11–12), including a careful specification of direct reciprocity in sexual relationship (1 Cor. 7:4). Straight away, then, couples are dissimilar from the emperor–subject relationship. Secondly, we find an instance where the word carries the clear sense of *cooperation*. An amazing plea to help hungry Christians sweeps readers up into Jesus' generosity (2 Cor. 8 – 9). No command appears in this argument. Readers are simply mesmerized by the imitation of Christ (ch. 32), and find themselves helplessly wanting to give. This participation is described as 'submission' to the story of Jesus.[3] It's a form of willing teamwork. Similarly, then, women are asked to *join in* when men seek to live their inalienable strength well.

That task calls for discernment (p. 312), to be sure. A distinction is made between a child's obedience and a wife's submission (Col. 3:18, 20; Eph. 5:22; 6:1). Peter only connects obedience to submission illustratively (1 Pet. 3:5–6). Obedience isn't a dirty word (ch. 33), but to summarize this submission as 'obedience' limits our moral imagination. It may also rob women of a proper space for discernment, for many male acts cannot be endorsed, as when my wife Mary-Anne challenged my rage (ch. 28).

Women can celebrate and reinforce every moment when a man's power is used for good. (I remain amazed at Mary-Anne's capacity to encourage, shape and reinforce the best uses of my strength.) There may be overtones here of the help given by a woman long ago (Gen. 2:20). When the dynamic between

---

3. At the pinnacle of this argument (2 Cor. 9:13), many English versions translate the Greek term for 'submission' into 'obedience'. I believe this choice of word robs us of the opportunity to discover the *willingness* of 'submission' arising from a response of *affectionate participation in* the gospel. Translators may reply that 'obedience' can be joyful and willing (see ch. 33). I agree, but still believe that their choice of 'obedience' lacks imagination, and misunderstands Paul's argument.

men and women is seen in this light, the language of male 'headship' becomes the most honest label for the proper use of male strength (1 Cor. 11:3; Eph. 5:23). There's an implication of hierarchy in these texts, which deeply disturbs modern readers; but in both cases, the writer goes on to qualify it (1 Cor. 11:11–12; Eph. 5:28, 33).

Perhaps the most radical qualification is found in Galatians 3:28, where in a rhetorical flourish on another subject Paul declares that there's 'neither Jew nor Greek, slave nor free, male nor female, for you are all one in Christ Jesus' (NIV). I think this is his way of pointing to the *new future* (ch. 24), a place and time when the usual identity markers no longer define our social relationships (cf. ch. 36). Whatever the status of women in our broken and deranged world, in the coming future Christ will treasure women and men together. I think this new future formats Peter and Paul's present, enabling them continually to defend the parity between men and women. (Paul subversively calls *everyone* a 'son' in this new condition, Gal. 3:26, which serves in his time to dignify women; cf. p. 204.) But the new future doesn't overturn the structures of the present. Until then, men need direct tutelage in how to carry their strength.

So this way of thinking orders the use of inalienable male strength for service, while retaining and emphasizing several points of equity between men and women. This is a conception of hierarchy unlike any other. It may also follow from it that men who are not very strong, or who prefer not to use their strength, are now called to inhabit what strength they have as helpfully as they can. The strong man, and the not-so-strong man, are being shaped to live constructively.

Abusers do twist texts about headship, but these texts were written to correct abuse. Biblical texts are not defective just because they can be twisted. They're also generalizations: of course there are strong women who beat men, and weak men who connive to undermine. But these instances don't negate Peter and Paul's generalizations. By reflecting on Jesus' ethic of power, they give a way to accept inalienable male strength, and offer a way out of the most common conflicts between men and women.

So far I've offered my reasons for how the first strange practice could possibly be good. But what about the second, the leadership of churches by men? How can it be good? Defenders of this practice all speculate a little, due to some gaps in Paul's argument that men should hold the teaching authority in churches (1 Tim. 2:11–15). All letters have such gaps, and ancient hearers would easily have filled them. We, on the other hand, must imagine and weigh the possibilities. Rather than detailing them, I want to account for his command by way of *Peter's* writing, to suggest that Paul is extending what I've already said about inalienable male strength.

When Peter directs church leaders, he explicitly recalls Jesus' ethic of power. The metaphor of a shepherd becomes his preferred image. 'I exhort the elders among you: shepherd God's flock ... not lording it over those entrusted to you, but being examples to the flock' (1 Pet. 2:1–3). He then pictures *young* men – those testosterone-fuelled piles of strength who so easily bring disaster to all they touch – following the example and teaching of these 'shepherds'. 'Likewise, you younger men, be subject to the elders,' while the Jesus-shaped community learns its new method for relationships (ch. 25): 'all of you clothe yourselves with humility toward one another' (1 Pet. 5:5). (This text overlaps with others, where leaders exemplify *God's character*, ch. 21, by their 'godliness'.)

In this structure of Christian community, leaders *model* the best use of male strength. Male leadership of churches is inserted into human affairs to *show Jesus' alternative use* of inalienable male strength. Women are capable of every aspect of the role – except the *embodiment* of *male* strength in service. To have men inhabiting these roles, it seems, is something men need if they're to prosper as men, and so that women need if they're to prosper with men. Such 'shepherds' subvert and expose male domination of others. They also expose the opposite tendency of male 'flesh' to abdigate their responsibilities and languish passively in lazy and disinterested self-absorption, leaving care and service to women.

Of course, male leaders who revert to the usual bullying domination of male 'flesh' destroy the innovation of this practice. Or men may so divide various tasks as to avoid the harder kinds of care and service. Or men can forget that women have parity in their capacity to contribute gifts and skills as 'co-heirs' in Christ. But these mistakes don't overturn the excellence of the practice at its best. (My circle of churches attempts to avoid errors like these, and to express interdependence between men and women, by practising what we call *complementarianism*.)

Other schools of moral formation (ch. 8) have taught us to reject formal distinctions between men and women. Any formal recognition of men's physical strength is regarded as highly dangerous to women. So I don't under-estimate the clash between the male leadership of churches, and other social arrangements between men and women. I think other churches have adopted the dominant culture's conception of how to be male and female together. They would disagree, and would offer arguments to show that their practice is truer to the gospel. Whoever is correct, the churches' competing visions and different practices regarding men and women can exist only in parallel. Our freedom to assemble around these different visions and practices is an achievement of the modern West.

But I hope to have shown how the practice of churches like my own might not be evil, and may even be good. I recognize, though, that many modern people would need more reasons to associate with such a church. I believe we find these in Jesus himself (Part 3), and in the deeper logic of Christian community (chs. 18, 25, 34).

43. SEX

In Part 7 we're looking at some moral 'hotspots' — areas of conflict that often arise between Christians and others. This chapter's title will surprise no one; you've probably turned here first! It overlaps with chs. 36–37 and 44.

'The burden of such a great weight cannot be borne by the weak,' complains one Firmus to the theologian Augustine, nearly 1,600 years ago.[1] Firmus is a Roman aristocrat, and Augustine his evangelist. The 'burden' Firmus refers to is the 'burden', if he becomes a Christian, of having sex *only* with his *wife*. (Men like Firmus took it as their right to have many mistresses.)

I'm regularly told how 'unrealistic' it is for Christians to promote chaste singleness (ch. 36) and faithful lifelong marriage (ch. 37). A letter to a newspaper declares that to espouse sex as belonging to marriage is 'unrealistic'.[2] In an ambivalent discussion of chaste singleness and faithful marriage, my daughter's text on religion explains that the Christian account of marriage

---

1. Augustine, *Letters*, tr. Robert B. Eno (Washington, D. C.: Catholic University of America Press 1989). Letter 2* (Divjak collection, 1980), pp. 19–30.
2. Dr Muriel Porter, 'The Archbishop Is Wrong on Abortion', *Age*, 10 Aug. 2004. Online: <http://www.theage.com.au/articles/2004/08/09/1092022399318.html> (accessed 12 July 2010).

'may be seen as unrealistic' because Australian serial monogamy is 'generally accepted'.[3] An English publican once explained to me that lifelong faithfulness might have been reasonable at the time of the Ten Commandments, when people died young, but that this expectation is no longer realistic. These views are not new. Firmus evidently thought the same.

I also hear that Christians are obsessed with sex. Pundits regularly mock Augustine as the original church-obsessive on the matter. That I call 'sex' a 'hotspot', and that he appears in my first sentence, will be a bingo-moment for some. But this charge of obsession is a classic misdirect, of course. Clothing with a sexualized edge is common on my local streetscape. The public space I move through tells of herculean orgasms, and of how to augment them. I don't have to look far to find gymnastic repertoires of sexual technique diligently taught and learnt. I suspect I see plenty of people who enjoy happy episodes of sex; but I think I also see a sheen of witty and relaxed posturing about sex translucently hiding a lot of anxiety and disappointment about sex. I'm always relieved to escape back to the quietness of my happy marriage. If people need to believe that I, the Christian, am obsessed, then perhaps I should not question sincerely held beliefs if they bring comfort. However whenever Mary-Anne cuddles me, I now feel obliged to report that she's being 'unrealistic'.

Charges and counter-charges about who's 'realistic' or 'obsessed' mask what's really going on. Firmus, the doctor, the publican and the textbook all inhabit a gestalt (p. 72) in which sexual options meet sexual thoughts and feelings, and nature takes its course. In this awareness, the immediate recommendations of body and brain are the main consideration (ch. 9). There may be great complexities and anxieties of sexual etiquette, techniques, prowess and orgasming, but these are just necessary aspects of the terrain. For people in this gestalt, it remains weird to question its 'reality'. Long before Augustine's wrestle with Firmus, the apostle Peter observes this way of seeing sex: 'they are surprised that you do not plunge with them into the same flood . . . and they slander you' (1 Pet. 4:4). What alternative gestalt is at work to make someone's sexualized 'reality' seem more like a 'plunge' into a 'flood'? The 'unified field' (ch. 26) of the Bible's story arc (ch. 19) helps to articulate what Christians bring to sex.

Creation (ch. 22) brings an 'order' to sex that we accept, enjoy and protect. Many now want to reconnect with the natural order we inhabit. We exist on

---

3. Christopher Hartney, *Cambridge Studies of Religion: Stage 6* (Port Melbourne, Vic.: Cambridge University Press, 2008), p. 153.

the 'blue marble' that sustains us in interdependence with biodiversity. Every day brings to light more genetic and physiological connections to the planet. New habits of sustainable care are emerging (ch. 40). After the Industrial Revolution, we began to think we were like the machines we'd invented. But we were always more like plants than machines.

All along, Christians have upheld that sex is knitted into this wider order – that it bonds a man and a woman, and often makes them into parents (ch. 38). Yet despite the green era's rediscovery of our material aspect, most people spend a lot of energy evading the connection of our sexuality to this wider order. No one really argues that sex isn't a part of a natural order. But whenever people invent other uses for it, and augmentations that minimize its parental aspect and maximize its pleasure, we live as if the natural order is now irrelevant to sex. Christians simply think they've been put back in touch with that side of it.

We also think that when sex is split off from its natural aspect, we distort community and do each other an injustice. *Jesus-shaped community* (ch. 25) brings a method for relationships. It often surprises people that the New Testament's sexual ethic pivots on treating others justly (1 Cor. 6:8–10; 1 Thess. 4:6). Chaste singleness and faithful marriage are, in the logic of the New Testament, the way to a new and *just* Jesus-shaped community. That sexual laxity cheats others, and even does some sort of violence to my own body (1 Cor. 6:18), testifies indirectly to the natural 'grain' of sex.

This odd news of sexual justice reminds us of *God's character* (ch. 21), who deals in justice and steadfast love. People express steadfast love by keeping lifelong marital promises. Sex adorns and enables the promises, and keeping the promises makes sex safe. Apart from marriage, steadfast love takes the form of not sexualizing relationships, and so maintaining justice. In this way, a community of 'holy' character is formed.

The prospect of a *new future* (ch. 24) teaches us that we don't finally exist *for* sex. Christianity doesn't need to picture this future as endless sexual ecstasy. The intimacy of married sex advertises intimacy with Christ, even if we can't easily imagine what form it will take.

Commands (ch. 23) about sex unveil and uphold this bigger picture. There are times when these commands cut across us, particularly if we share in a gestalt where the quest for sexual pleasure has become a self-evident goal. When Firmus first hears that his desires need rearranging, it cuts like a hot knife. But a stance against 'sexual immorality' was a defining distinction between Christianity and Hellenistic paganism. Interestingly, we can track a pattern in the New Testament where sexual immorality reappears as part of a package of vices (ch. 30) that includes idolatry, greedy consumption, or both (e.g. 1 Cor.

5:9–11; Gal. 5:19–21; Eph. 5:3; Col. 3:5; 2 Cor. 12:20–21; 1 Thess. 4:3–6; Rev. 2:20; 9:21 and perhaps Acts 15:28–29).[4] In this literature, sexual immorality and greedy consumption flow together as an entire gestalt. If we're unwilling to interrogate our sexual desires, we're not likely to interrogate many of our desires. It then becomes convenient to control our own gods. We're content for good things to mesmerize us, and we become lost among our loves (ch. 7).

Our culture has decided that sexual thoughts, feelings and experiences are essential to human identity. If we're older and a virgin, we're somehow incomplete. If we've unmet sexual yearnings, then our lives haven't been full. We think we're like a machine that 'needs' sex, just as a car 'needs' fuel, and so we speak of our sexual 'needs'. In this 'sexual essentialism', erotic intimacy or sexual ecstasy is the pinnacle and goal of human existence, and sexual acts complete our humanity.

If we hold this philosophy, it colours everything we think and do. Marriages are automatically under threat if there's any sexual shortcoming. Singleness is necessarily incomplete, and the *absence* of sexual yearning somehow becomes weird. Friendships are confusing, for at the first sign of intimacy, we wonder if it should find a sexual expression. This philosophy undergirds a great deal of our interpretation of our world. We hear this essentialism at work when we presume to bestow sexual and sexualized identity labels, such as *ladies' man*, *hottie*, *slut*, *gay*, *lesbian*, *bi*, *stud*, or even *family man* or *frigid*. All of these assume that sexual desire and its expression defines who we are.

Into this view appears the gospel, which unveils how we can 'find ourselves' not in sexual essentialism but 'in Christ' (ch. 14). We can live in the chaste singleness lived by Jesus, or in the faithful lifelong marriage he affirmed. We cannot believe at first that Christ's way is thinkable. Sexual feelings do seem like final truth. Yet in Jesus-shaped community, we find men and women forging contented marriages, and single people learning the art of a network of intimate, non-sexualized friendships.

In the two-millennia 'experiment' in community called 'churches' (chs. 18, 25), we hold each other to chaste singleness and faithful marriage. This community doesn't publicly endorse anything other than chaste singleness or faithful marriage. But this hospital for sick sinners (ch. 34) is full of those who are still 'catching up' with their identity in Christ (p. 98). Some singles are angry and discontent. Some men want to have sex with other men. Men repulse some women, and they allow intimacy only with other women. Some

---

4. See further, Brian S. Rosner, *Greed as Idolatry: The Origin and Meaning of a Pauline Metaphor* (Grand Rapids: Eerdmans, 2007), pp. 152–153.

of the married are so revolted by each other, or so caught in cycles of pain or misunderstanding, that it seems impossible to believe marriage can be good. Some people think constantly about sex, or are addicted to pornography. Others cannot stop thinking wrongly about children. On and on it goes in the sad pantheon of sexual brokenness we all bring to the community. The credibility of the experiment seems compromised when sexual failures or church sexual abuse occurs (ch. 34).

But just as in other areas of our lives, Christ's Spirit attends the dark episodes in our journey (ch. 17). Meanwhile, we find friends across our differences, who sustain each other (ch. 39). And so the experiment continues, with more unpublicized successes than are suggested by the public failures.

The wrestle between Augustine and Firmus remains current. According to an anonymous hate-mail correspondent, a community like my own is oppressive and ridiculous. As far as I can tell, the writer considers it an offence against humanity to hold any view other than sexual essentialism. Another man tells me that the notion of chaste singleness is 'infinitely cruel'. We see so differently that our vast disagreement can only result in different *groups*. Such divergent views of sex are mutually exclusive: they cannot operate within the same group. People will coalesce around different visions of what sex is for, and how best to practise it. A group may be mocked for 'excluding' anyone with the other view, but that's unfair. In a free society, there's no other way to navigate our differences than by free assembly.

I can only shrug as we stare across the chasm Peter once described. But when Firmus complained that 'the burden of such a great weight cannot be borne by the weak', I find myself giggling at Augustine's reply:

> You do not seem to notice, O men who dread this burden so, how easily you are surpassed in bearing it by women, by the religious multitude of those faithful and chaste women whom mother church produces so faithfully. . . . One of this multitude in particular . . . is your wife.

In other words, many now abstain from sexual immorality and are doing well. Many I travel with have begun to find peace. There are singles who would enjoy sex, yet are content. There are those whose homosexual thoughts and feelings no longer define or control them. People who were once promiscuous, or who sold their sexuality, are finding a different way. Married people love their spouse again after times in the sexual wilderness. We don't pretend it's easy or simple, but it *is* good.

'Some of you were like this,' Paul writes to people who had lots of sex, stole, and went with their desires as easily as breathing. 'But you were washed, you were sanctified, you were justified in the name of the Lord Jesus Christ and by the Spirit of our God' (1 Cor. 6:11). As Augustine says tantalizingly to Firmus, 'the mysteries of rebirth are rightly and properly made known only to those who accept them'. So we'll keep inviting people to find rebirth in Jesus, and to join the experiment with us.

Further reading

** Kuehne, Dale S., *Sex and the iWorld: Rethinking Relationship Beyond an Age of Individualism* (Grand Rapids: Baker, 2009).
(Also see further reading under chs. 36, 37 and 44 in this book.)

44. HOMOSEXUALITY

In Part 7 we're looking at some moral 'hotspots' — areas of conflict that often arise between Christians and others. This chapter is related to other chapters addressing our sexuality (chs. 36–37). It considers the disagreement between 'conservative' Christians and those who identify as gay and lesbian.

If you've immediately turned to this chapter, either it represents a pressing personal concern, or you're using it to test my general position. I did invite you to dip into this book as you please (p. 11). However, I believe it will help you to look at other chapters I mention. Perhaps this is a polite way of asking you not to fling the book aside if I fail your test.

I recognize that many don't like the clinical tone of the term 'homosexuality', but I didn't want to camouflage the chapter. To do so spotlights particular people in a way that now seems unfair. I live in a wider political community committed to upholding and accepting those who self-identify as gay, lesbian, bisexual and transsexual (GLBT). My wider political community considers it deeply unacceptable to challenge or question their self-identity. But as everyone knows, many Christians do just that. So I do need to address the controversy over Christian disagreement with same-sex sexual practice.

It's fairly obvious that the disagreement arises from the Bible's command structure (ch. 23). I've already rejected a wrongheaded use of Old Testament commands about homosexual practice (ch. 19), but I've also argued that biblical commands cast light on various aspects of our life (ch. 23). In Christian thought, sex belongs to faithful marriage (ch. 43), and chaste single-ness is good. Logically, then, the biblical authors exclude other uses of sexual-ity to buttress their promotion of marriage (ch. 37) and of chaste singleness (ch. 36). The negative mention of homosexuality in New Testament vice lists (Rom. 1:26–27; 1 Cor. 6:9; 1 Tim. 1:10) is a subset of this wider discourse.

Many suggest that this material doesn't preclude loving, sexually exclusive same-sex relationships. I think that unlikely, but I won't dig into these argu-ments (see the readings below). That may seem like a fudge, but I think it more useful to outline how we find it thinkable to challenge such a relation-ship. I'll also touch on how we may all share cultural space, when we have such profoundly competing moral visions of sexuality.

It's politically powerful to attack Christian challenges as 'homophobic'. The label creates a suspicion of the other, where the only possible escape is via wholehearted affirmation of same-sex sexual practice. We can persist in this melodrama of suspicion, or we can try to find one another, across our differ-ences. I think I speak for other Christians when I observe that 'homophobe' puzzles me. It doesn't engage with who I think I am – an ironic mistake, because people who identify as gay or lesbian know quite a lot about others not engaging with who they think they are.

I live near an openly gay community. As my son and I once walked down the street, we came across two beautiful men dressed in silver. The first was dressed as a fairy, and the second wore a simple silver loincloth. They made us giggle, which I think was the intended effect. They spoke kindly to us; we felt no threat. These silver men obviously lived differently to us. They handed me an invitation to a sex party, which completely disoriented me. I was amazed that they should do so with my young son next to me, yet they did so with such complete innocence that I did not think to be angry. Clearly, these men had participated for a long time in a school of moral formation (ch. 8) where it's normal to make such invitations to people like us. My attention to them was not phobic. I was concerned that they appeared to have no other options for how to perceive themselves and their sexuality.

Our disagreement is about our most basic stories of humanity – of how to be good, of what our humanity is meant for, of how to join up our lives. Gays and lesbians describe powerful and persistent desires that they yearn to express, whether in sexual practices or in a relationship of intimacy. When they meet with similar others, these experiences coalesce into a shared story, and into a moral community that describes their best humanity in terms of a freedom to express love sexually without what they take to be arbitrary and artificial limits. Their sexual thoughts and feelings become necessarily central to a true description of them, and these need to be expressed openly and without shame if they're to inhabit an authentic human life. That aspiration then becomes a central feature of this community's political activism. When a Christian suggests that some act or feeling or thought or relationship doesn't express how we're meant to be, it represents a most direct attack on someone's entire sense of self. Like all of us, they respond to such attacks with anger, and their moral community mobilizes to refute, marginalize or minimize the source of the attack. (Diatribes against homophobia then function as a *genealogy*, or 'likely story', to explain the difference of opinion without testing and with little prospect of rebuttal.)

It grieves me to think of all that has gone wrong between moral communities called 'GLBT' and 'conservative Christian'. Each community battles for hearts and minds; each has its articles of faith; and we both have the capacity to hurt each other terribly. At our worst, these communities become each other's evil twin – two warring gangs (ch. 8) locked into cycles of verbal violence and reverberating with recriminations over who fired the first shot. In this milieu, those Christians who sound like they hate others should repent, and the Christian community should challenge their bitter, angry and hostile modes of speech. It goes both ways, as when I saw a budding Christian church in a pro-gay 'village' suffer a media vendetta. The only privileged topic was sexual self-identity. Whatever might have been good about identifying with Christ, and what that might have offered the village, was considered irrelevant. The journalists (and several villagers) could imagine only that the Christians were setting up shop specifically to condemn their way of life. It reminded me of an episode where the apostles were almost killed because the locals couldn't think past their immediate investments (Acts 19:23–41).

But we've simply discovered Christ, and have found that the identity we thought we had was alienated and incomplete without him. Whatever story we once told about ourselves, we begin to find a new version of ourselves 'in Christ' (ch. 14). Christ's death, and a kind of 'resurrection' for us, has meant we view even our sexuality differently (chs. 15–16). We begin to question *all* the once-obvious recommendations of our 'flesh' (ch. 9), as by his Spirit (ch. 17) even what we love begins to change (ch. 7).

The New Testament texts that mention homosexuality address the tragic downfall of all human desire. (In a letter not noted for its subtlety, Jude alludes to Sodom's homosexuality: v. 7. Yet he's not particularly interested in it. He's far more interested in the way human desire sabotages news of grace: vv. 4, 8.) But none of us is very reflective about why we love what we love. To experience sexual desire, and even to enact it, goes a bit deeper than simply making a choice (cf. ch. 17). At the same time, none of our desires is as fixed as the pro-gay community around me likes to imagine. I don't mean I agree with Christian ministries that work to change sexual orientation, as if to be in Christ is to 'become straight'. I refer to the way that in Christ we find that *our sexual self-identity isn't an adequate summary of who we really are, and of who God intends for us to be.* We discover reasons to believe that both chaste singleness and faithful marriage are liveable and good. We relearn how to be friends (ch. 39).

So we simply want others to have the same opportunity to find *their* new identity in Christ – the Jesus-shaped version of themselves. When we practise church well (chs. 18, 25, 34), people with homosexual thoughts and feelings are most welcome. We want for them to enjoy and keep the best of friendships. We don't want them to be lonely (cf. ch. 36). Their journey in relation to sexuality may be hard, with some unpredictable twists and turns; but we've all found that as we 'catch up' with our new identity (p. 98). Meanwhile, we support each other across our differences. Church becomes the place where we each find our loves renovated by Christ.

A different kind of church is now emerging, which defends homosexual practice when expressed in a lifelong same-sex relationship. I don't agree with what these churches say, but it's an achievement of modern Western life that communities may freely assemble and attempt to find peace in their own way. So now two opposing kinds of church community (pro-marriage-and-singleness and pro-gay) conduct alternative 'experiments' in how to be human. They may continue in parallel for some time. Their 'experiments' may go on for decades, or even centuries. (We've seen such splits in Christian history before, as when parallel Christian communities couldn't agree about the human nature of Christ.)

During this time, those who identify as GLBT are not victimized when conservative communities promote chaste singleness and faithful marriage, just as conservatives have to join the delicate political task of learning how to live alongside the other community in relative harmony. While the disagreement remains, *free assembly* is our only way to share cultural space peacefully. We can share cultural space peacefully *only* while each community has the legal freedom to say what it thinks, and to employ those who think it.

Further reading

** Bonnington, Mark, and Bob Fyall, *Homosexuality and the Bible* (Cambridge: Grove, 1996). Online: <http://www.grovebooks.co.uk>.

*** Gagnon, Robert A. J., *The Bible and Homosexual Practice: Texts and Hermeneutics* (Nashville: Abingdon, 2001).

* Keane, Christopher, *Choices: One Person's Journey out of Homosexuality* (Brunswick East, Vic.: Acorn, 2009).

* Keane, Christopher, *What Some of you Were: Stories about Christians and Homosexuality* (Kingsford, NSW: Matthias Media, 2001).

*** Roberts, Christopher Chenault, *Creation and Covenant: The Significance of Sexual Difference in the Moral Theology of Marriage* (New York: T. & T. Clark International, 2007).

45. BIOETHICS

In Part 7 we're looking at some moral 'hotspots' — areas of conflict that often arise between Christians and others. This chapter suggests that at the core of our disagreements about bioethics is a disagreement about where humans are located in the cosmos.

The Australian Baptist ethicist Rod Benson thinks that Christian discussions of ethics have reduced to what he regards ironically as 'the sacred seven'. Three of these are bioethical — abortion, anything related to the human embryo, and euthanasia. (The other four are drug and alcohol abuse, homosexuality, pornography and gambling.) Like him, I think Christian ethics is about a lot more than this 'sacred seven' (cf. p. 279).

His comment highlights how the arena of life, health and death forms one gigantic 'hotspot'. It comprises several smaller hotspots that continually reappear in our society. This short chapter can act only as a tiny lifeboat in a sea of controversy. But I choose this gigantic hotspot because it elegantly illustrates how a joined-up Christian life entails strange practices that mystify people who act on the basis of rights (ch. 4) or results (ch. 6):

- We fight for an embryo to 'succumb', with no research conducted on it, when that embryo could yield good results for medical technology.
- We fight against abortion even when some quirk in a fetus hints that the child may have a disability, or even when a woman's future with the child may become harder.

- We fight for truer real freedom for a woman to bear her child, in a society that believes it's already won a woman's right to choose.
- We sometimes challenge irreversible cosmetic surgeries, which people pursue for the sake of their happiness.
- We fight for a few extra weeks of life when pain-free non-existence obviously seems like a better result.

Although many Christians wouldn't include themselves in this 'we', a lot would. Dr John Wyatt, a specialist in neonatal (newborn) care in a major London hospital, observes how Christians work alongside others who have a very different view of humanity's place in the cosmos. English people find it a bit impolite to mention these disagreements at work. But they must be quite powerful, since one floor below his multi-million pound neonatal facility he can find another expensive facility aborting fetuses not unlike those he strives to save. Two powerful, competing world views drive the construction of these different wards.

I've outlined how the joined-up life springs from the character of God, the order of creation, Jesus-shaped community and the new future, with some commands shaping that vision (Part 4). In contrast, the dominant culture has an alternative account of the material order, the community and the future. On this view the material order we inhabit is neither good nor bad. It randomly coughs up humanity onto the shores of the present, without rhyme or reason. A history of chaos is embedded in the very materiality of our bodies. The human systems that have emerged from evolution are respected; yet human medical ingenuity imagines it can 'improve' humanity.

Since the human will can improve our lot, the human community becomes a collection of individuals who choose what they want, with medical professionals giving it as they're able to. We impose our will upon our natures, and medicine colludes to give us what we want. It follows that at the end of our lives, with no future other than nothingness, medical professionals should also give us what we want: an end to our pain. There's no creator of nature, so no character of God impinges on us, and no commands are relevant. Rules (ch. 3) and values (ch. 5) can only derive from whatever we deduce about ourselves from this alternative account of creation, community and future. Modern medical ethics now revolves around vague values of beneficence, non-malfeasance (i.e. the avoidance of harm), autonomy (and informed consent) and justice. These have their place, but they say nothing about the good toward which we're beneficent, or about the evils that constitute harm. In the absence of agreement about these goods or evils, doctors must privilege the will, as expressed in the value of autonomy and in the practice of consent.

We see an extreme version of this trend in some forms of cosmetic surgery. The *apotemnophiliac* has a form of 'body dysmorphic disorder'. He believes his true identity (ch. 14) is to be an amputee. Some apotemnophiliacs have had healthy limbs removed by a surgeon.[1] Most other surgeons believe this surgical decision to be wrong, but they find it hard to say why. If we exist to improve random materiality by the power of our will, then it simply isn't wrong. The best a dissenting doctor can do in those circumstances is to point to *her own will* – that her professional judgment is such that she won't perform the requested procedure. What was once medical care is reduced to a battle of wills.

On the Christian account, we receive, uphold and defend an orderly creation (ch. 22) that includes our limbs. So we seek for the apotemnophiliac to discover how to receive his limb with gladness. We may even find that some construction in his brain makes that a hard quest. But we need not believe with him that his leg is an evil, or that he has imagined an improvement. (I often wonder if people will look back upon reconstructive surgery much as we now see lobotomy – a draconian intervention intended to bring relief; but a tragically mistaken intervention, because the real problem lay elsewhere.)

This Christian optimism about the good of creation doesn't instantly make everything easy. We know there's a dark side to our experience of the creation (p. 264). There are perplexing phenomena: the person born with male and female genitals; the sperm or egg cell that carries a known anomaly giving rise to a terrible disease; the baby born without higher cognitive functions. Christians can find it as taxing as anyone to discern and then argue for what's best in these hard cases. But even though we grieve these moments of brokenness, we're not being fanciful to receive the created order as good, and to protect it through medicine rather than improving it by medicine.

Interestingly, this Christian logic is similar to what propels modern green thinking. Industrial medicine's quest to improve the material order is precisely the kind of modernist fantasy that environmentalists reject elsewhere in the natural world. Irrigation, pest control and the draining of wetlands have often turned out to be mistakes, not improvements. One day we may think similarly of some medical interventions.

---

1. For a brief summary, see Carl Elliott, 'A New Way to Be Mad', *Atlantic Monthly* 286.6 (2000). Online: <http://www.theatlantic.com/issues/2000/12/elliott.htm> (accessed 15 May 2010).

Another element of the Christian account of creation is that everyone carries God's 'image' (Gen. 1:26). Scholars argue over what of God this image images (and tend to forget that Jesus' humanity solves this riddle; chs. 12, 14). But the 'image' makes every human precious (or, as some prefer to put it, this image gives us *dignity*). People are precious despite their state of mind about themselves (e.g. the old person in despair, or the body-dysmorphic person). They're precious even if they're not very productive, and cannot contribute much that we would pay for (e.g. someone with a challenging physical or intellectual disability; or someone weak and terminally ill).

Communities in Christ (chs. 18, 25, 34) practise care because they regard this 'image' so highly. We don't simply shrug and abandon people to their choices (e.g. the depressed person who wants to commit suicide, or the body-dysmorphic person who wants surgical reconstruction). Nor do we abandon people to false beliefs about their 'usefulness' or 'productivity' (e.g. the terminally ill person who no longer wants to be 'a burden', or the person with a disability who's wickedly told she's good for nothing – or that her mother 'should have done something about it' instead of letting her be born). To all of them, the Jesus-shaped community says, 'You matter; let's reflect together on your condition; we'll help.' In doing so, we seek to reflect God's faithful, just and merciful character (ch. 21).

I've pointedly ignored a fight many Christians engage in:

- We fight for machines not to be switched off, even when no doctor has the slightest clue how to cure the patient.

I believe this fight is often mistaken, because it hasn't properly apprehended the Christian logic of the new future (ch. 24). Where we currently stand in the Bible's story arc (ch. 19), death always wins (Heb. 9:27a). Death is only finally defeated when the new future comes (1 Cor. 15:24–26). Given this sad truth, there comes a time when death *has* won. Switching off life-support is often the recognition of this truth.

If death finally wins, it becomes possible to distinguish *euthanasia* and *assisted suicide* (where we act to kill a patient) from the *withdrawal of burdensome treatment* (where we recognize we cannot save a patient, and cease arduous treatments that offer no prospect of cure). But a huge culture war is raging over that distinction. For those who privilege human will and choice, both euthanasia and withdrawal of treatment are acts of will. Since human agency is at work in both, they say we kill when we cease treatment, and we do so because quality of life is poor. They conclude that we should honestly embrace our killing, and also kill those who wish to be euthanized.

In reply, this privileging of the will simply ignores the wider canvas: that we support people, and uphold and defend their lives. But we can also admit when death has effectively won; and so we withdraw *treatments* that are unnecessarily burdensome. We don't withdraw them because *life itself* has become 'burdensome'. (That people can 'share' in 'the sufferings of Christ', p. 105, shows that even a hard life is worth living.) Nor do we simply retreat into the quick fix that euthanasia offers, because general permissions to kill contradict the support of people and the defence of life. Christians seek a kind of discernment (p. 312) that neither overly extends life, nor consigns people to death.

We recognize that medical professionals regularly traverse the twilight intricacies between life and death. They possess the technical skills required to make a judgment about when death has won. We ask and trust them to guide us, to describe when a treatment may advance life and when it simply won't. We in turn seek to support them as they walk courageously in that twilight world, doing what they can. We seek to help them not fall into despair, so that they'll keep re-engaging and defending life. Philosophical musings designed to confuse them into accepting euthanasia in the name of human autonomy don't really offer much motivation to continue supporting people and upholding their lives. We also ask them not to end life simply because they predict a low 'quality' of life. Their predictions can be wrong. Also, people with disability regularly confirm the Bible's news that all are precious whether or not they can perform various tasks. Jesus-shaped communities continue to discover with them that we're at our best when we serve one another.

When Christians oppose the practices arising from the other world view, we're not enslaved to some rule system (chs. 3, 23, 33), and don't somehow get off on 'imposing our values' (ch. 47). We simply want society to join together in care, like Jesus Christ, for all sorts and conditions of people.

I've only offered a glimpse of how two competing world views, or moral visions, affect matters of life and death. But whether as health-care workers or as patients, we can become more alert when daily medical care expresses one moral vision or the other. Christians in health care need to discern when to cooperate with, subvert or challenge others – or where the two visions of humanity have become so mutually exclusive that they simply must part company (ch. 35). A day may come when different medical institutions will embody competing visions of true humanity. These institutions will fight over resources in a brittle, politically brokered peace (much as we now see in parallel systems of public and independent school education). But maybe, just maybe, we can avert that sad way of living together.

Further reading

** *Centre for Bioethics and Human Dignity*. Online: <http://www.cbhd.org>.

** Meilaender, Gilbert, *Bioethics: A Primer for Christians*, 2nd ed. (Grand Rapids: Eerdmans, 2005).

*** Swinton, John, and Brian Brock, *Theology, Disability and the New Genetics: Why Science Needs the Church* (London: Continuum, 2007).

*** Verhey, Allen, *Reading the Bible in the Strange World of Medicine* (Grand Rapids: Eerdmans, 2003).

** Wyatt, John, *Matters of Life and Death: Human Dilemmas in the Light of the Christian Faith*, 2nd ed. (Nottingham: IVP, 2009).

** Wyatt, John, *New College Lectures 2008*. Online: <http://www.newcollege.unsw.edu.au/newcollegelectures.html> (scroll to end).

46. DIVERSITY

In Part 7 we're looking at some moral 'hotspots' – areas of conflict that often arise between Christians and others. This chapter examines the claim that the Christian message and Christian communities are a 'hegemonic' threat to diversity.

'Diversity' has become quite a loaded word. It describes the many different kinds of domestic family arrangements in which people find themselves; sexual choices, identities and orientations that people express; ethnic, racial and cultural patterns that characterize various communities; and religions, philosophies and world views people espouse.

Likewise, 'biodiversity' describes the myriad natural species and their habitats. We now regard diversity as a good thing. It's been an insight of postmodernity that the uniformity isn't always good for us. Modern Western society has parleyed peaceful settlements among diverse people, so that we can share the planet together. 'Diversity' is meant as a peace-making word.

Yet along comes Christianity, and seriously contends that Jesus' humanity encompasses and 'decodes' everyone's diversity, all journeys and every vocation; and that to be truly human involves knowing him and participating with him (ch. 14). The claim sounds completely 'hegemonic' – a term used to describe pernicious ideas that seek to obliterate all the particular personal elements that contribute to diversity. So Christians now find themselves charged with being a threat to diversity, a threat to individuals (causing them to become insecure or guilty about their identity), and a threat to a fragile and hard-won social peace.

There's an irony to these charges, since previous societies once alleged that Christians threatened the *uniformity* necessary to society. (A lynch-mob drags some Christians forward, shouting, 'They are all defying Caesar's decrees, saying that there is another king, one called Jesus,' Acts 17:7.) There's a further irony when we track back into the history of diversity. Christianity first taught that even young women and servant girls could offer insights into God's word (Acts 2:17–18). Christians of the Reformation then demanded this freedom to think for themselves about the truth of the Bible, and contributed to a monumental chain of events that led eventually to our modern conceptions of free speech, free assembly and freedom of conscience: in other words, to our conception of diversity.[1]

But Christians do challenge some diversities. I don't mean to defend those pathetic moments in Christian history, where the attack on diversity has merely been a religiously packaged demand to conform to whatever random group norms are in vogue. (I've been in churches that opposed overdressing at church, only to create a new demand that we should underdress at church.) Christians will regularly do that, merely because we're human (ch. 8). The real attack on our diversity, like the attack on our conformity, comes from Jesus himself.

Jesus assaults the conformity and groupthink of his day. But his simple demand to follow him (ch. 13) certainly attacks diversity. 'Do not suppose that I have come to bring peace to the earth,' he declares. 'I did not come to bring peace, but a sword.' The sword is only metaphorical, but he's still very troubling:

> For I have come to turn a man against his father, a daughter against her mother, a daughter-in-law against her mother-in-law – a man's enemies will be the members of his own household. Anyone who loves his father or mother more than me is not worthy of me; anyone who loves his son or daughter more than me is not worthy of me; and anyone who does not take his cross and follow me is not worthy of me. Whoever finds his life will lose it, and whoever loses his life for my sake will find it. (Matt. 10:34–39)

Confronted with that, Christians tend to shrug a bit when we're accused that we threaten diversity. We know whom we now follow and won't change that

---

1. Oliver M. T. O'Donovan, *The Desire of the Nations* (Cambridge: Cambridge University Press, 1996), ch. 7.

for anyone. We'll continue to invite others to join us. Call that our contribution to diversity.

Yet it's interesting to see where this logic leads in practice. Emphatically unlike other religions, it doesn't result in a quest to rule nations, but in social experiments called 'churches' (ch. 34). Each church does have some expectations of what you do to participate in the group (although, ironically, different expectations by different churches also express diversity). But churches that continually interrogate their group norms against the Bible uphold different gifts and skills as being precious gifts from God (Rom. 12:4–8; 1 Cor. 12; Eph. 4:4–13). They learn to deal respectfully with different thoughts and practices, even when these seem wrong (Rom. 14; 1 Cor. 8; 10:23–33). They discover that all the usual markers of tribe, race and identity are less important than humans usually think (John 10:16; Rom. 3:29; 1 Cor. 12:13; Eph. 2:13–22; 3:6; Gal. 3:26–28). They look forward to a completely diverse gathering, where Jesus Christ is central to everyone's attention and identity (Rev. 7:9–10).

The allegation that Christians threaten diversity is simply an overstatement. There's a controlled subtlety to what diversities it challenges. There's the recognition that, ultimately, each person's identity is between them and Jesus Christ. There's also a deep awareness that only the Spirit of God (ch. 17) can bring about meaningful unity. So we say what we say, and do what we do, without needing to make others join us. When Jesus-shaped community (ch. 25) shapes our expectations about diversity, we're better at working with it than opponents admit.

47. IMPOSING IT

In Part 7 we're looking at some moral 'hotspots' — areas of conflict that often arise between Christians and others. This chapter responds to a charge that appears whenever Christians touch upon some controversial area of politics or law.

'You have no right to impose your values on others.' These words pop up regularly in discussions of politics and law, particularly when Christians want or don't want some law. It's interesting to reflect on how nutty these words would have sounded throughout most of human history. A Babylonian despot, a Roman emperor or a French king of *l'ancien regime* would have found the sentence utterly unintelligible. That doesn't mean the statement is wrong. It simply shows how much we take for granted when we think it's right.

The sentence has several layers to it. It's thoughtful about rules (ch. 3), implying that the impositions of law are serious, and some are evil. By warning me off what I have 'no right to' it highlights the rights of others (ch. 4). It assumes that values are only ever personal (ch. 5); there are no virtues applicable to all (ch. 30). It presumes a person's identity (ch. 14) is whatever they define it to be, and that diversity (ch. 46) is a result worth having (ch. 6). The Babylonian, Roman and French rulers would have found all this most curious. We've come a long way.

But unfortunately, the sentence often appears in contexts where no one really understands all it implies. It's become a kind of throw-down phrase, a conversation stopper when disagreement is in the air. All law represents the imposition of something on someone; most laws challenge someone's values; but this mantra isn't about that. It arises from a particular current in Western thought, loosely termed *political liberalism*. This way of seeing society seeks to maximize freedom for individuals to live without any interference by government. Therefore, it follows that we need extremely good reasons for a law. Anything less is an unwarranted imposition.

The sentence generally has no traction when those on the 'right' use it against those on the 'left' (e.g. 'you have no right to impose on others your values of climate-change mitigation, wealth redistribution through the tax system, or social inclusion'). So it seems to me the sentence is also a kind of code phrase used to raise the alarm when anyone with a religious or conservative bent advocates legislative change. Even more oddly, those who defend the status quo *against* legislative change are often said to be doing the imposing, even though they're not asking for a change. Given this 'religious' connection, let's pause to consider what Christians might be doing in these contexts. (I won't try to speak for what other religions are doing.)

If the Holy Spirit enables inner change (ch. 17), then people can only be informed of what Christians take to be true, and never coerced into accepting it. In the English-speaking world, the philosopher John Locke forcefully held society to this logic by using the concept of 'tolerance'.[1] Everyone has been exploring the implications ever since.

So, at their best, Christians don't argue for or against laws just to dominate others. They often hold *a different conception of society* to that of political liberalism. (It sometimes resembles liberalism's recent competitor, 'communitarianism'.) Having noticed the many-layered relationships of, say, a church community (ch. 25), we learn to notice that societies are more than mere collections of individuals who maximize their desires. We want governments to set the conditions under which relationships can prosper. We want the less powerful and the underincluded to find their place. So we argue for more freedoms in some areas, and more regulation in others.

Lately, 'imposing values' has become the code phrase to describe the motives of those who resist gay marriage. But this resistance seeks to retain cultural space for marriage as the lifelong, sexually exclusive, open-to-children thing (chs. 37–38) that men and women will largely continue to do. Resisters like me realize that same-sex couples care for one another, and that

---

1. John Locke, *A Letter Concerning Toleration* (1689). Online: <http://www.constitution.org/jl/tolerati.htm> (accessed 15 May 2010).

they sometimes care for children. Some of us accept that there are good reasons for governments to recognize these domestic arrangements. But we also think that society needs to do all it can to produce and keep a large proportion of families where stable, loving, harmoniously married men and women are open to bearing and raising children; and that there are likely to be good reasons for a child to have a kind mother *and* a caring father. We honour this activity by calling it 'marriage', and by indulging it with some positive discrimination in the form of marriage ceremonies and public registration. A good society must also accept, support and care for families that are not like that; but we can still aim to enable many more to become like that. To concede this cultural space to marriage doesn't compromise the freedoms of same-sex couples.

My point in using this example isn't to convince you of its truth. That judgment would require more than I've said. I'm simply offering a glimpse of how Christians think it reasonable to engage in social and political debate. I could make the same point about the other usual suspects, such as bioethical dispute (ch. 45). The Bible *has* affected our thoughts. Our identity *is* in Christ (ch. 14). *Of course* we understand that not everyone is with us at those points. Yet we remain interested in the good of our society; and as citizens, we'll offer our best shot at what might keep society good, or make it better.

All sorts of interesting discussions then follow about how 'publically accessible' Christian reason can be to others. We agree that people need to be able to follow some of our reasoning if our proposals are to be useful – although at times, we may also be pointing out blind spots no one cares about (chs. 7–9). For example, something like that's going on when Christians resist state-sanctioned adoption of infants by same-sex couples. Our society insists that there's little or no social significance in gender difference. We reply that gender difference, though somewhat mysterious, remains precious – especially from the perspective of a child. In this way, we draw attention to what we believe has become a cultural blind spot.

Our society is now so politically charged that it's become easier for opponents simply to shout about who's imposing upon whom. But our conflict doesn't have to be this bad. Done well, it can reveal what really matters to each of us. We can then find new ways of thinking about society that may surprise us at first, and may even delight us later. We can grow in the art of accepting one another, even while we disagree. In this way, we may be able to fumble toward finding peace together.

Further reading

** Beckwith, Francis J., *Politics for Christians: Statecraft as Soulcraft* (Downers Grove: IVP, 2010).

*** Bretherton, Luke, *Christianity and Contemporary Politics: The Conditions and Possibilities of Faithful Witness* (Chichester: Wiley-Blackwell, 2010).

** Chaplin, Jonathan, *Talking God: The Legitimacy of Religious Public Reasoning* (London: Theos, 2008). Online: <http://www.theosthinktank.co.uk>.

AFTERWORD: DILEMMAS AND DISCERNMENT

Near the start of this book (ch. 2), I pictured a bunch of decisions. Really, each of them hid a dilemma:

- 'Should we smack our toddler? She needs to stop that behaviour, but we don't want to damage her psychologically.'
- 'Should we send our child to a government school? We disagree with some of its messages, but want to connect with our local community.'
- 'Should we send our child to a non-government school?' We like the school's shared moral agreements, but the monetary buy-in excludes some and forgets the poor.'
- 'Should I stay with that difficult husband or wife? He/she is constant hard work. I don't feel very precious around him/her. But I want to reflect God's own faithfulness.'
- 'Should I buy a Pontiac Firebird? People own other nice things, and there's nothing wrong with enjoying beauty, but others will be envious and will assume I love myself.'
- 'Should a surrogate mother bear our child? We want the gift of a child so much, but we're not sure about bringing another person so intimately into our marriage, or about whether to include her in the child's life.'
- 'Should we turn off Father's life-support machine? Life is so precious, but death always wins.'

- 'Should we tax carbon emissions? The carbon economy keeps people clothed and fed, but carbon emissions are probably putting future communities at risk.'
- 'Should the Internet be censored? It's so loaded with foul material, but we don't want to give people the power to filter out good ideas and important critiques.'
- 'Should we turn away asylum seekers if they're "illegal immigrants"? We want a compassionate nation, but others are waiting in legal channels, and we haven't thought through how many our community can really care for.'

I haven't wrestled with dilemmas, because I don't think they best show how ethics works. In Christian thought, people are called to something better. We're called to become people who are *wise*, who can *discern*, who make canny *judgment calls* in the moment. Look at the following biblical texts. In comparison to talk of rules, rights, values or results (chs. 3–6), they feel extraordinarily 'open-ended':

And I pray this: that your love will keep on growing in knowledge and every kind of discernment, so that you can determine what really matters and can be pure and blameless in the day of Christ, filled with the fruit of righteousness that comes through Jesus Christ, to the glory and praise of God. (Phil. 1:9–11)

Walk as children of light – for the fruit of the light results in all goodness, righteousness, and truth – discerning what is pleasing to the Lord. Do not participate in the fruitless works of darkness, but instead, expose them. (Eph. 5:8–11)

Do not be conformed to this age, but be transformed by the renewing of your mind, so that you may discern what is the good, pleasing, and perfect will of God. (Rom. 12:2)

Test all things. Hold on to what is good. (1 Thess. 5:21)

Do not believe every spirit, but test the spirits to determine if they are from God, because many false prophets have gone out into the world. (1 John 4:1)

Discerning, determining and *testing* are the practices of people who've learnt to *recognize* things. These are difficult and frustrating ideas for us at first, particularly if we've thought that rules, rights, values or results are all we need. However, this is the language of an altered gestalt (p. 72), of wrestling with what's in front of our eyeballs, while remembering that not all is what it seems.

The 'mature', in this way of thinking, are 'those who have their powers of discernment trained by constant practice to distinguish good from evil' (Heb. 5:14, ESV). These New Testament texts extend and expand upon the great Old Testament category of a joined-up life – 'wisdom', an art of *pattern recognition and response* (ch. 10). It's a holistic way of *seeing* into complexity, *working out* what's needed, *making the call* and faithfully *managing the result*, while paying attention to *what we'll become* as we proceed. This book has attempted to refract discernment into some component parts and I've argued as follows:

1. Unseen undertows distort our attempts to apply rules, rights, values and results. The patterns of what we love, and our systems of group inclusion, affect us. The biblical authors summarize these undertows as our 'flesh' (Parts 1–2).
2. Christians mistrust this broken aspect of us, and so don't really 'do ethics'. We 'follow Jesus' and are 'in Christ'. *He* becomes our way into moral reality (Part 3).
3. Broadly speaking, those in Christ seek to uphold and protect the *created order*, to learn and mirror the *character of God*, to inhabit the ways of *Jesus-shaped community* and to become 'formatted' to fit the *new future*. Scriptural *commands* unveil reality and interrogate desire (Part 4).
4. In daily operations, we forgive and reconcile. We aim for virtue and practise freedom. We imitate Jesus and obey God. We learn true humanity at church, and take it to others when we cooperate, subvert, expose or separate (Part 5).
5. While we attend to the core aspects of our life-package (Part 6), ethical disagreements often highlight the different perspective that identity in Christ brings (Part 7).

Therefore, we seem to dodge and weave with those around us:

- We respect rules – until we notice that the rule is destroying freedom, demolishing discernment or becoming a loophole against community.
- We defend some right – then object when the right dismisses the weave of creation, or damages community.
- We uphold some values – and complain when a value opposes God's character, or is too vague or self- or institution-promoting to support community.

- We work toward results – only to protest when the quest for some result denies or displaces God's good future, or compromises community.

Now that all seems quite irritating – but we're only copying Jesus (if clumsily). He wreaked the best kind of havoc wherever he went. He upset everyone's moral categories all the time. To the law-stickler he said, go and discover some compassion (Luke 14:3–5). To the equal-rights activist he said, challenge your inner greed (Luke 12:13–15). To those who valued self-fulfilment he said, learn some faithfulness (Matt. 19:3–6); and to the seeker after self-improvement he said, learn some kindness (Matt. 19:16–21). To the goal-oriented security-seeker he said, lose yourself in God's abundant creation (Luke 12:22–34). To those wanting righteous judgment on others he said, stop it (Luke 9:52–55). To evaders of righteous judgment he said, wake up (Luke 13:1–4). For those deserving righteous judgment he prayed, forgive them (Luke 23:34).

He upset moral categories everywhere, yet he inhabited the most joined-up life imaginable. So Christians orient themselves to the cosmos 'in him'. Anything less – any adherence to some other code, set of values, consequences, principle or philosophy – would relegate Jesus merely to becoming a fellow traveller within that code or philosophy. That would be a horrendous error, because we would then miss all the signals that he's the human who *knew how to be human*. We would miss the opportunity for him to induct us into true humanity.

Of course, just claiming to be wise doesn't make us so. The New Testament also mentions poor discernment (Luke 12:56; Rom. 1:28; 1 Cor. 1:19; 2:14). People have constantly to test themselves and each other (1 Cor. 11:28; 16:3; 2 Cor. 8:8, 22; 13:5; Gal. 6:4; 1 Tim. 3:10), just as God tests us in various ways (1 Cor. 3:13; 1 Thess. 2:4; 1 Pet. 1:7). Testing and being tested by the Scriptures are integral to this picture (Acts 17:11; Heb. 4:12). Wise discernment doesn't grow in a vacuum. It's shaped in a matrix – in a relationship with the God who tests, and within a community where all are permeated by Scripture. But this delivers Christian wisdom – a creative, imaginative and somewhat free endeavour, because we seek to maximize as much good as we can, on all fronts. Here are some creative options that occur to me as I contemplate the first four of those dilemmas:

- 'Should we smack our toddler?' For a little one, a smack functions like a command (ch. 23), alerting her to the created preciousness (ch. 22) of another when she refuses to care. Tingling a child's nerve endings isn't the horrendous evil some portray it to be, any more than is telling an adult what they don't want to hear. But smacking can easily become the violent projection of an adult's rage (ch. 28). Smacking can also compromise the way of community (ch. 18) we call our family. In a society morally ambivalent about having children and treating them well (ch. 38), it sends a message too easily misunderstood. I'd experiment with just holding her, stopping her and repeating, 'No, we don't do that here.' In our current environment, that's my best guess at how to express my identity in Christ (chs. 14, 32).

- 'Should we send our teenager to a government or non-government school?' I'd deeply interrogate the desires, ambitions and systems of belonging (chs. 7–8) that generate our impulses. Is it really about the child, or is it about the parent's standing? All school communities are a bit toxic, whether government or non-government, and at various points live contrary to Jesus' new community (ch. 25). A child might learn a lot in such a place. It might be too toxic for a different child. A child's carer makes this call in freedom (ch. 31), and there may be more than one right answer.

- 'Should I stay with that difficult husband or wife?' The created good of marriage (ch. 22), the faithful character of God (ch. 21), the Jesus-shaped community's way of reconciliation (ch. 29), the hope of God's new future (ch. 24) and the work of the Spirit (ch. 17) are all powerful supports to marriage; and some suffering is a participation with Jesus (p. 105). Sadly, though, we may arrive at a point where our created preciousness is so insulted (p. 188) that we cannot continue. 'Divorce' names this state of affairs (ch. 37).

Try it. Try going through the other examples, using some imagination. Try asking, what would defend and uphold creation's good. What would best reflect the character of God? What would maximize and enhance Jesus-shaped community? What results would best prepare us for the new future? Which biblical commands, if any, illuminate the situation?

As I've presumed to describe a joined-up life, I've noticed how hard ethics has become for modern Westerners. We pay little attention to the effects of our desires and of our needs to belong. Meanwhile, we try to analyse good and evil in terms of the moral categories that surround us – various rights, values and results, as encapsulated by various codes, rules and laws (chs. 3–6). Yet our moral field is fragmented. It becomes hard to see moral patterns, and we've been robbed of wisdom.

I've also noticed how central Jesus becomes to those 'in' him. He gives us a better angle on life. We find an understanding of created good, a glimpse of God's character, a place to belong, the hope of a better future, and some changes to our desires by his Spirit. We don't live it very *well* – after all, we're just fumbling extras in the game he pioneered (p. 114). But he forgives and accepts us, and we're finding the Jesus-shaped version of ourselves.

We've begun to find, in him, a joined-up life.

SCRIPTURE INDEX

OLD TESTAMENT

NEW TESTAMENT

INDEX OF SUBJECTS AND NAMES

Main discussions are noted in **bold**.

Author names mentioned under each chapter's 'Further reading' are not listed.